GILDED RAGE

GILDED RAGE

Elon Musk and the Radicalization
of Silicon Valley

JACOB SILVERMAN

BLOOMSBURY CONTINUUM
LONDON · OXFORD · NEW YORK · NEW DELHI · SYDNEY

BLOOMSBURY CONTINUUM
Bloomsbury Publishing Plc
50 Bedford Square, London, WC1B 3DP, UK
Bloomsbury Publishing Ireland Limited,
29 Earlsfort Terrace, Dublin 2, D02 AY28, Ireland

BLOOMSBURY, BLOOMSBURY CONTINUUM and the Diana logo are trademarks of
Bloomsbury Publishing Plc

Copyright © Jacob Silverman, 2025

Jacob Silverman has asserted his right under the Copyright, Designs and Patents Act, 1988,
to be identified as Author of this work

For legal purposes the Acknowledgements on p. 275 constitute an extension of this copyright page

All rights reserved. No part of this publication may be: i) reproduced or transmitted in any form, electronic or mechanical, including photocopying, recording or by means of any information storage or retrieval system without prior permission in writing from the publishers; or ii) used or reproduced in any way for the training, development or operation of artificial intelligence (AI) technologies, including generative AI technologies. The rights holders expressly reserve this publication from the text and data mining exception as per Article 4(3) of the Digital Single Market Directive (EU) 2019/790

Bloomsbury Publishing Plc does not have any control over, or responsibility for, any third-party websites referred to or in this book. All internet addresses given in this book were correct at the time of going to press. The author and publisher regret any inconvenience caused if addresses have changed or sites have ceased to exist, but can accept no responsibility for any such changes

A catalogue record for this book is available from the British Library

Library of Congress Cataloguing-in-Publication data has been applied for

ISBN: HB: 978-1-3994-1998-7; TPB: 978-1-3994-2000-6; eBook: 978-1-3994-1996-3;
ePDF: 978-1-3994-1999-4

2 4 6 8 10 9 7 5 3

Typeset by Deanta Global Publishing Services, Chennai, India

Printed in the United States at Lakeside Book Company

To find out more about our authors and books visit www.bloomsbury.com and
sign up for our newsletters
For product safety related questions contact productsafety@bloomsbury.com

For my parents

Yep, and your Internet was their invention, this magical convenience that creeps now like a smell through the smallest details of our lives, the shopping, the housework, the homework, the taxes, absorbing our energy, eating up our precious time. And there's no innocence. Anywhere. Never was. It was conceived in sin, the worst possible. As it kept growing, it never stopped carrying in its heart a bitter-cold death wish for the planet, and don't think anything has changed, kid.
—Thomas Pynchon, *Bleeding Edge*

I'm not a paranoid deranged millionaire. Goddamnit, I'm a billionaire.
—Howard Hughes

Contents

Preface		ix
Introduction: You Could Make a Lot of Money Here		xii
1	December 14, 2016	1
2	Thiel and the New Alignment	5
3	Tech Libertarians Embrace the Security State	9
4	The Digital Authoritarian Style	23
5	Killing Twitter, Building X	33
6	The Saudi Influence behind Twitter and X	46
7	Learning to Hate the Place You Love	60
8	Billionaires v. The People of San Francisco	77
9	A Working Model	91
10	Finding The Exit	102
11	The Great Solano County Land Grab	113
12	It's Free Money	129
13	The Crypto Swamp	139
14	The Tap Turns Off	156
15	The Companies Suck	163
16	TikTok, China, and the Moneyman of the Moment	171
17	The Road to Vance	183
18	Didn't the Last Guy Go to Prison?	199

19	Best to Be Low-Key	224
20	Someone Has to Win	240
21	Election Day	259

Epilogue	271
Acknowledgements	275
Notes	276
List of Figures	297
Index	298

Preface

In early 2023, I started writing this book on a hunch. It seemed to me that some of America's most famous tech executives and venture capitalists were moving—often quite vocally—to the political right. The men (and they were mostly men) who were filling my timeline on social media or speaking on cable news and podcasts, were rich, angry, and motivated, and they seemed to be gearing up to play a big role in the 2024 election. The idea behind this book was that it would chronicle that coming political wave and ask where it came from, where it's going, and who's responsible. Having written about the politics of tech for a decade, and having spent a few years immersed in the world of crypto fraud, illicit finance, and political influence operations, I thought I had some understanding of the dramatic transformation underway. Some of my reporting on tech's political shift that appeared in articles published in *The New Republic, The Nation, Zeteo*, and other publications would end up informing this book. But I had no idea how far it would go.

I didn't know as I started writing this history of Silicon Valley's radicalization that it would end with Donald Trump re-elected in a landslide, with Elon Musk serving as practically his running mate. Or that Trump would be inaugurated surrounded by the tech oligarchs I had been reporting on, many of whom had showered his campaign and his family with cash. Or that Musk, already the richest man in the world, would celebrate inauguration day with what appeared to be a fascist salute as he established a position of political authority unprecedented in

American politics.[1] (Musk denied that the gesture had any fascist meaning.) I didn't think that it was possible for the country's richest industrialist and defense contractor to launch what looked like a coup against the administrative state. I might have seen Trump becoming amenable to crypto, but I didn't imagine him becoming arguably the country's leading crypto entrepreneur, creating several new companies that would bring in billions of dollars, some of it from sources overseas.

I did worry that the re-election of Donald Trump would be a disaster—from his promises of mass deportations to his obvious distaste for democratic governance to his economic policies that promised tax breaks for the rich and devastating tariffs for everyone else. It seemed to me that the inability of the political mainstream to articulate, much less enact, a genuinely populist economic program was one reason why American democracy was approaching the precipice. If given two competing visions of America as a bleak, hobbled country waiting for its strongman savior and a sclerotic liberal party trying to scold its disaffected base into compliance, the tech industry's leading lights understandably chose the former. And in the end it would make all the difference.

In the 2024 election, tech's bias for action—for moving fast and breaking things—met Donald Trump's complete disregard for what we euphemistically call "norms." Together they changed the political process with shocking velocity, merging corporate and government power, personal and private interests. In about five months on the campaign trail and six months in office as a "special government employee," Elon Musk enacted an extraordinary degree of disruption, becoming a dominant political force during what I believed to be America's slide into authoritarianism.

The MAGA-tech oligarch alliance has experienced its own internal discord and contradictions. Trump's aggressive tariff policy may harm the interests of some of his biggest donors—not to mention the national economy. The two sides bonded over shared resentments, but they have yet to inaugurate the "golden age" promised by Trump. But together, Elon Musk, his billionaire colleagues, and Donald Trump blazed a new path to power. America needs to find someone or something a lot better than the men named in this book to dig us out of the rut of decline, corruption, and mistrust that the 2024 election seemed to represent.

We'll have to figure out that project together. For now, I can show you how we got here, where we're going, and who's responsible. The authors of our political predicament left a long trail of evidence. And they're still at it.

Introduction

You Could Make a Lot of Money Here

On a chilly winter evening in January 2019, I took what, for me, was an unusual meeting. Getting off the subway near Madison Square Garden, I found a limestone-colored office building tucked next to a collectivist bookstore-slash-coffee-shop. Upstairs, I was greeted by the sandy-haired lieutenant of a biotech executive named Vivek Ramaswamy, with whom I was supposed to meet to interview for a job. What kind of job, I wasn't quite sure. I knew that this company, which was trying to apply new models to drug development, was looking to hire a writer. I didn't know much more than that.

I had learned by then that for America's richest executives, their acquisitive instincts extended to people, whom they collected as surely as they might snap up a midnight-blue Maserati or select a pied-à-terre from a luxury realtor's website. I think they wanted the modicum of journalistic authority I brought, along with the ability to write prose that sounded like it came from a human. Beyond that: TBD. I supposed I would sit and wait for orders. Maybe write an op-ed or two. Whatever I would do in the job, I imagined I would be a ghost, working to advance some yet-unspoken goal of decision-makers far above.

It was deep into the dinner hour, but a smattering of young employees in business casual remained glued to their computers in the office, some of them slurping down the free delivery meals that were offered to those who worked late. The startup was a biotech company called Roivant—obscure to most of the public, but it had raised more than $1 billion from SoftBank, a top-tier Japanese venture capital fund that had also lavished WeWork, the battered co-working startup, with ungodly amounts of money. I knew little about Roivant except that it was valued at $7 billion—a semi-fictional number, as most startup valuations were—and was headed by Ramaswamy, who was considered some kind of financial wunderkind, a mid-thirties, fast-rising business executive overflowing with energy and confidence.

Roivant was developing a model derived in part from private equity: they looked for drugs that had been abandoned or left on the shelf by big pharma—the drug-discovery equivalent of distressed assets—bought them, spun up companies around them, and then paid for the long and expensive testing process, which could take years and lead to nothing. It was a difficult business. At the time, Roivant hadn't brought any drugs to market, and they had had one notable failure in a hyped but ultimately ineffective Alzheimer's drug being developed by Axovant, one of an increasing number of Roivant subsidiaries (its "vants," each devoted to a specific class of drug). Ramaswamy was accused of profiting off the Axovant hype while his investors lost out.[2] Over time, Roivant was able to sell interests in other "vants," which further enriched investors and Ramaswamy himself, sending his fortune into the upper nine figures. At the time, Roivant didn't have much in the way of finished products (they would succeed in bringing several to market in the subsequent years), but they did have industry buzz, money in the bank, a rich charismatic founder, and their investors' understanding that drug development can take a decade. That gave them a long runway.

Roivant had assembled a horde of young analysts, scientists, and doctors, scouring the world for drugs that might have been overlooked, or that might be tested for efficacy against disorders or treatments other than those originally envisioned. In the biotech press, where I turned to educate myself about the company, there was skepticism around Roivant—a sense that it was mostly financial engineering, that it had received more hype, venture capital, and media coverage than it deserved. It hadn't yet delivered anything, really. But inside the company, it didn't matter. They were flush with cash and spent like it, lavishing employees with tech-company-style perks.

Finally Vivek walked in. He was 34 at the time (about my age), slim, and a touch under six feet tall. He was handsome and well groomed, fit from regular tennis games. He spoke with the directness and assuredness of someone who was rarely told no. His posture was much better than mine.

We sat down at a large oval conference table, along with the communications director who had met me by the elevator. To my surprise, Ramaswamy held a copy of my first book, a critique of big tech and the surveillance-saturated world it had made. It appeared that he had read it—the book was covered in post-its and annotations. Most Roivant employees passed through a rigorous interview process—the company prided itself on recruiting from elite institutions—but I had snuck in the side door. I was referred by a publisher I knew, the heir to an old American business fortune, who had gone to Harvard with Ramaswamy and the other staffer sitting there at the table. Many Roivant employees had attended Harvard.

I didn't go to Harvard. I went to Emory. But I had a friend who had. That's how I ended up in that room.

I still wasn't quite sure why. The company wanted to hire a writer at a six-figure salary, which, given my spotty freelancer's finances and my young child at home, was reason enough for me to take the subway to midtown Manhattan. Perhaps, I thought, it was time to take a break from reporting on tech and do some first-person immersion. Perhaps it was okay to make a little money for once. It might even be fun.

Ramaswamy had that vibrational intensity of someone who's up early and scheduled all day, a high achiever constantly checking off boxes. He radiated ambition and an impatience toward anyone who didn't serve his needs and his schedule.

INTRODUCTION

Our conversation is lost to the legal fog of a nondisclosure agreement. You're not missing much. What I took away was the fact that, no matter what role I had, I could make pretty good money at a well-funded biotech startup. Beyond that I might as well have been a piece of expensive furniture, like the stylish ivory-white sofa that sat unoccupied outside his private office.

I could try to get myself excited about drug development, I decided. I used the industry's products: I was as medicated as any red-blooded American. But really I knew little about it as a business. I had the instinctive leftist distaste for big pharma corporations, health insurance, and other aspects of our for-profit healthcare system.

The next day, I got a call: the job was mine. It seemed bizarrely easy, as if I had passed from the precarity of freelance journalism into moneyed startup life simply by saying the word "Harvard" a few times. Sure, my own body of work and ability to represent myself had got me past the finish line. But it was elite connections and social favors that got me in the door.

The job offer came with a low six-figure salary, a hefty potential bonus, and stock options, assuming I lasted long enough for them to vest. I asked the hiring manager what my title was. "What do you want it to be?" he said.

The delirious sense of having wandered into something strange but exciting came over me. Somehow we came up with the title "Director of Special Media Projects," an appropriately lofty and vague designation for a job whose duties still hadn't been fully enumerated to me.

And that was it. Within a couple of weeks I was "onboarded" into a massive startup with hundreds of employees on three continents and almost no products or revenue streams. Like a new deputy in a cop show, I was given my kit: laptop, swipe card, business cards to identify myself to new contacts, numerous forms and policy handbooks. I was directed to the amply stocked kitchen and, like a child on vacation, assured that I could have whatever I wanted.

My time at Roivant was undistinguished. I was nominally a ghostwriter, but I didn't seem to have a real mandate to do anything, and after a few meetings with Ramaswamy and other executives, they left me to while away time at my desk. I was pretty lost in the quantified world of venture-capital-funded, private-equity-inspired drug development. I enjoyed talking to the company analysts because they came from a foreign world, speaking a jargon I was barely starting to decode. In the open-floor-plan office, I sat at my computer and drank coffee and listened to the younger analysts chat about *The Bachelor* while I anticipated a call from daycare telling me that my toddler had another fever, which would allow me to rise with purpose from my chair and announce that I had to tend to my sick child.

I got accustomed to the relative luxury of my mostly do-nothing six-figure job—I probably ate my salary in free snacks and boutique oat milks—but the daily insecurity of simply having nothing to do, of waiting to be summoned into Ramaswamy's office to receive some vague, imperious directive, gnawed at me. I felt useless and overpaid. I was an inefficiency that someone would eventually deal with. And after two months, I was politely sent back into freelance life with some severance pay. I was upset, but I also knew the fit wasn't right. Neither of us knew what to do with the other.

Roivant wasn't the last time I dabbled in corporate life. Executives and startup founders often want to be known beyond the self-regarding industries of Silicon Valley, finance, or biotech. They want a certain gravitas that, if it can't be achieved organically, perhaps can be bought. (Or maybe it can be won through electoral politics—which, these days, is increasingly coming to resemble another extravagant purchase.)

Other wealthy people solicited me to do ghostwriting or creative work that would satisfy some urge that their lucrative day jobs had forced them to set aside. There was the late-career Texas energy-industry lawyer with literary ambitions who wrote religiously inflected short stories. A wealthy British couple who worked as corporate coaches and consultants on something called "digital transformation" thought it might be nice to do a podcast. Did I have any ideas? Here's a few thousand dollars for equipment.

Another biotech startup founder asked me if I could, in a series of essays, help explicate a political belief system that he believed to be quite novel. It ultimately sounded to me like a run-of-the-mill mix of social liberalism and libertarian capitalism. By then, I knew I made a poor ghost. It was less about morality than motivation. It was hard to write things I didn't believe. And most of my clients had only a hazy idea of what they wanted. I wasn't the instrument to give shape to their ideas. I appreciated the call, I told the biotech founder, but I declined.

Between my occasional work as a corporate ghost, and my freelance journalism on tech and politics, I learned about how wealthy people came into their money and the ego that seemed to come with it. I learned how the ruling class reproduced itself and who they decided to draft into their networks—people like Vivek Ramaswamy. Coming up professionally in the years after the Great Financial Crisis, I learned about who had gotten rich under ZIRP—the zero-interest-rate policy years that ran from about 2008 to 2021, when money was cheap and easy to borrow in fantastical quantities. And I learned about the failure of this new class of financiers, venture capitalists, and tech moguls to create anything enduring. So many of them, it seemed, had gotten rich via some form of financial engineering, a combination of insider connections, cunning use of the law and tax loopholes, and huge sums of cheaply borrowed cash that they could leverage on big bets. Risking other people's money, they really hadn't made much in the way of products or innovations that had mattered to—or even come to the attention of—the wider public. But now they were ready to translate their bankrolls into political power.

In his area of business, Vivek Ramaswamy was a young master of the universe—showered with industry praise, put on the cover of *Forbes* magazine at age 30, loaded with money and opportunity. But in the wider world, hardly anyone knew who he was. (*Forbes*' cover headline called him "Boy in the Bubble.") Ramaswamy wanted to change that. My mistake was thinking that he genuinely wanted some kind of intellectual prestige, earned through thoughtful, well-timed op-eds and original essays. That was low-stakes stuff. Ramaswamy wanted to be on the *Wall Street Journal* op-ed page and Fox News, sure, but that was a single tool in a larger arsenal geared toward one thing, what he had been accumulating ever since he was a precocious undergraduate at Harvard: power.

What happened next is something that I came to see repeat itself again and again over the coming years in American politics, especially as tech moguls stepped further into the political arena. After I left Roivant, I heard that Ramaswamy might run for governor of Ohio, which seemed like a ludicrous prospect, until suddenly, it wasn't. He wasn't yet a name-brand public figure, but he was making inroads into the top levels of media, finance, and politics. He started appearing on Tucker Carlson's highly rated Fox News show, where he inveighed against corporate wokeness and spoke in favor of cutthroat American capitalism. Tacking to the hard right, he became a reliable guest voice excoriating identity politics and environmental, social, and governance (or ESG) policies that take into account social and political issues in matters of corporate governance. In Ramaswamy's newly articulated worldview, America's corporations needed to stick to making money, not social policy. Passionate, confident, and a rapid-fire speaker, he found his footing as a budding right-wing firebrand. And perhaps he found another ghostwriter, because in just a couple of years, Ramaswamy churned out book-length jeremiads with culture-warring titles like *Woke, Inc: Inside Corporate America's Social Justice Scam*; *Nation of Victims: Identity Politics, the Death of Merit, and the Path Back to Excellence*; and *Capitalist Punishment: How Wall Street Is Using Your Money to Create a Country You Didn't Vote For*. They were bestsellers.

He was starting to arrive, but there was more to be done. Ramaswamy gave up Roivant's CEO chair, appointing one of his executives to succeed him and becoming company chairman. He moved home to Ohio, where he started a venture capital fund called Strive Asset Management. His new firm was explicitly anti-ESG— against the kind of liberal, environmentally and socially conscious policies that he thought were corrupting American business. Its mission statement read: "Strive's mission is to restore the voices of everyday citizens in the American economy by companies to focus on excellence over politics."[3]

Business is never apolitical, and it was easy to detect conservatism—and even some strains of MAGA thought—in Ramaswamy's new project. Strive had major investors, including Peter Thiel's Founders Fund, JD Vance's Narya Capital, billionaire financier Bill Ackman, and Palantir co-founder Joe Lonsdale—all of them politically active conservative donors, and all of whom we will meet in this book. JD Vance was Ramaswamy's friend from Yale Law School and a first-term senator from their shared home state of Ohio. In terms of political connections, it was an elite list of supporters and they had the cash to match. It seemed that Ramaswamy, then in his late thirties, was being drafted into Thiel's so-called PayPal Mafia network, the influential group of mostly right-wing political donors and investors that sprang out of the payments startup PayPal. In Ramaswamy, the ruling cadre of conservative tech oligarchs was preparing a member of the next generation.

In December 2022, the *New Yorker* published a profile of Ramaswamy, calling him "the CEO of Anti-Woke, Inc."[4] The article suggested that Ramaswamy might run for president, which seemed to me like an insane idea—less quixotic than hubristic. And yet, two months later, Ramaswamy did exactly that, announcing his run to be the Republican nominee for president in 2024.

On a personal level, I couldn't believe it. The swaggering CEO I had briefly worked for was now saying that he should be president of the United States. And then it occurred to me that it didn't matter that his chances of victory were almost nonexistent. For the ultra-rich, Donald Trump's successful runs had introduced the "why not me?" factor into the presidential calculus. If a one-time long shot like Trump could build up a movement around himself, why couldn't they? The present era of vanity presidential runs has shown that there's almost no downside, as long as you don't leverage too much of your own fortune. Simply by being theoretically in the running and doing a little political glad-handing, Ramaswamy would become far more famous than he was before. Maybe he would end up in Trump's cabinet. Maybe he and Peter Thiel would found the next big AI startup together. The exact outcome didn't matter. Ramaswamy had already won something, just by entering the race.

Ramaswamy spent months traveling around early primary states, but he didn't end up winning many votes. Observing the inevitability of Trump capturing the Republican nomination, Ramaswamy made a lot of noise as an America First true believer and then bowed out of the race just after the Iowa caucuses.[5] He immediately—and fulsomely—endorsed Trump. Within days, he was by Trump's side in New Hampshire, stumping for the presumptive nominee. Ramaswamy's plan worked: in less than a year, he had shot to notoriety, racking up social-media followers and colorful soundbites and generally establishing himself as a voluble presence on the conservative political scene. Some of his Republican colleagues, like Chris Christie and Nikki Haley, seemed to find him insufferable—he could have a smarmy debate-kid affect at events—but at times he polled in the low double digits in Iowa. There was even some vice presidential speculation. For a former unknown, it was a great achievement. It reminded me of his ability to spin huge fees and IPO paydays out of startups with no products. While he'd spent some $25 million of his own money on the campaign, his personal fortune had increased with the markets. It wasn't a path to electoral victory, but it led him to greater cultural attention, money, and political power. For a young oligarch on the make, those were just as important.

Cobbling together his tech–finance–politics power base, Ramaswamy embodied, in my eyes, an almost sociopathic millennial ambition. Seeking power for its own sake, he proudly denounced trans people ("there are only two genders") and argued that we should invade Mexico to go after drug cartels—an idea that found increasing purchase among Republicans as the political cycle went on.[6,7] In his more fascistic turns, he talked about curtailing voting rights and arming every household in Taiwan against a potential Chinese invasion. In short, he spoke like a full-blooded Republican, and he developed the requisite alliances. Silicon Valley figures with right-wing sympathies—especially Elon Musk and David Sacks—loved him.

It seemed to me this was a step-change in American politics. Once, corporate titans built libraries, museums, and universities; now, they build political and media operations designed to propagate their influence. That is not to sacralize JP Morgan, Cornelius Vanderbilt, or other Gilded Age robber-barons who laundered their reputations with lavish acts of philanthropy. They were deeply political figures, often malign ones, too. But they did also establish sustainable, public-spirited institutions. Their names may be on the buildings, but their legacy is larger than themselves.

Their contemporary analogs look far different.

THE REACTIONARY UTOPIANS

Progressive politics were always an awkward fit for tech and finance elites who would often be tweeting their political complaints from private jets. While some might claim liberal social views, in practice, the ultra-rich tend to focus on avoiding taxes, trimming regulations, suppressing union organizing, and other pro-business policies. They may claim populist sympathies, but the truth is usually they don't spend much time with people outside their class who aren't on their payroll. They zealously manage their public reputations and make heavy use of nondisclosure agreements. They might appear to mingle with ordinary people on social media, but their real lives exist at an Olympian remove from the public.

It's not just a matter of divergent class interests. In recent years, some of our wealthiest business elites have become far more vocal, and notably angrier, when expressing reactionary social and political beliefs. Today's billionaires trade in posting views on social media that are often anti-migrant, transphobic, bigoted, and wackily conspiratorial. Part of this book's project is to explain how and why that happened.

As this book's subtitle implies, Elon Musk is at the heart of this right-wing radicalization overtaking America's business class. During the 2020 election cycle, Musk sounded, at least in public, like a lot of other rich-guy CEOs: dispensing light observations on the race without betraying a rooting interest. He maxed out donations to a handful of elected Republicans and Democrats, but put nothing toward the presidential race. There were no massive PAC (Political Action Committee) donations and no grandstanding about the potential end of civilization on social media. On a *New York Times* podcast that aired that summer, Musk said that he was undecided about who he'd vote for. He spent election day 2020 reminiscing about the good old days when Tesla, then a small startup, teetered on the brink of bankruptcy. Musk was so politically indifferent that, as far as I could tell, he didn't mention Joe Biden in a tweet at any point that year. He tweeted once at President Donald Trump to thank him for calling for California governor Gavin Newsom to remove mask mandates. When election deniers rioted at the Capitol on January 6, Musk shared a couple of jokes about the QAnon shaman, and that was about it. (Like many people, Musk does occasionally delete some of his posts.)

During that fraught time, you might have found relief in Musk's goofy Twitter timeline, where he nerded out about engine torque, the scientific mechanics of Covid-19 tests, or his favorite video game. He tried to cast himself as a superhero—specifically Tony Stark, aka Iron Man, a rich inventor (and arms dealer) with a winking, populist touch. Musk even had a cameo in *Iron Man 2*. Every year, Musk liked to tout Tesla's perfect score on the Human Rights Campaign's measure of LGBTQ equality. "Don't buy our car if that's a problem," he tweeted in 2018. "People should be free to live their lives where their heart takes them." He followed it with a string of colorful heart emojis.[8]

But Musk hasn't made a declaration like that since 2022. Instead, he became the most high-profile example of a dramatic rightward political shift among top tech executives and venture capitalists, and his public persona utterly transformed. Dozens of times per day—and usually deep into the night—Musk posted dark fantasies on Twitter (which he later bought and rechristened X), about invading migrants, trans people, pedophile groomers and the infamous "woke mind virus," which he saw as a threat to human civilization. Musk has appeared to approvingly respond to tweets endorsing the Great Replacement Theory, some versions of which state that liberals and Jews are helping to bring in illegal migrants in order to change the racial demographics of American society and tilt the voting rolls towards the Democrats. Once a fringe belief that inspired mass murders such as the Pittsburgh synagogue and Christchurch mosque shootings, this racist and false conspiracy theory is now trumpeted by some of the richest, most powerful people alive. In real life, Musk was beset by enemies—Tesla skeptics, regulators, lawsuits, liberals. Online, he had all the supporters he could want, and in Donald Trump, he found the ultimate vehicle for his resentments.

Once Trump and his MAGA movement moved the window of acceptable political opinion firmly to the right, a wealthy class already predisposed to authoritarian beliefs readily followed. Something changed in the body politic, as societal elites seemed to become more brazen in their entitlement to wealth and power, and more contemptuous of everyday people, especially the homeless and other "unproductive" members of society. It wasn't just Musk—but he seemed to speak for a generation of tech moguls who lined up behind him—and it augured a grim reactionary turn in our politics.

In a sense it was simple. Musk and his peers were radicalized, embracing far-right movements and conspiracy theories that they might have dismissed a decade earlier. The political terrain had also changed. A leading candidate for president could be an attempted coup plotter and found liable for sexual abuse, a convicted felon with a backlog of legal proceedings awaiting him, a grifter by every measure—and his fans loved him all the more for it. So it was with Musk, who only found more adulation from his hardcore base of supporters as he fell down what appeared to outsiders to be a rabbit hole of extremism, funding lawsuits against Disney and palling around online with conspiracists like Mike Cernovich, who promoted the "Pizzagate" theory about a Democratic Party-run pedophile ring supposedly operating out of the basement of a Washington, DC pizza restaurant. (In 2016, a deluded gunman went into the restaurant—which doesn't have a basement—looking for children to rescue, and fired three shots. Fortunately no one was hurt.)

Through specific choices Musk ensconced himself in what looked like an echo chamber, where his darkest beliefs were always confirmed and amplified. After buying Twitter, he set about remaking it to boost the right-wing personalities he was beginning to correspond with. He removed blue checks from verified accounts and started selling the checks as a status emblem, which caused subscribers' posts to appear at the top of replies. People who didn't pay a fee—like the formerly verified journalists who turned into some of Musk's biggest critics—would see their reach diminish. In another important change, the new Twitter algorithm deprecated links to outside websites, which encouraged the viral spread of sensationalist, unverified, and unsourced information. The changes came as Democratic politicians and a good chunk of the public turned against him, but on Twitter-turned-X, Musk could feel as popular as ever as he received mass validation. "You are the media," he liked to tell his followers. He seemed to be granting them the freedom to believe the master narrative he was peddling: that the richest man in the world was on their side; that all the other elites were corrupt; that every expert was lying to them; and that it was okay to believe in conspiracies to which the mainstream media refused to give credence.

As a corporate titan with virtually unlimited resources and a massive media apparatus at his command, Musk had the potential to be a dominant political power player. His pop-cultural influence was vast, and his political conversion was welcomed by Republicans who liked his bitterly "anti-woke" perspective. When Florida governor Ron DeSantis decided to announce his

INTRODUCTION

entry into the 2024 presidential race, he did it in a Twitter Spaces event, hosted by Musk and his VC buddy David Sacks, who was a major donor to DeSantis. The Spaces event was a disaster, with the audio frequently cutting out. Amazingly for a political culture that thrives on optics, there was no video. Instead there was a choppy audio stream of two very rich guys talking to an obsequious governor about why he should be in charge of the country. It didn't do much to advance DeSantis's prospects. But Musk and Sacks presented the event as a success. "We broke the internet," said Sacks, awkwardly evoking a years-old Kim Kardashian meme.[9] In fact, they broke Twitter. But in their minds, it seemed to represent another marker of their growing political stature. And why not? DeSantis came to their turf and kissed the ring. The rest was mere details.

Although he isn't as well known as Musk, David Sacks offers another useful case study for the new style of billionaire political influence, and you'll encounter him a few times in this book. A longtime tech executive, Sacks together with his wife Jacqueline became a big-money donor in California politics, especially for recall efforts targeting Democrats, with the recall process becoming a tool for an increasingly politicized tech class to directly shape government to better suit their desires. Sacks once donated to Hillary Clinton's presidential campaign and Gavin Newsom's gubernatorial run, but only a couple of years later he donated to the failed recall effort against Newsom—along with successful recall campaigns against the San Francisco school board and progressive district attorney Chesa Boudin. After advising his friend Musk on his takeover of Twitter, Sacks, who had written culture-warring conservative columns in the 1990s with his college pal Peter Thiel, emerged as a vocal social-media commentator. He bashed the Biden administration for its foreign policy and offered doom-ridden prophecies about how Democratic politicians were destroying San Francisco and other liberal cities. By the time the 2024 presidential campaign began in earnest, Sacks had placed himself close to the seat of power, hosting fundraisers for DeSantis, Ramaswamy, and Robert F.

Kennedy Jr. He began speaking more sympathetically about Donald Trump—mostly about how Democrats were driving frustrated voters into his arms. Like a good venture capitalist, Sacks was spreading out his bets, knowing that one of them could hit down the road. But it was clear that his political passions would eventually land him in Trump's camp.

Any time a class of wealthy elites begins to intervene in politics, we should be looking at where their money goes and to what ends. Musk, Sacks, Ramaswamy, and their colleagues were chipping away at an already fractured democracy, pouring money into recall efforts, funding extremist politicians, and running firebrand campaigns demonizing marginalized social groups. Armed with Koch-like fortunes and MAGA-inspired cultural resentments, speaking in a populist register, they claim to be refugees from liberalism—sometimes literally so, for the millionaire and billionaire techies who "fled" San Francisco for Austin and Miami during the height of the Covid-19 pandemic. Notably, they found refuge in liberal cities in conservative states where there was no income tax—precisely the kind of political bargain that appeals to very rich people seeking liberals' social tolerance without the attendant fiscal priorities.

As I explore in this book, there had always been a current of conservatism running through Silicon Valley and a close union with the defense and intelligence establishment, but this was something different. The political realignments of the Trump years crashed up against a tech industry that, fattened on zero percent interest rates and billions of dollars in government contracts, became increasingly reactionary and alienated from the people who were supposed to be its customers. Covid-19 quarantine restrictions came to represent another deep-state power grab, rather than a bumbling, if mostly good-faith effort by politicians and bureaucrats to keep more people from dying. In time, the resentment over Covid protocols helped catalyze an antisocial worldview that saw baroque conspiracies around every corner.

Tech billionaires led the growing backlash against urban homelessness and criminal justice reform. They funneled money to right-wing politicians and bloggers trying to breathe life into the phony bigotry of race science. Elon Musk and his venture-capitalist buddies led a political revolt that at times included a rejection of basic democratic governance. On X, Musk expressed his desire for a Roman dictator to cleanse, perhaps literally, the body politic.

Playing the role of market fundamentalists, these tech titans preached crypto, artificial intelligence, space travel, and life extension while most people just wanted messaging apps, free healthcare, and affordable housing. Once, they aspired to solving real material problems; now, they seemed more concerned with monetizing them.

In the minds of some tech leaders, the problems facing us were less material or political than about some vague menacing notion of "wokeness," with each viral story about overwrought identity politics adding fuel to a fire that only grew on Elon Musk's X.

Along with directing huge flows of investment money, often solicited from Middle Eastern dictatorships—such as the Saudi cash which helped with Musk's purchase of Twitter—these lords of techno-capital are rich in opinion and growing in influence. In social-media posts, TV interviews, podcast appearances, and the occasional congressional testimony, they rage against liberal politicians, homeless people, San Francisco's social ills, and a broader civilizational decline that one week may be caused by the war in Ukraine and the next, by sudden panic over AI chatbots. The rising political sensibility among today's venture capitalists can be summarized as an impatient selfishness, an exhaustion with liberal-democratic mores. They want control to remake the world according to their impulses. These titans of industry might be fabulously wealthy, but they can come across as deeply unhappy and eager to break the existing political order. They seem to have no vision for how to put it back together.

Gilded Rage is my guided tour through America's self-designated innovator class. It's a reported history of how the last decade's economic policies, social disruptions, inequality, Democratic fecklessness, and Trump-led resentments shaped an industry's politics and its role in public life. And it's about how this industry's leading lights ultimately helped return Trump to the White House—with Elon Musk in tow.

Ridiculing their own employees on social media, laying off masses of workers to preserve declining profit margins, and backing vulgar culture warriors like Florida governor Ron DeSantis before lining up behind the authoritarian Donald Trump, tech industry leaders have, it seems to me, become their own threat to democracy, clawing at society's threadbare fabric rather than working to mend it. They have looked for ways to "exit" normal civilian life: to flee from democracy, from financial regulation and the rule of law, and even from Earth itself, for which they've predicted various versions of apocalypse. They have gotten into bed with undemocratic regimes, supported right-wing political parties around the world, and sought to create their own tax havens and self-governed polities, where they can rule like Venetian doges. They've bought up media platforms in order to shape public opinion, boost their stock portfolios, and enact a political program of minority rule, of oligarchy. Their networks of influence helped reelect Donald Trump and ensured that one of their own—JD Vance—is now vice president.

We are a long way from Silicon Valley's long-held problem-solving ethos, much less its civic-minded, if rarely elaborated upon, mission of "changing the world." More often the tech industry seems focused on the ways they could wreak creative destruction. The catastrophic promise of AI has practically become part of the sales pitch. In their ominous warnings of unchecked artificial intelligence escaping Pandora's box, industry luminaries can sound like Robert J. Oppenheimer and the Manhattan Project scientists who wondered if a nuclear bomb test would ignite the Earth's atmosphere. Executives like OpenAI CEO Sam Altman talk about buying guns and prepper gear, and some of the industry's leading figures can seem almost delighted by the prospect of some apocalyptic event that would unleash a more exciting world. It makes one wonder: Do we need these supposed innovators, these secretive alchemists toying with Armageddon? Or is there another way? How did they become so powerful? And why do they all seem so angry at the world they've come to dominate?

There's something recognizable in this reactionary swerve. In an era of political stagnation, a lot of people are mad, dissatisfied, and alienated, even those who are materially comfortable. The Covid years hit some of us hard. But for these men, their resentment comes with the power to do something about it, to enact a different social and political order than the one that supplied their wealth.

This change in mindset was also powered by something of a historical economic one-off: the zero-interest-rate policy (ZIRP) era, when interest rates remained for many years close to zero. It minted numerous millionaires and billionaires in tech and finance, even when some appeared to produce little in the way of public value or even viable businesses. Think of insanely well-compensated WeWork CEO Adam Neumann or the now-fallen FTX fraudster Sam Bankman-Fried. Buoyed by the gains of cheap capital and a rising stock market, this new class of the ultra-rich could also convince themselves of their exceptionalism. With entitlement seemed to come a belief that perhaps they will be the ones to save humanity from existential risk. "Our whole civilization is at stake," Musk posted on X in February 2024, regarding a scandal over Google's generative image AI miscasting white historical figures as non-white. "The woke mind virus is killing Western Civilization."[10,11]

Musk seemed to really believe this. A few months later, he told the kooky Canadian psychologist turned right-wing influencer Jordan Peterson that the woke mind virus had killed his son. Musk's child wasn't dead. She was living happily as a transgender woman who said she wanted nothing to do with a biological father who she said had harassed her for being queer.

For Musk, it appeared that the woke mind virus was a very real infection that had colonized everything from AI to the federal bureaucracy. He was determined to excise it and to reelect Donald Trump to help him do so.

Something had gone very wrong. The tech elites who got rich in the last 20 years have the world at their fingertips, but they can't stand the touch. The rest of us are already contending with the consequences.

I

December 14, 2016

If there's one date that might demarcate this new political era, it's December 14, 2016. That winter day, 14 of the tech industry's most powerful executives—including leaders of Apple, Cisco, IBM, Intel, Google, Microsoft, Tesla, Amazon, and Facebook—traveled to Trump Tower in Manhattan and made nice with the newly elected president-in-waiting, Donald J. Trump. They were joined by the president-elect's two sons and daughter Ivanka; several future presidential appointees and political advisors, including Jared Kushner and Steve Bannon; and venture capitalist Peter Thiel. Indiana governor Mike Pence was there, though as he noted when he introduced himself to the group, he would only be governor for a few more days. The assembled notables laughed as if one of the more wooden politicians in the country had just delivered an epic punchline. It was that kind of meeting: a convivial show for the cameras, with everyone acting solicitous in a "looking forward to working with you to move America forward" kind of way.

It was an astonishing agglomeration of wealth and power—enough money and influence to move markets, to shape a nation's industrial policy, or to provide a crucial stamp of approval for a controversial new president. Trump needed the support of the country's economic elites, especially socially liberal Silicon Valley, which had until that point largely supported Hillary Clinton. And today he was getting it. Quite easily, in fact. As the executives introduced themselves one by one for flashing cameras, Trump, whose election victory was reportedly a shock even to himself, sat with a pursed-lip grin, his hands resting on the conference room table. Trump, too, was a CEO, but of a much less successful, occasionally bankrupt firm—a veritable penny-stock hustler in a room loaded with Wall Street darlings. But that day, they were there for him.

Thiel was responsible for bringing together this particular group. His authority was signified by the presence of Alex Karp—the bristly, roguish CEO of data analytics company Palantir, which Thiel co-founded. Palantir was already a valuable startup, with lucrative and strategically important contracts with the Pentagon and intelligence agencies, but it was a far smaller concern than any of the other companies represented at the table, some of which had bigger government contracts of their own. It would be almost four years before Palantir went public, reaping a windfall for Thiel, Karp, and other government-connected company insiders. But that was years off, and the still-unprofitable Palantir had nothing on networking giant Cisco or on Oracle, an enterprise software stalwart whose first customer, in the late 1970s, was the CIA. Karp was there because Thiel wanted him there, because Thiel was an investor in Palantir (as was In-Q-Tel, the CIA's venture capital arm). Palantir's core government-contracting business had the potential to take off under a Trump administration.

As if Thiel's influence weren't obvious enough, Trump decided to acknowledge it early on. In his remarks, Trump said that Peter Thiel had helped determine the guest list and the fact that some large companies were unworthy of inclusion. Then Trump offered some superlatives for the billionaire venture capitalist and top campaign donor, who served as a crucial conduit to Silicon Valley.

"I want to start by thanking Peter, because he saw something very early, maybe before we saw it," Trump said. "He's been so terrific and so outstanding." The two men awkwardly joined hands and smiled.

Thiel had bet on Trump when the tech industry, at least publicly, had turned against the former *Apprentice* host. So had large swaths of America, who assumed that with his crude, abusive behavior and proud disdain for anyone he saw as beneath him, Trump could never be elected president. On October 7, 2016, the *Washington Post* published a video of Trump bragging about assaulting women—"I grab them by the pussy,"—while filming an episode of *Access Hollywood*.[1] It was one month before the presidential election, and many observers assumed that the tape's release would put an end to Trump's political career.

Eight days later, Thiel donated $1.25 million in support of Trump's campaign. It was a large donation demonstrating that deep-pocketed backers like Thiel weren't going anywhere. In line with Thiel's truculent contrarianism, it was also a rebuke to a self-regarding liberal establishment understandably repulsed by Trump's behavior. The donation could pay for some ads, sure, but more than anything, the money demonstrated Thiel's stubborn commitment to a candidate who he hoped would disrupt political institutions the same way that Thiel and his colleagues had disrupted whole industries from Silicon Valley.

The *New York Times* called Thiel "the only prominent supporter of the Republican candidate in the high-tech community," which wasn't quite accurate.[2] Doug Leone, a billionaire investor and partner at leading venture capital firm Sequoia, was a Trump supporter. (He later denounced Trump after January 6, before embracing him again during the 2024 election cycle.[3]) Oracle co-CEO Safra Catz was part of Trump's transition team. Other corporate leaders and financiers had given Trump huge sums, including, as the *Times* noted, hedge fund magnate Robert Mercer and his daughter Rebekah Mercer, who together gave $15.5 million while also investing in ideologically motivated tech and media projects, such as Cambridge Analytica and Breitbart.[4] Oracle CEO Larry Ellison—one of the ten richest people in the world—emerged as a major Trump backer, to the point that he would later participate in a strategy session about overturning the 2020 election results.[5]

Trump's vulgar populism didn't make him an obvious favorite for Silicon Valley—something that he would try to change in private meetings with Mark Zuckerberg and other CEOs—but he had an enormous amount of big-money support. Some of that support expressed itself quietly. At other times, it played out for the cameras in Trump Tower.

"They're all talking about the bounce, so right now everybody in the room has to like me at least a little bit," said Trump at that December 2016 gathering—referring to the stock market, his preferred metric for assessing the success of just about anything—before laying on some flattery. "There's nobody like you in the world," he said. "You call my people, you can call me. It makes no difference."

As Trump said, Thiel had a reputation for being early to things. He was a co-founder of PayPal and the first venture capitalist to invest in Facebook. He'd had some notable failures as an investor, particularly as a hedge fund manager, but his portfolio brimmed with the riches yielded by making early commitments to future tech unicorns. Gay, philosophically libertarian, with politics that might generously be described as authoritarian, he was known for veering right when his colleagues herded left. He had chafed against liberal pieties since he was a flame-throwing undergrad at Stanford, where he founded the conservative publication the *Stanford Review*. It seemed in his nature. And now, Thiel's bet on Trump had paid off.

2

Thiel and the New Alignment

Seven years after that December pow-wow, the scorecard read differently. Thiel would describe his support of Trump in 2016 as not quite a mistake, but more like an experiment gone haywire. "Voting for Trump was like a not very articulate scream for help," Thiel told the journalist Barton Gellman in 2023. "It was crazier than I thought. It was more dangerous than I thought."[1] (Thiel didn't describe what kind of help he was crying out for.)

Thiel wanted out of the morass of politics. Or at least he claimed to, saying in interviews that he wouldn't donate to anyone in the 2024 election cycle. "There's always a chance I might change my mind," Thiel said, but his husband was asking him to sit it out, and Thiel thought it was best that he did.[2]

Thiel seemed to indicate a personal exhaustion with the fracas of big-money politics. Later in Trump's term, Thiel refused a request for a $10 million infusion of campaign funds, which eventually led to a rift between the tech industry's most famous right-wing venture capitalist and the president.

An impression formed that the tech billionaire who had bucked his liberal peers to give a defiant speech at the 2016 Republican National Convention had had enough of politics.

Yet while Thiel was sticking to the political shadows, his fingerprints would be all over the 2024 election, from Trump's choice of JD Vance as his running mate to the former Thiel staffers who worked on Project 2025, the right-wing intellectual, policy, and personnel handbook for a second Trump term.

Some of Thiel's wealthy colleagues were ready to take his place as loud and proud Trump supporters. By the time of the 2024 election cycle, Elon Musk, the Tesla and SpaceX CEO and industry controversialist, had trolled, bought, and tweeted his way to the kind of media ubiquity that was rivaled only by Trump. He was now as well known for his online tirades against trans people or telling X advertisers to "go fuck yourself" as he was for presiding over a genuinely innovative rocket company.[3] While nominally controlling six companies, he was a full-time culture warrior, erratic and unforgiving in his frequent pronouncements about the woke rot overtaking America and a supposed migrant invasion.

It was a huge change from the electric-car evangelist who, early in President Trump's first administration, quit a climate advisory board in response to the president pulling the US out of the Paris Climate Accords. The two men had reconciled. Now, Trump and Musk seemed perfectly aligned in their blustery public attitudes, their loose relationship with the truth, their furious resentments against those who didn't sufficiently appreciate them, and their apocalyptic warnings of an America on the verge of collapse.

Musk was joined in his grievances by a raft of executives, venture capitalists, Wall Street financiers, and other alienated members of the business overclass who together reflected a political realignment that had coalesced in the Trump years. This new political formation was motivated variously by reactionary disgust for the #MeToo movement against sexual assault and rape culture; the restrictions and perceived conformity of Covid-19 lockdowns; and opposition to Black Lives Matter, left-wing social justice movements, and anything that might be dismissed under the increasingly broad pejorative of "woke." Musk and his cohort had thrived on zero-interest-rate policies that made borrowing cheap, generally positive public sentiment toward tech, light regulation, and valuable government contracts. But all those were at risk, and the cultural and political terrain had moved underneath them in a way that had become intolerable.

Musk's fear of a "woke mind virus," which initially seemed like some kind of dorm-room joke, turned out to be quite real. In Black Lives Matter protests and college encampments in support of Gaza, he and other billionaires who claimed to identify as socially liberal saw a form of progressive politics threatening the familiar sociopolitical order.

Some billionaires expressed personal resentment against Covid-19 quarantine measures, which were cast as an extension of the bureaucratic, nanny-state, professional-managerial class politics so despised by people like billionaire venture capitalist Marc Andreessen and Vivek Ramaswamy. They bridled at not being allowed to run their businesses—and their employees' lives—as they liked, even during a major pandemic.

Throughout the spring and summer of 2020, Musk battled with California politicians and health officials over reopening his Fremont Tesla factory, which was closed to mitigate the spread of Covid. On March 19, 2020, Musk, who had said that "the coronavirus panic is dumb," predicted that Covid would be gone by the end of April. He wrote that "kids are essentially immune" and that Tesla was making ventilators, "though I think there will not be a shortage by the time we can make enough to matter."[4] Instead of furnishing actual ventilators, he bought 1,000 BiPAP and CPAP machines for hospitals while Tesla's ventilator design never graduated beyond a prototype.[5]

As Covid cases climbed, Alameda County kept the Fremont factory running at minimal staffing levels while Musk fumed. In late April, when Texas, which was increasingly becoming a center of Musk's operations, announced that it would be lifting some lockdown restrictions, Musk celebrated. "Give people their freedom back!" he wrote, complaining that quarantine measures had "put everyone under de facto house arrest."[6] On May 9, Musk announced that he was moving Tesla's operations to Nevada and Texas and would sue Alameda County health officials.[7] "If we even retain Fremont manufacturing activity at all, it will depend on how Tesla is treated in the future," wrote Musk. Two days later, he said he would reopen the Fremont factory anyway, daring public health officials to do something. "I will be on the line with everyone else," he wrote. "If anyone is arrested, I ask that it only be me."[8] Within days, Alameda County approved Tesla's plan to reopen the Fremont factory.[9]

Other business leaders felt the financial sting of Covid policies: work-from-home politics led to a decline of the commercial real-estate market, which was rationalized as another signifier of Democratic dysfunction, especially in San Francisco. David Sacks, whose Craft Ventures firm had invested in several real-estate-related startups, mused about the toll work-from-home policies and elevated interest rates were taking on the property market. After an investor posted lamenting the state of San Francisco and Portland's office markets, Sacks responded, "Working hypothesis: the magnitude of CRE collapse in a city is proportional to how progressive that city is. Thoughts?"[10]

These were some of the material and cultural antecedents for a political shift that was moving from billionaires' angry social-media posts to actually being expressed through the more forceful language of six-figure donations, recall elections, public demagoguery, and political favor-trading.

But there was an even bigger transformative force coursing through Silicon Valley: the opportunity to become a paid-up member of the defense-industrial complex, building surveillance tools, databases, and weapons for the biggest military on Earth. It would prove tremendously lucrative while connecting tech leaders to the highest levels of political power. It would also further catalyze an authoritarian shift that was years in the making.

3

Tech Libertarians Embrace the Security State

This new political reality didn't start with Elon Musk or Peter Thiel or the 2016 election. Beyond the personal computer and smartphones, the history of Silicon Valley is just as much the history of the Cold War defense industrial base, from radar research to early microchips in Minuteman missiles to the CIA's own investments, via its In-Q-Tel VC firm, in startups like Palantir and Keyhole, which eventually became Google Maps. All of that is deeply political, often tied up in nationalistic, militarist policies and, by extension, moral choices about how our society props up war profiteers.

President George W. Bush's global war on terror brought some tech companies, especially those specializing in telecoms, surveillance, and data analysis, deeper into the lucrative national-security embrace. The war on terror also generated a stunning list of scandals and abuses as the Bush administration began prosecuting an unbounded, global war against an amorphous enemy abroad and established a massive, indiscriminate surveillance apparatus at home. That required the cooperation—sometimes voluntary, sometimes compelled—of powerful players in tech. But it brought potential legal liability. On July 10, 2008, President Bush signed a law retroactively granting immunity to telecoms companies that assisted the government in its warrantless wiretapping program.

With the stroke of a pen, Bush validated years of lawless surveillance and assured future corporate collaborators that they probably had little to fear by yielding to the coercion of a government on a permanent war-footing. The message seemed clear: if they broke the law in the service of fulfilling US policy, then they would be taken care of.

If they didn't play ball, they might end up like Joseph Nacchio, the former CEO of Qwest, a large telecommunications company. According to Nacchio, in February 2001, National Security Agency representatives asked Qwest to cooperate with a wiretapping program that allowed the NSA to siphon data from company cables transmitting internet communications and phone calls. Qwest refused to cooperate without a court order. The company lost a government contract, said Nacchio. Four years later, Nacchio was indicted on insider trading charges and convicted on 19 counts, receiving a sentence of six years in federal prison. Nacchio claimed that his prosecution was retaliation for not cooperating with the NSA.

During Barack Obama's presidency, the growing union between tech and the security state became defined by a revolving door of personnel, industry-friendly policy, and the singular example of Eric Schmidt, who worked as Google's CEO and later its chairman. More than any other tech leader, the mild-mannered engineer turned CEO positioned himself as a political operator thinking on a global scale—writing books with Henry Kissinger and former State Department official Jared Cohen, influencing tech policy, forming deep relationships with the Obama White House, investing in lethal drone companies and data analytics startups that worked for political campaigns he supported. The Tech Transparency Project (TTP), an industry watchdog group, called Schmidt "Obama's chief corporate ally." Writing in 2016, TTP summarized the relationship: "Eric Schmidt has enjoyed virtual open-door access to the White House during the Obama administration, records show, meeting with the US president and top White House officials on at least 18 separate occasions from 2009 to 2015, not counting large meetings and social events like state dinners."[1] His access would also extend to the Biden administration, with which he consulted on AI policy.

Schmidt demonstrated a comfort with the US as a global military power—a power increasingly reliant on digital surveillance, data analysis, cyberattacks, drones, special-operations forces, and targeted assassinations. With his professional network, startup investments, and political activities, Schmidt developed a "unique position as a link between the tech industry and the Pentagon," according to *Wired*.[2] Schmidt was the first chair of the Defense Innovation Board, a new DoD advisory organization established in 2016. He served on government advisory groups for NASA, AI, and biotechnology policy. He created a think tank called the Special Competitive Studies Project (SCSP) and loaded its board with prominent Department of Defense officials like Michèle Flournoy and Robert O. Work. The SCSP published reports and policy recommendations urging government officials to leverage AI for military purposes and to "beat China"—the kind of vague but seemingly urgent goal that can drive billions in tech and military spending, potentially enriching companies in which Schmidt was an investor. "We are in a decisive decade of military competition with China," an SCSP official wrote in 2023. "Generative AI should be used to help invalidate the PLA's investments, increase their uncertainty, reduce risk, and ultimately, help prevent conflict."[3]

While nominally a liberal, Schmidt's politics, like many of the tech leaders discussed in this book, are better understood along the axes of authoritarianism and the fusion of corporate and state power. Along with supporting Democrats, Schmidt made substantial donations to Republican organizations and politicians. Some of his ideological preferences may not neatly line up with Thiel, Musk, or the other moguls discussed here, though like them, he thinks the tech industry should help ensure that the US remains the world's preeminent military power. And like many in the Valley, he appears to think that the tech industry should be unfettered by regulation, left to innovate to its delight.

"Why don't we wait until something bad happens and then we can figure out how to regulate it?" Schmidt remarked about AI.[4]

He said that humanity's only hope for stymieing climate change was a breakneck pursuit of AGI, or artificial general intelligence, a greater-than-human intelligence that will be able, somehow, to solve the problem for us.

Schmidt represented a Silicon Valley variant of an increasingly prominent type: the politically connected defense contractor, comfortable with the broad exercise of US power, seeking to form deeper relationships between tech startups and the security state. Like the right-wing executives who straddle the increasingly connected domains of Silicon Valley and the US military, Schmidt was zealous about confronting China—and an advocate for making Silicon Valley a profit-making partner in that competition. "In many ways," *Politico* noted, "Schmidt paved the way for Silicon Valley hawks to come roost in DC."[5]

Not all Silicon Valley hawks were the same. Some liked to show off their plumage a little more fiercely—like Alex Karp, the CEO of Palantir, the data analytics startup, who we have seen managed to snag a seat at Trump's table thanks to his business connection with Peter Thiel. (It probably didn't hurt that the CIA was also a Palantir investor and customer.) Karp had endeared himself to some journalists for his offbeat intellectual history (before becoming CEO of an intelligence contractor, he studied with the German philosopher Jürgen Habermas), his shock of wild silver and black curls that gave him a resemblance to the filmmaker Taika Waititi, and his ability to riff in fulsome terms about the profound importance of ensuring continued American global hegemony or personally droning his enemies.[6] Confident, jingoistic, even belligerent, Karp was a regular on TV and the elite business conference circuit (Sun Valley, the World Economic Forum, etc.), and he had proven highly quotable.

Like many CEOs of publicly traded companies, Karp hated short sellers, who bet against a company's stock price, hoping to profit from its fall. After Palantir's stock spiked in March 2024—potentially causing some short sellers to lose money—Karp was exultant. "Almost nothing makes a human happier than taking the lines of cocaine away from these short sellers," said Karp in a

CNBC appearance. "The best thing that could happen to them is we will lead their coke dealers to their homes after they can't pay their bills."[7]

In May 2024, Karp was a featured guest at the Hill and Valley Forum, a private meeting on Capitol Hill for tech luminaries and lawmakers to talk about defense issues. In the years since that 2016 meeting at Trump Tower, Palantir had accrued major defense contracts, received hundreds of millions of dollars to run a data platform for Britain's National Health Service, and sold technology used in the wars in Gaza and Ukraine. Karp claimed that 20 percent of US hospitals were using its software.[8] Palantir was by then a publicly traded company with a market capitalization of almost $50 billion dollars—about the size of the retailer Adidas or the oil company Hess. Its success had catalyzed a consequential shift in Silicon Valley culture and investment: working on behalf of an intelligence agency or an illiberal foreign ally like Israel was no longer something forbidden or done quietly. In a few short years, "defense tech" had become a hot new investment sector. (Palantir's business would continue to soar: a year after this meeting, its market cap had risen to about $267 billion.)

At the Hill and Valley Forum, surrounded by influential tech leaders and high-level government officials, Karp was in his element, riffing about violently punishing his enemies. "I historically have been one that would rage against Silicon Valley venture people," said Karp. "And I had all sorts of fantasies of using drone-enabled technology to exact revenge—especially targeted—in violation of all norms."[9]

Karp said that student protests against Israel's war in Gaza were "pagan," "unforgivable," and "incomprehensible."[10] He suggested that protesters should be sent to North Korea and forced to eat tree bark. The theatrics seemed like an authentic reflection of Karp's worldview. But far from provoking any controversy, his remarks were welcomed as eccentric reflections from a maverick chief executive.

Karp spoke onstage opposite Jacob Helberg, whose official job title was advisor to Palantir's CEO—that is, to Karp. In practice,

Helberg's remit seemed far larger than Palantir. He had organized the Hill and Valley Forum. A former policy lead at Google, he had held positions at top think tanks and published a book about geopolitical strategy and technological competition. Former President Bill Clinton blurbed it, along with members of Congress. An unapologetic China hawk, Helberg was credited with being a leading influence behind the legislative effort to ban TikTok (or induce its sale). He described himself as a disenchanted Democrat, and by spring 2024, he had emerged as a full-throated Trump supporter. Helberg's transformation was described in a *Washington Post* profile that highlighted his $1 million donation to Trump's campaign.[11] (Helberg touted the article on X.) Like Peter Thiel, Helberg was a Stanford graduate. He was married to the venture capitalist Keith Rabois, one of Thiel's Stanford buddies, who had recently left a position at Thiel's Founders Fund.

The event was supposed to be nonpartisan, but Helberg had a surprise for his audience: a short pre-recorded video from Donald Trump. The video opened with Trump thanking Helberg by name, followed by a reference to a private meeting the two had in Mar-a-Lago. "Our meeting was very productive, talking about AI and all of the ramifications—both good and bad," said Trump.[12] The video was practically substance-free, but its existence offered a crisp example of the growing alignment between Trump and militaristic tech executives. And it was a direct endorsement of Helberg's rising position in the Silicon Valley-meets-MAGA power structure.

Despite the Trump cameo and the political alignment of the event's organizers, the Hill and Valley Forum attracted a bipartisan crowd of senators. The increasingly symbiotic relationship between Silicon Valley and the defense establishment that began under Bush and became codified under Obama had survived the rigors of Trump's shambolic rule—and might benefit from his return to power. Under President Joe Biden, the tech industry and the US government were arguably closer than ever, though their policy preferences diverged on antitrust matters. But on core issues of national defense and the tech industry's role in it, there was little daylight between the two sides. The Biden administration had also dispensed billions of dollars in subsidies for companies like Intel to build semiconductor factories in the United States, a level of industrial capacity the country desperately needed. Still, for some in Silicon Valley, the lucrative status quo wasn't good enough.

The shifting political conditions could be usefully observed in how an industry titan like Google dealt with matters of war and peace. In 2018, after an outburst of employee protest, Google announced that it wouldn't renew a contract with the Department of Defense for Project Maven, an initiative to use artificial-intelligence tools to analyze images and video for potential targets for air strikes. The decision was seen by some as a tech company taking a moral stand, or at least offering a sop to the 4,000 Google employees who signed a petition against the program. At the time, Project Maven was bringing in less than $15 million. Pennies for Google.

Google's sensitivity to the ethics of military contracting work dissipated quickly. It won awards for other contracts from government agencies. In December 2022, along with Amazon, Microsoft, and Oracle, Google received a piece of a fiercely contested, $9 billion DoD cloud-computing contract. In April 2024, Google received government authorization to store top-secret information, expanding the range of services it could offer to intelligence agencies and the DoD. Its cloud division created a sales page—"Solutions for Department of Defense"—that offered everything from machine-learning tools to AI document processing to cybersecurity protection. "Since our early years Google has partnered with the U.S. government," the site read.[13]

By spring 2024, as the IDF razed much of Gaza and killed tens of thousands of Palestinian people, Google had hardened its policy toward employee protest. In public statements, Google focused on its work for Israeli civilian institutions. But as *Time* magazine reported, Google had a cloud-computing contract with the Israeli government, including with the country's Ministry of Defense, which had expanded its use of the company's technical resources after the Hamas attacks on October 7, 2023.[14] Other reporters found that Amazon and Google provided services to Israeli weapons manufacturers and to an entity dedicated to expanding illegal settlements in the West Bank.[15]

When a few dozen employees staged sit-ins protesting Google's work for Israel, they were removed by company security and immediately fired, as were some other organizers and supporters. Google eventually fired 50 employees for speaking out against the company's work for the Israeli government.[16]

The political environment had changed dramatically since the Project Maven protest. Large tech companies marketed themselves like utopian college campuses but governed themselves as ruthless surveillance states with offices devoted to tracking potential "insider threats." In tandem, the American college campus was also losing its sheen, returning to an era of 1970s-like tumult, with violent police crackdowns against students protesting Israel's war in Gaza. As with public political protest in many US cities, the space for acceptable dissent had shrunk, becoming highly monitored, policed, bureaucratized—neutered. The workplace was no different.

In tech, as in any large industry, truly countercultural expression tended to be rare or quickly metabolized by corporate concerns. Or, as in Apple's famous George Orwell-inspired ad from 1984 and its longtime slogan of "Think Different," a sense of rebellion was reconstituted as a pledge of brand loyalty. Think different. Buy Apple products.

If tech's leaders, then, reflected some kind of opposition to the establishment, it wasn't coming from a techno-hippie left. It increasingly was coming from a corporatist, techno-fascist right that was the natural ideological province of cosseted billionaires who once thought they could remake the world in their image, only to find that their proposed revolution received some unwelcome pushback from privacy and labor activists, regulators, journalists, and people who simply did not buy into the proffered vision.

At the same time, a new generation of engineers, venture capitalists, managers, and executives openly embraced far-right and nationalistic politics that a few years earlier seemed to be rarely expressed in public. Trollish forums on 4chan, Reddit, and

Something Awful had helped engender a reactionary tendency that could border on nihilism. There were a lot of angry men displaying little ability to process, or usefully direct, their grievances. On social-media platforms like X, their histrionic provocations—women shouldn't work or vote; race science and genetic differences in IQ are real; Covid-19 vaccines don't work—produced dopamine hits of engagement and attracted an audience who shared their politics of resentment. It was less about truth-seeking than wanton destruction. Their rebellion was against a status quo they resented as woke, censorious, and judgmental.

They liked the US military and the CIA, and had no interest in morally equivocating over working for them. They were often indifferent about Russia, which they saw as a doddering power brutishly guarding its interests in Ukraine, but not really an immediate threat. They were deeply concerned about China, which they saw as an inchoate technological and military powerhouse bent on exporting its totalitarian vision of governance.

China policy tended to unite hawks from across the political spectrum. The US government was deep into a years-long trade war focused on denying China access to the most advanced semiconductor technology and manufacturing systems, and the blunt language of tariffs resonated with Donald Trump. At the same time, TSMC, the world's most important semiconductor manufacturer, was based in Taiwan, about 100 miles from the Chinese mainland. While the chip industry had a major presence in Japan, South Korea, and other countries, TSMC had become a fixation for China hawks who seemed almost excited by a possible war. In May 2023, Democratic representative Seth Moulton suggested that the US could blow up TSMC if Chinese forces invaded the island. "Of course, the Taiwanese really don't like this idea," said Moulton, who explained that the bombing plan had become a real question debated by policymakers.[17]

Elbridge Colby thought it was a good idea. A former intelligence official who had held positions in the George W. Bush and Trump administrations, Colby had become a prominent Beltway China hawk, speaking at national-security conferences, issuing strategy papers, and touting the threat of China on social media—sometimes in conversation with his counterparts in the tech industry, who would support his presidential appointment to a Defense Department position in Trump's second term. "Disabling or destroying TSMC is table stakes if China is taking over Taiwan," Elbridge once posted.[18] After Moulton mused about bombing TSMC, Colby posted that the congressman was right. A pseudonymous account replied to Colby saying that such a serious decision should be left to the government of Taiwan. "Sorry but that's not just a Taiwanese decision," said Colby. "Far too important for the rest of us."[19]

These beliefs were always part of the Silicon Valley substrate, but now they emerged as an essential part of the structure. They became reflected in op-eds, political donations, investment decisions, and social-media posts. Electoral victories can legitimize any belief system, and it was no longer unusual to see MAGA-aligned software engineers and top venture capitalists stumping for the tech industry to elevate its role in the military-industrial complex.

During this period, Silicon Valley also saw the creation of startups explicitly designed to do military and intelligence work. Palantir, with its proudly jingoistic CEO, had paved the way. Palantir and its backers at Peter Thiel's Founders Fund helped spawn Anduril Industries, a military-minded startup founded by five young tech entrepreneurs (which, like many Thiel-connected ventures, took its name from the fantasy series *The Lord of the Rings*). Working off the idea that the next Raytheon should be a tech startup, Anduril aimed to compete with the big "prime" defense contractors. At first, the company said it wouldn't build lethal weapons; that would change.

One of Anduril's co-founders was Palmer Luckey, who created the Oculus VR headset and sold the company to Facebook for $2 billion. Luckey was also one of the tech industry's most prominent Trump supporters. In 2017, Luckey left Facebook, claiming that he was forced out due to his support of Donald Trump. Some of his Facebook and venture-capitalist colleagues would later publicly apologize for not doing enough to prevent his Facebook ouster. In interviews, Luckey described the affair as a defining experience, generating an almost inexhaustible well of rage that would drive him for years.

Luckey became Anduril's co-founder and CTO. He started to tout a future of overwhelmingly powerful, American-made weapons that would dissuade the country's enemies from acting against it. Peace through fear of immediate annihilation. With his penchant for Hawaiian shirts, a distinctive chin scrub of facial hair, and a proudly militaristic attitude, he became the face of the company. He also became one of the faces of a new kind of Silicon Valley nationalism, where making weapons was cool because America was righteous and worth defending, and overwhelming strength and technological might were seen as more effective than diplomacy.

"Societies have always needed a warrior class that is enthused and excited about enacting violence on others in pursuit of good aims," Luckey told an audience at Pepperdine University. "You need people like me who are sick in that way and who don't lose any sleep making tools of violence in order to preserve freedom."[20]

Brash chauvinism was part of Luckey's pitch. "When we started Anduril, it wasn't just about the United States. It was explicitly around defending the west, and you know I think that even goes back to the name of the company," he told an interviewer from Founders Fund, an Anduril investor. Anduril, which meant "Flame of the West" in Tolkien's Elvish language, was Aragorn's sword, the hero's Excalibur. Luckey continued in his tone of manifest destiny: "We wanted to take this position that, you know, countries aren't just different, that there are countries that are better or worse, that we were going to be on the sides of the ones that were better, as determined by the handful of values that still remain true between those countries today."[21]

The cohort of millennial and Gen Z founders who pushed this simplistic, might-makes-right ideology had come of age in a country engaged in a seemingly endless and unbounded global war on terror. They played *Counter-Strike* and *Call of Duty* while the government issued color-coded daily terror alerts and Vice President Dick Cheney talked ominously about the need to work in the shadows. For many, it was a dark time as the global hegemon showed a corrupt appetite for militarism, domestic authoritarianism, torture, indefinite detention, mass surveillance, and drone warfare. The moral and strategic failures of the war on terror and the war in Iraq were object lessons in imperial hubris. For Palmer Luckey and his tech peers, they inspired business ideas.

Another notable hawk raising his voice was Luckey's Anduril co-founder Trae Stephens, who began his career working for an unnamed US intelligence agency. (He refused to disclose which one.) From there Stephens moved to the private sector, working as an analyst at Palantir before becoming a partner at Thiel's Founders Fund. After Trump was elected in 2016, Stephens advised his transition team on Department of Defense appointments.[22] As a tech investor, Stephens embraced the defense industry in a way few venture capitalists had. The tech publication *Newcomer* described Stephens as the person "who's done as much as anyone to bring military technology into the venture capital mainstream."[23]

In 2023, the VC firm Andreessen Horowitz (aka a16z) gave this nascent ideology of tech-inflected nationalism a name: American Dynamism. Andreessen Horowitz established an investment fund under that moniker, loaded it up with $600 million, and announced that its new fund represented a formalized effort to put defense contracting—and the overall "national interest"—at the forefront of the firm's investment decisions.

It wasn't just a16z and Founders Fund backing military contractors. The industry bloomed with defense startups and VC funds devoted to nurturing them. "Defense tech" became a promising new investment category—and a conduit for former intelligence officers, generals, and government officials to enter Silicon Valley.

The Defense Department established an office in the Valley. By the end of the Trump administration, there was hardly a major tech company that wasn't drinking from the spigot of government contracts. The FBI used a facial-recognition tool from Amazon. Salesforce provided cloud services for the Border Patrol. Microsoft was building mixed-reality goggles for the US Army, though that just scratched the surface of its government work. In 2020, the researcher Jack Poulson found that Microsoft had accrued "more than 5,000 subcontracts with the Department of Defense and various federal law enforcement agencies since 2016."[24] By subcontracting projects, tech companies could better conceal military work from the public and from their own employees.

In this new paradigm, where tech moguls' abundant self-regard met the military's bias for violence, unvarnished jingoism was practically an asset. It got Palantir CEO Alex Karp to the halls of Congress, and it made his advisor Jacob Helberg a leader in the war against TikTok. Helberg had a like-minded colleague in Josh Wolfe, a co-founder of Lux Capital, who said that China was using TikTok as a "mind control" weapon.[25] (Wolfe also suggested that Gaza solidarity protests were funded by the Chinese Communist Party.)[26]

You'd have to search hard to find liberal countervailing forces in Silicon Valley. Some de rigueur donations to the Democratic Party didn't seem to suffice—not when progressive activism at tech companies got employees summarily terminated. Tech's authoritarian instincts had become essentially bipartisan.

The tech industry saw occasional labor agitation but few examples of successful union drives. In 2022, hundreds of employees at Activision, a video game company owned by Microsoft, unionized. Some cafeteria workers, security guards, and other low-wage workers who helped furnish the luxuries for well-paid engineers and product managers belonged to unions. For some time, the largest tech union was the Times Tech Guild, which represented more than 500 tech workers at the *New York Times*.

There have been notable examples of tech workers speaking out against contracting for the DoD and the Border Patrol, particularly under President Donald Trump. Campaigns like #TechWontBuildIt and #NoTechForICE helped highlight the role of large-tech concerns in supplying the digital infrastructure that powered the country's deportation machine. But they did not dissuade tech companies from working on these systems. And for workers at these companies, any form of protest became a risk to their careers.

In 2017, I spent a couple of afternoons with some activist friends outside a Palantir office in Manhattan's West Village, handing out leaflets explaining that the nearby glass-walled office housed a cutting-edge software company providing tools to help apprehend and deport people, as part of Trump's pledge to cleanse the country of undocumented migrants. It was New York City, so most passersby threaded their way around us as if we were part of the scenery. A van arrived with the day's lunches for Palantir's employees. A security guard filmed us with his phone from inside the office building. Someone I went to college with, now a fintech startup founder, happened to walk by. I hadn't seen him in years. I mentioned what I was doing. "That's so funny," he said, laughing, before moving on. He didn't take a leaflet.

4

The Digital Authoritarian Style

There are many proper nouns in this book, and you may be wondering who some of these people are and why I'm insisting on the importance of a bunch of ornery California billionaires to the future of democracy. It's okay if some of these names and companies run together. They're less important as individuals than as representatives of a rising sociopolitical class of venture capitalists and financiers. On core matters, their fortunes are linked: they're friends, they invest in the same companies, they donate to the same political candidates, they party together on private islands where visitors have to sign NDAs. Theirs is a small, exclusive club. If you can't tell some of them apart, remember that it's what they do, and where their money goes, that matters most. This book is a group biography with a shifting cast of characters, but they are all headed in the same troubling direction.

We are dealing with a certain type of personality, whose authoritarian beliefs and interests align with his nearly socially identical friends and business partners. (Women are typically underrepresented at this echelon of the tech-finance power structure.) Three of the key figures in this book—Elon Musk, Peter Thiel, and David Sacks—spent parts of their youth in apartheid South Africa, where they belonged to the privileged white minority in one of the most racist, socially engineered societies ever conceived.[1]

Ultimately this is a story about class involving people who, since they stand atop the economic pyramid, don't wish to acknowledge its existence. This became practically a tic for Elon Musk, who despite his incredible wealth, adopted the same mantle of false populism worn by Donald Trump and other social-media-addicted billionaires. They may have had unbelievable sums of money, we were told, but they shared common people's resentments. And while they had seen the rot consuming their fellow elites and every marble-floored institution they'd passed through, these dissident billionaires claimed to have nothing to do with that corruption. They were here to infiltrate and overthrow it, just as we might have been. That's how someone like Vivek Ramaswamy could receive a fellowship from George Soros while later denouncing him,[2] or how Ramaswamy could have business dealings in China while politicking as an extreme China hawk, suggesting that the US provide guns to every civilian in Taiwan.

Extreme wealth becomes ennobling, affording these populist moguls a supposed immunity to the corruptions surrounding them. They are portrayed as class traitors, funneling truths about the deep state and power elite via Fox News and X to the MAGA masses. But their supposed betrayal of their peers is performative, never material. They won't actually give up their wealth for the common good. They'll dedicate their enormous resources to projects that they control—a politically influential foundation, perhaps, or a quixotic plan to travel to Mars. They will sell the venture to the public under the mantle of charity, civic progress, or as Musk called it, "extending the light of consciousness" to the red planet.[3]

According to one line that quickly calcified into cliche, people like Trump and Musk were actually so rich that they couldn't be bought. For those who believed it, it was a heartbreakingly naive analysis, when the obvious truth was that these men had acquired their tremendous wealth precisely because they put their monetary interests and will to power at the forefront of every pursuit. That's how they got to where they were (often with a big boost from inherited wealth). But we were repeatedly told by people who handed out NDAs like breath mints that they were pretty much just like us. They believed in free speech. They didn't seek dominion over anyone.

"I disagree with the idea of unions," Musk once said. "I just don't like anything which creates a lords and peasants kind of thing."[4]

Given the well-chronicled record of Musk imposing brutal work schedules and firing subordinates (one happened publicly on Twitter), this proposition of an egalitarian Musk was hard to take seriously.[5,6,7] In 2023, the Equal Employment Opportunity Commission sued Tesla, claiming that it "violated federal law by tolerating widespread and ongoing racial harassment of its Black employees and by subjecting some of these workers to retaliation for opposing the harassment."[8] The following year, Tesla settled a lawsuit with a former employee over claims of racial discrimination.

The billionaire CEO who didn't like "a lords and peasants kind of thing" gave himself the title of Tesla's Technoking and fought for a $50 billion-plus pay package. Tesla fought unionization efforts at factories in California and New York. The National Labor Relations Board (NLRB) charged that the company used illegal union-busting tactics. Its relationships with European unions were similarly adversarial.

Musk responded to the NLRB's enforcement action against Tesla through one of his other companies. SpaceX sued the NLRB, challenging the constitutional basis of its in-house courts and its very ability to act as a labor regulator.

By every conceivable measure, Musk stood against "the peasants." And yet, like any insecure sovereign, he needed their adulation, as he also demonstrated on X. Musk's billionaire-nerd populist act played well for a certain audience, but it disappeared when there was anything substantive at stake. In practical terms, Musk acted as an authoritarian confident of his power.

But he was not alone.

We have already briefly met Marc Andreessen—a pioneer of the web browser, Netscape founder, Facebook board member, and a top venture capitalist. He was Silicon Valley royalty, personally worth an estimated $1.7 billion. His wife, Laura Arrillaga-Andreessen, was the daughter of John Arrillaga Sr., a property developer who made billions developing office parks for tech companies and later donated $151 million to Stanford University. Arrillaga's name was all over Stanford's campus. Andreessen's eponymous venture capital firm, Andreessen Horowitz, also known as a16z, controlled billions in capital and became a major force in guiding the next generation of influential startups. Regularly lionized as a titan of the tech-mogul class, both an OG innovator and an astute investor, Andreessen helped to lead the Web 3 charge as his firm plunked down billions on crypto companies during the ZIRP years. While the 2022 crypto bubble burst, taking crypto prices and dozens of companies like FTX down with it, a16z profited. When crypto markets seemingly rose from the grave in 2024, as the crypto industry became an influential player in the US presidential election, a16z was right there, ready to benefit. Andreessen Horowitz would also supply a number of high-level appointees to the second Trump administration.

Once a year or so, Andreessen published a new manifesto about how only the heroic technology industry could revive American prosperity and greatness, whether through the wonders of Web 3 or by embracing defense contracting. The manifestos were animated by an extreme faith in markets and innovation and a blistering resentment for critics of any kind, who weren't considered "builders," a word that Silicon Valley treated with the kind of reverence also afforded to "founders." In October 2023, Andreessen published what he called "The Techno-Optimist Manifesto," in which he wrote, "Our enemy is the ivory tower, the know-it-all credentialed expert worldview, indulging in abstract theories, luxury beliefs, social engineering, disconnected from the real world, delusional, unelected, and unaccountable—playing God with everyone else's lives, with total insulation from the consequences."

Andreessen didn't consider that the archetype he most despised—unelected technocrats remaking the world in their image from a luxurious hilltop redoubt—might have been an accurate description of Silicon Valley venture capitalists.

Andreessen seemed to live well. In a period of about six months, he spent $255 million on three mansions in Malibu. He also owned a $33 million estate in Atherton, California, where he and a number of other wealthy tech professionals opposed a plan to build multi-family homes, which would have helped ease the city's housing crunch.[9] He ticked some of the tech-celebrity popularity criteria: a million social-media followers, a regular on the conference and speaking circuit, a member of the Internet Hall of Fame. He had the ear of fellow billionaires like Elon Musk. He had donated hundreds of thousands of dollars to Democrats and Republicans, and would donate millions more to pro-Trump and pro-crypto PACs in 2024. Andreessen was a big deal—a tech, business, and political power player—by any metric.

For Andreessen, it didn't seem to matter all that much. This putative titan of industry argued that he and his fellow billionaires were less powerful than one might think. In fact, they might not even count as "elites," that most hallowed signifier of political and economic influence. "The elite ruling class in our society is based on power, way more than money," Andreessen posted on X. "Our oligarchic elite ruling class freaks out about Elon precisely to the degree they think he's not onboard with their program."

Musk was America's leading oligarch, but Andreessen didn't care to recognize that.

In subsequent posts, Andreessen attempted to position himself as a member of the professional-managerial class, or PMC, a swath of middle- and upper-class corporate paper pushers who occupied their own politically anemic, if decently lucrative, position in the societal power structure. Andreessen saw himself as belonging to this separate class, one that reinforced his narrative of victimization. He posted a series of quotations, links, and comments on various PMC theorists and his own interpretations of where a billionaire venture capitalist might fit into this arrangement. Quoting everyone from George Orwell to James Burnham, the author of *The Managerial Revolution*, Andreessen held court online with a retinue of followers willing to engage with the idea that his sociopolitical role did not differ much from that of, say, a highly successful corporate lawyer.

Since the 1970s, said Andreessen, "the PMC has eaten up most of the power and most of the money in our society while feeling rebellious and aggrieved the entire time."[10] Asked how he, a billionaire VC, could be a member of anything but the capitalist class, Andreessen responded, "Ah! But most of the capital I speak for is not my own," referring to the institutional backers, like Saudi Arabia's sovereign wealth fund, which poured billions of dollars into Andreessen Horowitz's coffers. "That is what makes my current role classic PMC."[11]

It's useful to step back and examine the move he was attempting here. Andreessen was basically hawking an upmarket version of Trumpian populism. It was the same "I'm not like the other elites" brand of dissent honed for years on Fox News by Tucker Carlson, an heir to the Swanson Frozen Foods fortune who at the time was pulling down an eight-figure cable news salary. In this vision, real power dwelled with *them*—some other, possibly hidden power elite, be they woke progressives letting San Francisco fall to pieces or the menacing globalists of Trumpist lore or the destitute migrants coming over the border. It was all the same. The incredibly rich, well-connected guy talking to you, the one who might have helped create the very interface through which you were consuming his thoughts, was actually pretty powerless, culturally marginal, easily canceled. Same went for the billionaire ex-president, unfairly kicked off Twitter before having his megaphone restored by a sympathetic owner.

Andreessen would hardly be the first billionaire to claim he was somehow powerless or even persecuted. In 2014, Tom Perkins, a billionaire co-founder of Kleiner Perkins, a major VC firm, compared San Francisco's treatment of the rich to an early episode in Nazi Germany's genocide of the Jewish people. In a letter to the editor of the *Wall Street Journal*, he wrote, "Kristallnacht was unthinkable in 1930; is its descendant 'progressive' radicalism unthinkable now?"[12] Given a chance to walk back his comments, Perkins apologized for the Kristallnacht reference but stood by the Nazi comparison. At the time, Andreessen denounced Perkins, who died two years later, calling him an industry relic who was also "the leading asshole in the state."[13]

But like Perkins, Andreessen and Musk seem to lack much political perspective—that is, if we were to take them at their word. It simply goes against any reasonable notion of what power means that the richest man in the world, who was able to get to the captain's seat of a major communications platform, was not counted as a member of the "oligarchic elite ruling class." Musk's wealth was built on billions of dollars in government subsidies and contracts. His corporate decisions influenced the war in Ukraine. His every utterance had the potential to move markets and make headlines. That was power.

Andreessen's anti-PMC riffs might have seemed a little academic, but they reflected a line of thinking that bled into wider political discourse. In his run for the Republican nomination, Vivek Ramaswamy repeatedly railed against an administrative state that he said was ruining the country and acting like "a wet blanket on the economy."[14] Were he elected, Ramaswamy promised, he would immediately fire a million federal employees—with little regard, it seemed, for what government employees actually did or the variety of often essential roles they filled, from food inspectors to meteorologists. This was, somehow, part of Ramaswamy's populist promise: putting a million middle-income government workers out of a job was a good thing. Moreover, its goodness was taken as practically a given. Why *wouldn't* you want to fire a bunch of "government bureaucrats"? They had it coming. This would actually happen later under 'DOGE'.

"The real divide isn't black vs. White or even Democrat vs. Republican," Ramaswamy posted on January 21, 2024. "It's the managerial class vs. the everyday citizen."[15]

I admit that I found this post hilarious because I had been directly hired and fired by Ramaswamy. For two months at Roivant, he was my manager. He also had his own fortune of hundreds of millions of dollars. No shift in attitude could make him an "everyday citizen."

Ramaswamy's post was widely re-shared, receiving more than 2.4 million views. Of course, only one person's attention really mattered, and the biotech mogul turned political firebrand got it. The top reply to the post was from Elon Musk, who had this to say: "True."

Fiery political-media operative Andrew Breitbart was famously devoted to the idea that "politics is downstream of culture." Political influence flowed from pop-cultural ubiquity and popularity; it was necessary to seize control of the zeitgeist. A decade-plus later, feeling that they had lost the culture—that a slippery wokeness had infiltrated corporate life, that not everyone on X wanted to genuflect before them, that some people wanted them to pay more taxes, that public reputation couldn't be easily stage-managed—some billionaires adopted a false modesty that bordered on self-pity. As Andreessen described the members of the PMC, they were "aggrieved" that they were not properly recognized and appreciated. It was not enough that they had accumulated vast wealth and the resources to enact their authoritarian dreams. They wanted to be recognized as builders, as great capitalists contributing to History through their visionary work.

The vision was paltry, as exemplified by Andreessen Horowitz's lucrative but socially regressive investments in crypto exchanges, NFT markets, digital-ape collectibles, and other forms of Web 3-enabled gambling and speculation. It was a bit of a fall from helping invent the web browser, which Andreessen did decades earlier while working at a public university.[16]

If billionaires weren't elites, or if managers and stewards of capital weren't much different from you and me, then real power distinctions wouldn't exist. But they still do. Most of us know what it is like to be on the receiving end of an impossible-to-fulfill edict from a capricious boss. Or maybe you have dealt with the knowledge that you don't have full control of your working life. Sometimes you have to show up for that 8 a.m. shift. Sometimes you get laid off when you've been a great employee. Corporations don't love us back, and power distinctions can't be wished away, which is why managers often aren't allowed in rank-and-file unions.

A general lack of class consciousness meant that some still subscribed to the fiction that a tech billionaire could be a populist threat to the establishment, just as Trump supposedly was. As a result, a range of political and cultural figures treated Musk's purchase of Twitter as some sort of righteous moment of outsiders crashing the corporate ball. In fact departed Twitter CEO Jack Dorsey was a leading influence in Musk's takeover bid, calling Musk "the singular solution I trust" to steward the company.[17] Borrowing billions from Middle Eastern sovereign wealth funds and Wall Street firms to finance his takeover (and receiving a $400 million investment from Andreessen Horowitz), Musk was in this way of thinking not an elite. He was the man challenging the establishment's censorious dominion over free speech and social media. "A whole giant edifice of preference falsification is wobbling," Andreessen wrote, "and all the right people are nervous."[18]

Projection, perhaps.

As a political ideology, this nascent movement lacked a name or a coherent program, but its corporatism and anti-wokeness produced a convenient alignment with the Republican Party, to which David Sacks had become a major donor. On economics, they were united—tax cuts for the rich, dismantling the regulatory state, and protectionism against an increasingly competitive Chinese tech sector.

Over the course of 2023, Sacks auditioned a series of Republicans, both on Twitter and at private fundraisers, as potential Biden challengers. (Some of his peers also gave money and promotional energy to Dean Phillips, an obscure Democratic congressman trying to challenge Biden.) First among them was Florida governor Ron DeSantis. Sacks then had political dalliances with Robert F. Kennedy Jr. and Vivek Ramaswamy, before settling on what by now seemed inevitable: a commitment to back Donald Trump. By late April 2024, political media was reporting that Sacks planned to host a fundraiser for Trump. He made it official on June 6 in a lengthy social-media post listing the reasons—foreign policy, the economy, the border—that he would support Trump.[19]

Sacks and Musk had been convening secret dinners to strategize against Biden. In attendance at one of them: Michael Milken, Steven Mnuchin, Rupert Murdoch, Peter Thiel, and Travis Kalanick. The group represented the alliance of bitterly anti-Biden tech billionaires and financiers coalescing behind Trump. Their combined fortunes would be a huge asset for Trump in the general election. So would the media assets at their disposal, which would soon include Twitter. Except, when they were done renovating it, the platform formerly known as Twitter, rechristened as X, would look and operate very differently. And they had big plans for it.

5

Killing Twitter, Building X

Elon Musk's decision to buy Twitter seemed impulsive and almost trollish, a rich guy buying another toy for his collection just to show he could. But he was acting in a familiar tradition—a multibillionaire making an aggressive play for an influential but slightly tarnished media asset that he happened to be personally obsessed with. Like Robert Maxwell's pursuit of the *New York Daily News* or Rupert Murdoch overpaying to pry the *Wall Street Journal* from the Bancroft family, Musk had to have it. In the process, he mobilized a potent tranche of public opinion, drawing on the culture-warring right. This particular media platform had already been an effective force in burnishing the very cult of personality that had boosted the stock price of Musk's prized company. It was also where he had clashed with regulators for writing posts that may have had similar market-manipulating effects. Taking over the entire platform was for him a no-brainer, at almost any price. If he decided to make it a more overtly political platform—dedicated to his interests—the payoff could be tremendous.

Musk's purchase of Twitter played out with all the drama and histrionics that had come to attend anything involving him. First it was a silent takeover, with Musk quietly accumulating a large ownership share of Twitter stock in early 2022. When Musk announced his intent to buy Twitter and take it private in April 2022, it became a spectacle—and a potentially disastrous one as Twitter's stock price declined and Musk realized he might have vastly overpaid for a politically important but financially unprofitable platform. Soon, Musk was trying to renege on the deal. Twitter sued Musk to force him to go through with the purchase at the agreed-upon price, which had started to seem like a great deal for Twitter's executive team, who would be paid handsomely to go away. Musk resisted and the suit went to court in Delaware. After the court released Musk's text messages with friends and colleagues who had been subpoenaed, he decided to drop his opposition to the deal he had initially agreed to, and went forward with the purchase. The deal was officially consummated in late October, relying on billions of dollars in debt. Twitter, the ostensible public square of social media, was now privately owned by Elon Musk and a raft of investors, some of whose identities were unknown.

In an attempt at humor, Musk posted a video of himself showing up at Twitter HQ carrying a porcelain sink with the caption "Entering Twitter HQ—let that sink in!" It was the first act of renovating Twitter in his image. Bringing in family members, trusted confidants, dozens of Tesla engineers, and executives from The Boring Company and SpaceX, Musk began mass firings and cutting costs to the bone. He boasted about sleeping at Twitter's office. In Trumpian fashion, Musk stiffed vendors, deciding that paying his bills had become optional. "Elon doesn't pay rent," one transition team member allegedly told a Twitter employee, according to one of the many lawsuits filed against Twitter in the wake of Musk's takeover. "Let them sue" was apparently a frequently invoked Musk mantra, and in the wake of his Twitter acquisition, more than two dozen companies did just that.[1] (Musk's alleged distaste for paying his bills seemed to extend to SpaceX, which had more than $2.5 million in liens filed against it in Texas by contractors who hadn't been paid.[2])

In frequent updates on Twitter, Musk portrayed his takeover as both a restoration of free-speech fundamentalism and a cleanup job. Musk soon found what he was looking for: he posted about finding a pile of T-shirts emblazoned with the hashtag "#staywoke," which had been made to support the Black Lives Matter movement. Former Twitter CEO Jack Dorsey once wore one.

In those early months of Musk's "hardcore Twitter," the new owner tweeted lots of bold, middle-of-the-night promises to his growing army of fans. It became participatory theater for Musk's audience, who seemed to think they had crashed the ball with him. (Admittedly, it also became a reliable font of material for journalists to mine for content.) He fired employees who criticized his chaotic management—publicly, on Twitter. He released caches of company emails to select journalists and activists, who, using the brand-friendly moniker The Twitter Files, dutifully posted about the censorship and government interference they allegedly revealed and which Musk was here to excise.

During this chaotic period, Musk relied on longtime advisors, venture capitalists, family members, and dozens of engineers and other staffers from his companies to implement his edicts, choose survivors, and pore over the Twitter code-base. Musk's "war room" was staffed by venture capitalists David Sacks, Jason Calacanis, Sriram Krishnan, and Antonio Gracias, lawyer Alex Spiro, and Musk family office manager Jared Birchall. Musk also drafted numerous employees of the companies in his vast portfolio—supposedly as volunteers—but their identities were largely unknown.

A list of names subpoenaed in a case brought by six ex-Twitter employees who left or were fired after Musk's takeover offers a better picture of who, exactly, was working on Twitter in the fall of 2022. The subpoenas asked for a wide scope of records and communications about the transition, the decision-making process in firing incumbent Twitter employees, and people's duties at Musk's Twitter and at their other jobs in the Musk imperium.

The plaintiffs in the case, *Arnold v. X Corp*, alleged that they were fired and then not paid their "contractually required severance." The employee who was forced to resign said that he did so after "being repeatedly and specifically directed to violate California's building codes—in ways that potentially put Tweep lives at risk." Overall, the complainants painted a picture of impulsive decision-making focused on relentless cost-cutting, no matter the result: "Led by

Musk and the cadres of sycophants who were internally referred to as the 'transition team,' Twitter's new leadership deliberately, specifically, and repeatedly announced their intentions to breach contracts, violate laws, and otherwise ignore their legal obligations."

The list had 91 names on it. At least 70 of them worked for Musk directly or at one of his companies. It's unknown if this is a full roster of everyone Musk drafted during his crash takeover; there may be more people or entities subpoenaed in other filings. I relied on LinkedIn and public reporting from the time to determine who worked where. In the case of two people subpoenaed, I wasn't able to confirm their identities. A few names in the subpoena list were apparently misspelled.

Among the venture capitalists subpoenaed were Randy Glein (DFJ), Chris Shanahan (DFJ), Samuel Pullara (Sutter Hill Ventures), Pablo Mendoza (Vy Capital), and four employees of Valor Equity Partners, including its CEO and President Antonio Gracias, who had become close to Musk in recent years. Case filings indicated that a number of law firms were subpoenaed. So were Andrew and James Musk, cousins of Elon.

The Musk employees came from SpaceX, Musk's family office, The Boring Company, and Tesla. In the case of SpaceX, Musk brought over 11 employees, mostly senior executives, including top people from finance, human resources, IT, facilities, and real estate. More than 50 engineers joined from Tesla, many of them from the autopilot division. The Boring Company supplied two people from its operations department along with Steve Davis, its CEO and president. Davis, who was tipped as a potential future Twitter CEO, was one of the Musk loyalists who slept at the Twitter office—except that Davis was accompanied by his wife and a newborn baby. As a result, Davis's wife was also included on the subpoena list. (The baby was spared.)

Musk painted the Twitter transition effort as a volunteer process. Talented engineers from his companies responded to a call for help and offered their time and expertise—gratis. The implication seemed to be that if Musk ordered top engineers from a publicly traded company like Tesla to drop what they were doing and go work at Twitter in San Francisco, that could be a matter of concern for company shareholders. It could be a breach of Musk's fiduciary duties, especially because these people were paid by Musk's other companies while, by his own admission, Twitter teetered toward bankruptcy. But if they were just donating some extra time, then shareholders likely had no grounds for a legal complaint.

As he shuffled around top executives and engineers, Musk's behavior during the Twitter takeover revealed something about how he managed his vast portfolio. Few, if any, of the people he brought in to overhaul Twitter had experience at social-media companies, but that didn't matter. They were smart and loyal. Silicon Valley elites tended to dismiss expertise. "Everything you read makes sense if you simply translate 'experts' as 'crazy people,'" according to Marc Andreessen.[3] That attitude provided broad rhetorical and ideological cover for tech moguls to refashion any industry in their image, from taxis to healthcare to real estate to the entire federal government. Their worldview upheld the pretense that creative destruction and technological innovation were synonymous with progress. If expertise was worthless—because the experts themselves represented the corruption of the *ancien régime*—then tech was a salvific force. And the people leading the tech vanguard were the ones doing the saving.

In practice, it seemed like Musk didn't acquire Twitter to reform the place or listen to its longtime employees, whom he fired in droves, about how to fix the platform's problems. He was there to destroy it—a job made much easier if he thought that none of Twitter's employees knew what they were doing. Musk took things a step further, arguing that some Twitter employees were acting with malice, especially anyone working on content moderation or trust and safety. These departments work on interlocking, perhaps intractable, problems related to free speech, harassment, privacy, platform manipulation, and disinformation operations. Some of these disciplines are pretty new. Some of these issues don't have clear answers, especially when dealing with hundreds of millions of users scattered across the globe, living under different political regimes and cultural contexts. That ambiguity and uncertainty didn't fit with Musk's militant vision of a new Twitter, where anything resembling content moderation was immediately consigned away as censorship. It also meant that people who worked in these roles were inherently suspect.

Yoel Roth, Twitter's head of trust and safety, survived the initial culling that followed Musk's takeover. But a few weeks later, Roth decided to leave, writing in the *New York Times* that "Musk has made clear that at the end of the day, he'll be the one calling the shots"—a kind of impulsive, authoritarian leadership that Roth couldn't abide.[4] Neither could advertisers like Apple, Disney, Coca-Cola, and Microsoft, which decided to abandon Twitter in the wake of the anti-Semitism, racism, and other bigotry that surged on the platform. Musk told fleeing advertisers to "go fuck yourself" and sued a trade group for colluding against him.

Roth was involved in a number of high-level policy and enforcement decisions, including the suspension of Donald Trump's account after the January 6 Capitol riot. The Twitter Files supposedly revealed the company's censorious collusion with government agencies, and Roth's name was all over them. Six weeks into Musk's Twitter reign, a right-wing account tweeted at the company's new owner a link to Roth's PhD dissertation and misconstrued a passage to imply that Roth endorsed pedophilia. Musk took the bait and helped smear Roth, who was gay, as a predator. "Looks like Yoel is arguing in favor of children being able to access adult Internet services in his PhD thesis," wrote Musk, posting a screenshot from the thesis examining the culture, safety, and design of Grindr, a gay dating and hookup app.[5]

A wave of threats and harassment followed. Representative Marjorie Taylor Greene claimed that Roth had allowed child porn to appear on Twitter—one of many homophobic accusations seemingly inspired by Musk casting a withering spotlight on his former executive. Roth and his family fled their San Francisco home and were forced to sell it.

Roth didn't see Musk's tweet as an accident. It was part of a larger effort to attack the systems and individuals working on internet governance and to force companies to accommodate conservatives' self-interested demands. Two years earlier, Donald Trump had called out Roth by name, claiming that he determined what could be posted on Twitter. Roth was inundated with death threats and derogatory comments. "What happened to me was part of a calculated effort to make Twitter reluctant to moderate Mr. Trump in the future and to dissuade other companies from taking similar steps," Roth wrote.[6] The strategy was successful, causing Twitter CEO Jack Dorsey to overrule the trust and safety team's recommendation to ban Trump's account for encouraging violence on January 6, 2021.[7]

The effects, wrote Roth, were potentially broad and corrosive to civil society. "Private individuals—from academic researchers to employees of tech companies—are increasingly the targets of lawsuits, congressional hearings and vicious online attacks," he said. "These efforts, staged largely by the right, are having their desired effect"—chilling speech, undermining research into disinformation, and making companies unnecessarily risk averse, especially when it came to addressing threats from the political right and online trolls.[8] These aggressive, coercive measures had been built upon by authoritarian political leaders in India, the Philippines, Russia, and Saudi Arabia, where social-media companies found themselves pressured to abide by local censorship rules, put government agents on their payrolls, or tolerate government-run troll farms.

The Yoel Roth episode ultimately became one of many dramatic incidents at Twitter under Musk. It would be reduced to a footnote, along with the various defamation lawsuits against Musk, his banning of the account that tracked his private jet via public data, and his decision to suspend journalists who reported critically on his activities.[9,10,11] There are many other revealing anecdotes one could cite—demonizing migrants, amplifying far-right ideologues, happily engaging with Nazi accounts, and promoting salacious material that seemed obviously untrue.[12,13,14,15] Musk so frequently violated his own stated ethics, including his supposed free-speech absolutism, that few incidents had much time to stick in the public consciousness or to disabuse his fans of their admiration for him. Like Trump, Musk flooded the zone. You could only hope to keep up.

What happened to Yoel Roth was representative of what Musk had apparently become: capricious, and eager to conspiracize. Around the same time, Musk tweeted a link to *The Santa Monica Observer* that spread in false rumors concerning Paul Pelosi's sexuality after he was attacked by an intruder at his home.[16] The tweet was later deleted. For Musk, the human stakes didn't seem to matter. It was a good time, a jab in the eye of the media and political establishments he treated with Trumpian disdain. And his fans ate it up. The more Musk elevated tweets that accused his political enemies of being communists or child abusers, the more his following grew.[17,18]

Firing more than half of Twitter employees, Musk transformed how the platform operated. He chiseled away at content moderation, disbanding teams working on trust and safety, and then claimed he was doing more to protect children from sex trafficking and abusive material than the last managerial team. (Protecting children from allegedly rampant predation was an obsession of the conspiratorial online right.) He restored many once-banned accounts, including those belonging to "Groyper" leader Nick Fuentes, whose followers littered their feeds with content denigrating Jews and women and glorifying Adolf Hitler.

Acting on his billionaire populist, establishment-hating persona, Musk removed blue checks from verified accounts, since they were supposedly an elitist status marker and not a way to make sure that prominent people weren't being impersonated. In a misguided act of redistribution, he then made blue checks available to anyone who paid a new monthly subscription fee. Like YouTube, Twitch, and other social video sites, Twitter introduced profit-sharing for subscribers whose posts attracted a lot of views. The result was that a symbol that had been associated with verified identities and more reliable sources of information was now widely used by parody accounts, Nazis, trolls, and influencers, all of whom were motivated more by generating as many monetizable views as possible than by telling the truth or linking to reliable sources.

To encourage people to sign up for subscriptions, Musk made it so that blue-check replies showed up first under all posts. He was amplifying the speech of his paid-up fans while deprecating everyone else's. It also ensured that the most visible replies under any popular post—especially Musk's—would be largely from people who shared Musk's increasingly reactionary worldview. More than any other change, this one act cemented Twitter's new identity as a right-wing media platform that acted as an extension of Musk's own political beliefs, midnight musings, and personal interests.

Musk was "obsessed with the amount of engagement his posts [were] receiving," according to *Platformer*. He fired a company engineer who told him that engagement on his tweets was down because people weren't as interested in him.[19]

During the 2023 Super Bowl, Elon Musk tweeted that he was rooting for the Philadelphia Eagles. President Joe Biden also tweeted that he was supporting the Eagles on behalf of his wife Jill. Biden's tweet generated about three times the number of views as Musk's. That apparently was unacceptable to Musk, who deleted his tweet and flew to California after the game to demand changes to Twitter's algorithm.[20]

James Musk, one of Elon's cousins, posted an all-hands message on Slack at 2.36 a.m. Monday morning: "We are debugging an issue with engagement across the platform. Any people who can make dashboards and write software please can you help solve this problem. This is high urgency. If you are willing to help out please thumbs up this post."[21]

Thanks to the middle-of-the-night participation of 80 company engineers, the "high urgency" issue was quickly solved. In a fashion. The engineers tuned Twitter's systems to privilege Musk's posts above all others, boosting his tweets "by a factor of 1,000."[22] Many users started seeing Musk in their "For You" feeds, even if they didn't subscribe to his posts. The For You feed became a mirror of Musk's interests, containing the right-wing accounts he followed. Users found their timelines defaulting to For You, rather than the feed of accounts they had chosen to follow. On Twitter, Musk posted a popular meme that he altered to show a woman (labeled "Twitter") being forced to consume his tweets.

In July 2023, the transformation became official: Musk rechristened Twitter as X, "the everything app" that he had aspired to make years ago when he was a PayPal executive. Gone was the winsome blue bird logo, replaced by a swaggering black X. Musk promised that the new X would include "comprehensive communications and the ability to conduct your entire financial world."[23]

Buoyed by his ownership of a news-cycle-driving media platform, Musk seemed to believe—and was willing to amplify—noxious rumors in his timeline, including one arguing that hordes of illegal migrants were invading the country as part of a Democrat-controlled plot.[24] He suggested that a mass shooter was a government psychological warfare operation.[25] He said that George Soros wanted to "erode the very fabric of civilization" and that an anti-Semitic conspiracy theorist was speaking the "actual truth" when he posted that Jews encourage "hatred against whites."[26,27] He brought in popular right-wing commentators like Tucker Carlson, who after being fired from Fox News began posting his new show on X.

Musk began a lawfare campaign against his enemies. "Tesla is building a hardcore litigation department where we directly initiate & execute lawsuits. The team will report directly to me," he announced.[28] "Looking for hardcore streetfighters, not white-shoe lawyers like Perkins or Cooley who thrive on corruption. There will be blood."[29] After months of bad-mouthing Disney's leadership, he funded a fired actor's lawsuit against the media giant. He sued Media Matters, a liberal media watchdog group, which forced Media Matters to eventually lay off a number of staffers to cover legal fees.

Musk became practically a full-time litigant. The legal battle over his attempt to wriggle out of his Twitter takeover was widely reported. He also faced lawsuits over a $56 billion Tesla pay package, working conditions at his companies, SEC investigations into his social-media use and potential stock market manipulation, and various casual acts of alleged defamation. Meanwhile, scores of fired Twitter employees sued for unlawful termination or not receiving legally required severance payments. While being cross-examined during the trial over his mammoth Tesla compensation package, Musk appeared unsure of where he was. "Are we in the Tesla trial or the Twitter trial?" he asked. "I'm slightly confused."

However busy it kept him, legal pugilism was a sideshow. With his friend David Sacks, a politically active Republican donor who backed Governor Ron DeSantis for president before ultimately settling on Trump, Musk posted frequently about the apocalyptic damage being wrought on the country. Although violent crime had largely declined in America's urban centers in recent years, Musk embraced propaganda about violent Democrat-run cities. After one of his children came out as trans and legally disowned him, Musk became vocally anti-trans, promoting a transphobic film and supporting accounts like LibsOfTikTok, which specialized in shining a bright, potentially dangerous spotlight on gay teachers, trans children, and queer government employees. LibsOfTikTok was known for helping popularize the "groomer" slur against gay people, and for calling out institutions that provided gender-affirming healthcare. Many of these hospitals and clinics became the target of protests or bomb threats.[30] Like his peers, Musk engaged frequently with LibsOfTikTok and its creator Chaya Raichik.[31] Raichik soon became a top MAGA personality.

Musk and Sacks, again plowing the same field as Donald Trump, frequently described the mainstream media—and pretty much everyone in it—as corrupt liars. At the same time, Musk's apparent lack of discernment was staggering for someone so wealthy and supposedly brilliant.

In full public view, it seemed to many observers as though Musk was being radicalized by the online right, being baptized into their ranks. And some of his friends and peers followed. On X, they engaged with the same Nazis and boutique far-right subcultures—misogynist gamers, ultra-libertarian techies, and incel-worshiping Groypers (a subgroup of white-nationalist internet trolls led by Nick Fuentes). One could see it every day (and late into the night, in Musk's case). It was in the posts they shared, the people they talked to, and the reactionary ideas they promoted around Covid-19 mitigation, DEI programs, climate change, trans rights, and social justice. They posted far-right memes, promoted propagandistic documentaries, and went on podcasts that catered to the same audience. Every official narrative was a manipulative "op" crafted by elites pulling the wool over the masses' eyes. Meanwhile, they were increasingly funding one of the two main political parties that made up the ruling class they claimed to resent.

In April 2024, Edward Perez, who had worked at Twitter as a director for civic integrity, decided he had had enough and could no longer use X. Other people had made similar vows before, both public and private. It had become almost fashionable, an emblem of a sincere, conscious consumerism to say, "No more. I won't support an Elon Musk-owned business." (Some Tesla owners had taken to buying bumper stickers saying they bought the car without knowing his politics.) Before Perez left for calmer social-media pastures, he wrote a postmortem for the platform formerly known as Twitter that, building on his insider's view, astutely described the malign forces at work—financial, political, and personal.

"Musk is a poster child for divisive racist, sexist, and plutocratic tendencies that undermine democracy's commitment to equality for all," wrote Perez, describing the mogul as throwing a perpetual tantrum. "Musk's willingness to burn down[32] what he purchased suggests that he's motivated by a perverse righteousness, not profit."

It was hard to disagree with that. Even when Musk told the *New York Times*' Andrew Ross Sorkin that advertisers critical of his posts could "go fuck yourself" Musk seemed to be acting more out of pique than any true devotion to free speech.[33] Musk even waded into the furore surrounding the *Dilbert* cartoonist Scott Adams when Scott said in a video that Black Americans belonged to a "hate group" and that white people should "stay the hell away" from them. According to Musk, it was the media who were racist against white and Asian people.[34]

As Perez wrote, Musk's free-speech absolutism was a fiction perpetuated by a pliant media. In practice, Musk told advertisers to fuck off because they didn't like *his* posts and the Nazi-friendly environment *he* had created. It wasn't about principle; it was about Elon Musk.

"When one of the richest men in the world uses his own private global media platform to selectively amplify anti-democratic voices, and to prey on those he does not like, that is not 'free speech,'" wrote Perez. "That's personal psychological weakness, enabled by systemic plutocracy."

Perez nailed the troubling political and economic dynamics behind the world's richest man exercising control over a major media platform. He seemed to understand that, for Musk, it could be personal to a toxic degree. "Ownership of a platform like this cannot be online therapy and acting-out to soothe the grievances of insecure, immature, thin-skinned billionaires (yes, note the plural) who desperately want & need to be liked (because they are psychologically damaged)," he said.

Yes, I noted the plural. They were the people who had invested in Musk's Twitter takeover, supported his lawsuits, went to bat for him in the media, and echoed his increasingly outré views. Their names are strewn throughout this book.

With his fantastic wealth, his enthusiasm for memes and conspiracy theories, and his outright refusal to moderate his expression, Musk represented the distillate of the personality type that's been described here: authoritarian, impulsive, supremely entitled, insecure, and vain. His extreme example gave his peers the rhetorical freedom to say what they wanted. Whatever they believed, Musk had probably already said it, provoking a thousand chin-scratching think pieces. It was a type, and a set of underlying values, that Musk enthroned with his slapdash overhaul of Twitter.

But for some users of the platform, Musk's Potemkin populism and insincere free-speech absolutism did nothing except hang new drapes in the same smoky backroom.

6

The Saudi Influence behind Twitter and X

Ali Al Ahmed didn't think that Elon Musk was responsible for the decline and fall of Twitter. That disaster had long preceded the mercurial mogul's arrival. Musk was another face representing an old regime. Twitter, or X, wasn't special. It was like any other company. And its sins began well before Musk bumbled into Twitter HQ carrying a porcelain sink.

Al Ahmed was a Saudi journalist and analyst living in the DC area. He was a founder of the Gulf Institute, a Saudi-focused think tank with an emphasis on human rights reporting, and was the kind of expert—passionate, principled, always glad to hop on the phone—that journalists loved having in their digital rolodex. For Al Ahmed, who over the years had many family members imprisoned by the Saudi royal family, the pursuit of human rights was a solemn task. But Ahmed also had a kind of garrulousness—breaking into asides about his children or the talking gadget he'd invented to remind them to wash their hands—that reminded one of the deeper human stakes.

"Twitter is no different than Boeing or those military companies," Al Ahmed told me. "They care about making money. Twitter and Facebook are not champions or models for human rights. These people are nothing but money grabbers."[1]

I first spoke to Al Ahmed in 2021, when reporting on the Saudi government's use of Twitter to unmask and arrest people posting critically about the regime. It was a major issue for Saudis, for whom Twitter had become a popular online forum where free expression came at the price of serving oneself up as a target to Saudi security forces, which ran troll farms that propagandized and harassed anyone who criticized the regime.

For Saudi authorities, Twitter was an asset in every sense. The billionaire Saudi businessman Prince Alwaleed bin Talal was Twitter's largest outside shareholder, and the site had become a key tool in the government's apparatus of surveillance and control. The Saudi government had also managed to recruit two Twitter employees, Ali Alzabarah and Ahmad Abouammo, to spy for them—something that the company seemed unaware of until alerted by the FBI.

Al Ahmed believed his Twitter account had been compromised by Saudi Arabia's spies inside Twitter. He worried that their access to his account endangered dissident Saudis with whom he exchanged private messages. Twitter had also banned Al Ahmed's Arabic-language Twitter account, which had 36,000 followers. One of those dissidents he worried about was Abdulrahman Al Sadhan, an aid worker who, in 2018, was abducted by Saudi security forces for running a satirical Twitter account that parodied members of the Saudi government. Al Sadhan, who was then 37 years old, was sentenced to 20 years in prison. Al Ahmed and Al Sadhan had spoken via direct messages on Twitter.

"Saudi Arabia is carrying out more repression" than ever, said Abdulrahman's sister Areej Al Sadhan, who lived in the US when we spoke in 2021. In the first three years after her brother was arrested, her family had received only two brief phone calls from him. Saudi prisoners were frequently tortured and killed. Saudi crown prince Mohammed bin Salman, or MBS, had zero tolerance for dissent, especially in the form of mockery. "They are ruthlessly going after anyone who exercises their freedom of speech," she said.[2]

They wouldn't hear from him again after that. In a 2023 court filing, Areej Al Sadhan said that she wasn't sure if her brother was alive.

The notion that Saudi Arabia was engaging in transnational repression—with an assist from its Western tech investments—was contrary to the wise reformer image that MBS had spent untold amounts of money burnishing. The gruesome 2018 assassination of *Washington Post* columnist Jamal Khashoggi was the best-known instance of the Saudi state's penchant for brutality; Saudi officials said the journalist was killed in a "rogue operation" by a team of agents sent to persuade him to return to the kingdom, while Turkish officials said the agents acted on orders from the highest levels of the Saudi government. But there was also a larger crackdown that saw thousands of people, including some of MBS's own family members, rounded up and sent to prisons and black sites. That crackdown continues to this day. Despite his attempt to portray himself as a modernizing reformer, MBS could appear every bit as repressive as past Saudi rulers, turning the country into a surveillance state where arbitrary arrests and disappearances were routine. As the Khashoggi murder demonstrated, the Saudi state pursued vigorous methods of transnational repression, allegedly sending hit squads after enemies abroad, even in friendly countries, like Canada.[3] And he used his country's bottomless reserves of oil and capital to flood Silicon Valley, politics, sports leagues, and other power centers with cash and influence.

In the decades since the Sept. 11, 2001 attacks, corporate America welcomed huge infusions of capital from Saudi Arabia and other Gulf dictatorships. The UAE, with five sovereign wealth funds totaling more than $1.4 trillion in assets, became a player in everything from renewable energy to artificial intelligence to real estate. Saudi Arabia poured billions of dollars into American venture capital firms and tech startups through its Public Investment Fund and Sanabil, the PIF's VC firm. Andreessen Horowitz and Founders Fund were among the most notable recipients of Saudi money, but they were just two names among hundreds.[4] In 2016, Uber received an astonishing $3.5 billion from the PIF.[5] The SoftBank Vision Fund, a massive investment fund that invested billions in companies like WeWork, Slack, and FTX, received about $45 billion. Blackstone's infrastructure fund got $20 billion.[6] By fall 2018, the *Wall Street Journal* reported, Saudi Arabia had become "the largest single funding source for U.S. startups."[7]

The Saudi–Silicon Valley relationship represented a convergence of shared interests. The Kingdom of Saudi Arabia (KSA), like other Gulf dictatorships, wanted to wash its money, diversify its investments, deepen influence with its most powerful ally, extend soft power, and counter its image as a repressive state responsible for a devastating war in Yemen. Silicon Valley offered all of that, along with access to cutting-edge technology and a business elite coming into its own.

"They're surveillance states. They're police states," said Nader Hashemi, a Professor of Middle East and Islamic Politics at Georgetown University. "They want to use the latest technology in order to continue to remain in power and surveil their populations. So they have another interest in trying to sort of be the beneficiaries of high-tech developments, hoping that that will help them internally with their own political rule."[8]

The Saudi government had vast assets held in the names of senior members of the royal family, like Prince Alwaleed bin Talal. Through his Kingdom Holding Company, Prince Alwaleed had interests in businesses like Lyft and Snapchat. And until Elon Musk came along, he was Twitter's largest outside shareholder.

In March 2018, six months before the murder of Jamal Khashoggi, MBS visited the United States for a whistlestop tour that feted him as a young monarch on the make, ready to dispense billions of dollars in investment capital as he implemented his program to diversify the Saudi economy. English-language media covered the visit like a royal affair—and not part of an influence campaign by an autocrat. American Media, the company that owned the *National Enquirer* tabloid, printed 200,000 copies of a 97-page propaganda rag touting MBS as "transforming the world at 32." The one-off publication promoted MBS as an economic visionary fighting terrorism and seeking peace.[9] It was an especially unctuous example of MBS worship but not unusual for the time. The American relationship with Saudi Arabia had never been premised on democracy or human rights.

MBS's American tour was abundantly documented, but it projected an image that the crown prince, his advisors, and his business contacts wanted the world to see. I obtained a document purporting to lay out the media strategy for the crown prince. The 36-page PDF was heavily redacted, listing only the cities and some of the attendees at various meetings—venture capitalists, politicians, CEOs, political donors, national-security officials past and present, journalists, celebrities, and every living US president, except Jimmy Carter. Each meeting was categorized under Political, Security, Economic, Cultural, or Media. The document covered March 20 to May 8, taking MBS through DC, Boston, New York, Seattle, Los Angeles, San Francisco, and Houston. The redactions turned out to be poorly done—just some large white squares covering each page, which were easily removed in Adobe Acrobat. The full document showed how each meeting was, as might be expected, highly choreographed: the attendees, the strategy, the messaging, the photo op, even the planned tweet celebrating a successful encounter. Oprah would get a tweeted photo of herself with the crown prince; the meeting with "prominent political donors" would go unphotographed. With Elon Musk, MBS would tour a Hyperloop model—a proposed rapid-transport system using pressurized pods—and offer the following "key message": "This is a very exciting time for Saudi Arabia and for Hyperloop. I am confident that KSA will play a major role in bringing this revolutionary technology to the world." As of 2025, the Hyperloop remained only a concept.

For MBS, the trip was a triumph, allowing him to be feted by everyone from Bill Clinton to The Rock. The tech industry stood to benefit as well. MBS had dinner with Peter Thiel, John Doerr, and other top venture capitalists; lunched with Bill and Melinda Gates; and met with the CEOs of Amazon, Apple, Boeing, Google, IBM, Lockheed Martin, Microsoft, Uber, and too many other companies to name. The media coverage was well coordinated, from the press pool to pre-booked interviews with Saudi officials. For a discussion with women tech executives, the document stated that MBS's team should "offer an exclusive to a female San Francisco tech reporter."

Nader Hashemi, who had recently spoken at a conference of Saudi dissidents and exiles, saw the Saudi–Silicon Valley relationship as reflecting a fundamental rot in American governance. He described it as "a reflection or a microcosm of our deeper democratic problem here in the United States, where you have private interests with a lot of private capital, being able to effectively influence politicians by virtue of their wealth and dominate the political system, while the vast majority of the population are sinking into greater despair and greater poverty."[10]

We were speaking about the specific role of one foreign dictatorship, but it was a system leveraged by a range of malign corporate and government actors. "Lobby groups from different countries—they're all playing the same game," said Hashemi. "I'm just reminded of the fundamental, deeper crisis of American democracy that is impoverishing many people and forcing people out of despair to turn to Trump because they see no alternative."

Long before MBS was taking victory laps through America's power centers, his regime had embraced Twitter in its toolkit of repression. The service was extraordinarily popular in Saudi Arabia—Twitter's largest Middle Eastern market—where it initially seemed like "a great equalizer," said Al Ahmed. With no independent media and most political expression verboten, Twitter and other social media became a place for people to speak more frankly, especially when they could be pseudonymous. "That did not last," Al Ahmed told me.

Independent media didn't exist in Saudi Arabia, so it was important for the regime to be able to properly police and manipulate new social-media platforms like Twitter. The Saudi government established cubicle farms full of paid pro-regime trolls, who threatened dissidents, spread nationalist propaganda, and tried to game trending topics to emphasize government-friendly stories (and suppress critical stories and hashtags). Over time, Twitter became as popular with members of the Saudi ruling family and its extensive intelligence apparatus as the public. The sense of relative freedom evaporated. Ordinary Saudis no longer felt comfortable speaking freely on Twitter. Saudis living abroad worried that their posts would imperil their family members back home. Saudi dissidents and exiles spoke of constant harassment, death threats, and attempts to hack their accounts. In their view, Twitter bore some responsibility for how its service was abused. "There was no real step taken by the company to take care of and protect these activists," said Areej Al Sadhan.[11]

Saudi Twitter became a place for the kingdom's rulers to propagandize, track dissident thought, and identify victims for MBS's personal team of enforcers. Regime officials were even known to chat with their future targets. Ali Al Ahmed told me that after he'd exchanged some direct messages with MBS's advisor Saud Al Qahtani, someone who claimed to be Al Qahtani sent Ahmed a phishing email, attempting to steal his login information. (Al Ahmed messaged Al Qahtani, who was later banned from Twitter after being linked to Jamal Khashoggi's murder, but he received no response.)

Many Saudis knew better than to post on Twitter under their real names. But the Saudi government was able to unmask pseudonymous accounts and trace their owners, who, like Abdulrahman Al Sadhan, were then arrested. For a long time, dissident Saudis wondered how exactly government security forces had unmasked their friends and family members, and whether there were any countermeasures they could take. Surely the Saudi government had access to the finest Western security contractors and advanced spyware software. Perhaps that allowed them to de-anonymize and trace Twitter users.

They didn't yet know that MBS and his henchmen had something better: a spy ring inside Twitter.

In June 2014, a Saudi official named Bader Al Asaker—the secretary-general of MBS's personal charity, the Misk Foundation, and head of the crown prince's private office—took a tour of Twitter's San Francisco headquarters. The tour was jointly arranged by a man named Ahmed Almutairi, who operated a social-media marketing company that contracted to members of the Saudi royal family and the Misk Foundation, and a Twitter employee named Ahmad Abouammo. Al Asaker was grooming Abouammo, who worked on media partnerships in the Middle East, to spy for him, according to US prosecutors. In the months to come, Abouammo would receive more than $100,000 in cash and gifts as he gathered information—including email addresses, phone numbers, and private messages—relating to Saudi dissidents, journalists, and other accounts of note.

In 2015, Abouammo got a new job at Amazon, but the Saudi regime found a worthy replacement in Ali Alzabarah, a Twitter engineer whose position and technical skills gave him access to more user data than Abouammo. Soon enough, Alzabarah became an even more productive spy for Al Asaker and the Saudi regime, tracking dissidents across borders and providing IP addresses that could reveal people's locations.

In December 2015, an FBI agent visited the Twitter headquarters in San Francisco to tell them that they had a Saudi espionage problem. While Abouammo had left for Amazon, Alzabarah had siphoned data from thousands of Twitter accounts and passed it to his handlers. And he was still working at Twitter's HQ.

The FBI asked that Twitter refrain from taking immediate action but, reportedly suspicious about the intentions of government security agencies, which are known to pressure tech companies for private user information, Twitter decided to confront Alzabarah and suspend him. According to a federal indictment against Alzabarah, the engineer turned spy frantically called Al Asaker, who, along with the Saudi consul general of Los Angeles, helped spirit Alzabarah away to Saudi Arabia. After finding refuge there, Alzabarah was named the CEO of the Misk Foundation. He was just outside the frame of the famously strange photo of Donald Trump, Egyptian dictator Abdel Fattah el-Sisi, and MBS touching a glowing orb. Almost a decade later, Alzabarah was still on X—where his account was locked for privacy—and on the FBI's most-wanted list.

Ahmad Abouammo, now working for Amazon, was duly arrested and indicted. A jury found him guilty on six criminal charges related to his spying. A judge sentenced him to three and a half years in federal prison.

As Saudi Arabia became the preeminent source of Silicon Valley capital, Prince Alwaleed bin Talal emerged as the country's most recognizable mogul, taking the role of leading shareholder in Rupert Murdoch's News Corp. By 2015, the prince owned an estimated

5.2 percent of Twitter—more than Twitter co-founder Jack Dorsey. In November 2017, bin Talal was arrested and confined to the Ritz-Carlton Hotel in Riyadh as part of a sweeping "anti-corruption" purge that forced numerous wealthy Saudis and members of the royal family to sign over their assets to MBS. That may well have included bin Talal's Twitter shares.

"Since late 2017 or January of 2018, MBS has exercised control over more Twitter stock than is owned by Twitter's founder," according to a civil complaint filed against Twitter and the consulting firm McKinsey by Omar Abdulaziz, a Saudi exile who said that the consultancy helped finger him as a prominent online dissident, leading to his Twitter account being hacked. (In 2020, Canadian authorities warned Abdulaziz that he was a target of a Saudi kill team.)

According to Abdulaziz's original complaint, "Because of the tremendous wealth of key figures in [the Kingdom of Saudi Arabia], major corporations have enabled, collaborated with, and turned a blind eye to KSA's efforts to suppress, torture, falsely imprison, terrorize, and murder dissenters both within Saudi Arabia and around the world." Other exiles similarly argued that Twitter gave the Saudi government a reach well beyond its borders. Areej Al Sadhan's civil complaint noted that it was America's "authoritarian allies," not enemy states, who seemed to have intensified their practices of transnational repression. (India, which assassinated a Sikh separatist in Canada, is one prominent example.)[12]

In short, a murderous autocratic government abused its close relationship with Twitter to cultivate spies who provided information that got innocent people thrown in prison. That government continued to be one of Twitter's largest outside shareholders, harassing and monitoring its citizens via the service. After initially criticizing the brash Musk, Prince Alwaleed bin Talal supported his takeover effort, announcing he would roll his $1.89 billion worth of shares (presumably controlled by MBS) into the new venture.

For their roles in corrupting Twitter/X, MBS didn't suffer so much as a public warning, while Bader Al Asaker—who spoke multiple times with the Khashoggi hit squad on the day the journalist was murdered—continued to use the site to propagandize to a huge audience.[13] On X, where he often posted in praise of MBS, Al Asaker appeared like just another member of the global elite, mingling with royals, politicians, and business executives. He had more than 2.3 million followers. One of them was Jack Dorsey. The US tech CEO and the Saudi royal fixer appeared to at least have a passing relationship. In June 2016, six months after Twitter's management learned about the spy ring from the FBI, Al Asaker tweeted a photo of Dorsey meeting with MBS in New York. The tech billionaire and the dictator shook hands and grinned.

For Al Ahmed, the relationship was difficult to explain. "If somebody was spying on my company, would I be his friend?" Al Ahmed asked. "This is very serious. People died, people are in jail. Abdulrahman, this beautiful young man, is going to spend 20 years. This is sick, honestly."

In the years since Dorsey and MBS shook hands, little changed. Twitter's management never took public responsibility for the spying or for the outrageous fact that one of its biggest outside investors regularly arrested people who posted even mildly political remarks on the platform.

Despite Musk swooping into Twitter HQ with a promise to liberate users from the shackles of Silicon Valley technocrats, the user experience got worse. Free speech isn't just a mantra. You can't feel secure in your right to speech if the surrounding sociopolitical conditions are terrible—if your biggest investor is scouring the platform for people to imprison; if the place is overrun by Nazi trolls whose paid blue checks mean their posts are elevated, amplified, and monetized; if submitting reports about hate speech seems to do nothing while suspensions and outright bans arrive with the suddenness of an act of god. With no customer service line and its media relations office replaced by a poop emoji (yes really), someone trying to appeal an X account suspension might as well have turned to the power of prayer.

Musk seemed openly transactional in his dealings with foreign governments. Whatever universal principles he claimed to hold appeared secondary in practice to his business concerns and his personal whims. The free-speech absolutist said nothing about Saudi Arabia's abuse of his platform. Perhaps he was simply unaware.

The Saudi spy story remains important because it's part of the true story of Twitter. The company that once called itself "the free speech wing of the free speech party," which was run for years by a head-in-the-clouds, Bitcoin-obsessed billionaire anarcho-capitalist CEO who spent part of the year on mystical retreats abroad, did some things well. It created a raucous public forum that, with mixed results, became the assigning editor for the media industry. It also was a messy, money-losing, occasionally censorious business chasing viability via personal data collection, surveillance advertising, and an uneasy relationship with the US security state. It did not protect its users from data breaches and it made devil's bargains with foreign governments. Like Ali Al Ahmed said, it was a typical US corporation. Except that this one had charged itself with a higher purpose and, in bumbling into foreign markets under autocratic governments where its product basically invited local people to break the law, it set up its users for trouble.

For Al Ahmed, the conviction of one Saudi spy, without any larger reckoning over the kingdom's role at Twitter and in Silicon Valley, was a failure. Bader Al Asaker wasn't even named in the court proceedings, Ahmed noted. As possibly the only known victim of the spy ring living in the United States, Al Ahmed offered to testify at Abouammo's sentencing. After a video chat with representatives of the Department of Justice, he never heard back.

"It was very clear that they were just trying to close this matter," said Al Ahmed. "Imagine if this guy was doing it for the Iranians. Oh my god. He would get twenty."

He emphasized that the Biden administration recognized MBS as having sovereign immunity in a lawsuit filed regarding the murder of Jamaal Khashoggi. The US government also intervened in a lawsuit against MBS filed by Saad Al Jabri, a former spy chief with a brutal record who had defected to the US.

"I really think it was a betrayal of justice here," said Al Ahmed. "It's part of this foreign influence and the corruption that's also now in the court system."

Twitter's relationship with the Saudi government revealed how the company really operated as a political entity. It wasn't just a place for silly memes or catty media discourse or an attention-obsessed billionaire to cultivate his flock. It was an informational battleground, a crucial node in the broader media ecosystem, and one of many entanglements between Silicon Valley and Gulf dictatorships. It revealed the company's politics as riddled with the same kind of false populism and political opportunism embraced by Musk, Trump, and MAGA radicals. Twitter's authoritarian posture—its willingness to overlook horrific behavior by a major investor—wasn't unique. It's the default for most large corporations, the equivalent of a Western oil giant paying bribes to operate in a foreign country. But the tech industry had long tried to paint itself as a bearer of progress, where technological innovation was synonymous with human flourishing. Twitter's Saudi scandal showed that this wasn't true at all.

Twitter fought lawsuits brought by the Al Sadhan family and Omar Abdulaziz without formally commenting on the spy ring. A judge dismissed Ali Al Ahmed's lawsuit. Jack Dorsey, the former Twitter chief executive who shook hands with MBS months after the FBI told him he had an espionage problem, continued to hold himself out as a Bitcoin-worshiping libertarian disillusioned by the direction Silicon Valley had taken. In fact, Dorsey helped usher the industry down this very path, to the point of delivering Twitter into the hands of his friend Musk.

It's possible that there were other spies working at Twitter, just as there were likely foreign agents working throughout Silicon Valley. Economic espionage is an old story. But using tech companies' surveillance-based business model to repress dissent at home and practice transnational repression abroad was a relatively new, grimly novel phenomenon. Commonly, when tech companies operated in foreign markets—often with minimal local staff— they faced political pressures that could be difficult to resist if they wanted to continue doing business there. Formerly idealistic tech firms tended to make painful compromises over censorship if it meant having access to tens of millions of users in Turkey, Egypt,

Pakistan, India, or China. The cybersecurity specialist known by the mononym Mudge, who consulted for Twitter, testified before Congress that India and China had agents working inside Twitter who had broad access to user data.[14]

A month after Mudge testified, Elon Musk completed his harried acquisition of Twitter. The $44 billion purchase price required him to take on a lot of debt and to solicit support from friends and allies from Hawaii to San Francisco to Riyadh. By buying Twitter, Musk inherited the Saudi spy scandal and the still-unresolved litigation associated with it. He inherited a major shareholder who had committed espionage against their own asset. Yet there was still a lot we didn't know about Twitter, Saudi Arabia, and Musk.

I wanted to know more about who helped Musk take Twitter private and who now owned a piece of X. Who was this powerful, volatile billionaire potentially beholden to?

It wasn't something that Musk wanted to talk about. The company had done away with its PR department, first replacing it with a poop emoji and then hiring a head of communications who seemed to share Musk's derision for the press. In the public imagination, Elon Musk was X—he owned it, he was its most popular user, he set its policies, he intervened personally when one of his favorite accounts encountered issues. He owed nothing to the media. He was enjoying its death throes.

When Musk acquired Twitter, he fired thousands of people and, with his blithe disregard for the tenets of employment law, provoked numerous lawsuits. By early 2024, these lawsuits—by ex-employees who said they didn't receive severance, were coerced into quitting, or were encouraged to break the law in order to implement Musk's edicts—were winding their way through the courts. In some suits, the plaintiffs wanted X to submit a list of its shareholders to answer some of the same questions that have been raised here. Who were Musk's partners? Who might be materially affected by a lawsuit against X? Did the judge own shares in Tesla or another Musk company?

This was a legitimate concern. It turned out that a judge in a North Texas district where Musk liked to file his lawsuits was a

Tesla shareholder. US district judge Reed O'Connor owned as much as $50,000 in Tesla stock when he took on Musk's lawsuit against Media Matters. Judge O'Connor made a series of rulings in favor of Musk, and the case's accumulating legal fees led to Media Matters laying off staff. In November 2024, X added a provision to its terms of service stating that all legal disputes would be settled in Judge O'Connor's Northern District of Texas.[15]

These kinds of shareholder document requests are common, and a corporate defendant may request to submit the information under seal, making it unavailable to the public (and potentially even the plaintiffs). In one of the cases I followed, *Anoke v. Twitter*, X submitted a list of shareholders under seal.

I wanted to file a motion to have the list unsealed but was unequipped to do it on my own. I reached out to Reporters Committee for Freedom of the Press (RCFP), a First Amendment organization that offered pro bono services to journalists. Born out of the Nixon administration's attempted censorship of the Pentagon Papers, RCFP had a distinguished history of First Amendment litigation. They agreed to represent me.

Together we found a few cases where it might be possible to unseal X's shareholders list. The cases varied in their particulars, and some seemed more promising than others. But the public-interest claim was consistent and straightforward. The RCFP attorneys deployed precedent-laden arguments about X as a public square, media ownership, and foreign influence and national-security concerns. They contacted the many high-powered lawyers X was employing to fight these cases to formally let them know we would be filing motions to unseal. And by early July, they had completed the necessary filings. We officially filed a motion in the Northern District of California asking a federal judge to unseal a disclosure list of X's shareholders in *Anoke v. Twitter*. Soon, my lawyers found another case with a sealed disclosure list and filed a motion to intervene in that case as well.

And then I waited.

7

Learning to Hate the Place You Love

While Elon Musk was leading an elite counter-revolution at Twitter, a similar process was playing out in local politics, especially in San Francisco, where tech leaders had been using their formidable bank accounts to start dark-money political advocacy groups, fund political campaigns, recall elected officials, and attempt a veritable takeover of a city whose liberal-democratic governing class, they thought, had gone dangerously astray. One of the chief architects of this operation was one of Musk's close friends: the venture capitalist David Sacks.

For a long time, San Francisco was good to David Sacks. Born in South Africa in 1972, Sacks immigrated to the United States with his family as a child. He graduated in the early 1990s from Stanford, in nearby Palo Alto, where he was friends and writing partners with Peter Thiel and where he immersed himself in conservative politics, interning for Judge Robert Bork.

At Stanford, Thiel and Sacks worked together on the Thiel-founded *Stanford Review*. In 1992, the *Review* published "The Rape Issue," which included a piece by Sacks defending a student who had pleaded no contest to statutory rape. Sacks considered the crime "a moral directive left on the books by pre-sexual revolution crustaceans." According to Thiel biographer Max Chafkin, "Sacks included a graphic description of the encounter, noting that the 17-year-old victim 'still had the physical coordination to perform oral sex,' and 'presumably could have uttered the word, "no."' Keith Rabois, who later became Sacks' PayPal colleague, was also a contributor to "The Rape Issue." In 2013, Rabois resigned as Square's COO after being accused of sexual harassment.

After college, Sacks and Thiel wrote op-eds about economics and politics for the *Wall Street Journal*, *National Review*, and the *San Francisco Chronicle*. In 1995, they published a book called *The Diversity Myth: Multiculturalism and Political Intolerance on Campus*. Angry, trollish, homophobic, fixated on identity and campus politics, *The Diversity Myth* could easily be produced today with panic about "woke" culture substituted for every mention of multiculturalism, which was wielded throughout as a bitter epithet. In the book, Sacks and Thiel revisited the Stanford rape, writing that "a multicultural rape charge may indicate nothing more than belated regret." (In the authors' moral universe, almost anything could be derisively labeled as "multicultural.") When the line resurfaced in *Forbes* in 2016, both Thiel and Sacks apologized, although the book contained plenty of other similarly minded sentiments. They accused sexual-assault activists of vilifying men and promoting fraudulent "'advocacy numbers, not real facts,'" writing that "the rape crisis movement transmits its exaggerated fears to freshmen yearly."

The Diversity Myth was a deeply political book—not only in its screeds against multiculturalism and sexual-assault education, but also in its production. It was sponsored by the Independent Institute, a libertarian think tank, and it was helped by Republican operatives and politicians of the era. The authors acknowledged the advice of Tom Duesterberg, who was Vice President Dan Quayle's chief of staff; a former FCC commissioner; congressional staffers; and conservative political theorists, think tankers, and economists. They also wrote that "a special thanks goes to Keith Rabois and the other victims of multiculturalism interviewed for this book."

In 1992, while a first-year law student at Stanford, Rabois and two friends stood outside the home of a university lecturer and yelled homophobic slurs. Representative comments included: "Faggot! Hope you die of AIDS!"[1] Afterward, Rabois wrote by way of explanation to the *Stanford Daily*: "The intention was for the speech to be outrageous enough to provoke a thought of 'Wow, if he can say that, I guess I can say a little more than I thought.'"[2]

Stanford's administration basically conceded the point. The school condemned Rabois's behavior, while at the same time saying that "this vicious tirade is protected speech."[3] There was a lot of outrage, letter writing, and some campus struggle sessions about misogyny and bigotry within Stanford's institutions—genuine attempts at social critique that were duly made fun of in *The Diversity Myth*. But there was no formal effort to punish Rabois. Instead, after becoming locally infamous, Rabois transferred to Harvard Law School, before moving on to PayPal and a successful tech career, including many years as a partner at Thiel's Founders Fund, making him fabulously wealthy. In the long tradition of conservative victimology, that made Rabois a martyr.

Meanwhile, after cutting his political teeth at Stanford, Sacks joined Thiel and some of their friends in founding PayPal, which they would eventually sell to eBay for $1.5 billion in 2002. Sacks amassed a fortune as PayPal's chief operating officer, followed by stints as CEO of Yammer and Zenefits. Sacks then founded a venture capital firm called Craft Ventures, which raised the kind of billion-dollar funds from the Saudi government and other deep-pocketed backers that placed it in the upper tier of the industry. Sacks acquired a number of mansions around the country, including one on San Francisco's Billionaires' Row.

Sacks was a core member of what's frequently referred to as the PayPal Mafia—the web of influential PayPal alumni that included Sacks, Thiel, Elon Musk, Keith Rabois, Ken Howery, and a handful of others, most of them conservative white men, who became dominant players in Silicon Valley. Like their peers, they were motivated by making money, but their right-wing ideology was a constant, finding expression in conference keynotes, startup investments, and political fundraising.

"It's important to say that the genesis of the PayPal mafia is a political network, not a business network: It's the *Stanford Review*," journalist Max Chafkin told the *Los Angeles Times*' Sam Dean.

"This political project has been integral to the development of the tech industry as it exists today."[4]

Silicon Valley, and San Francisco in particular, was the backdrop for this project. The country's center of tech entrepreneurialism, however steeped in cultural liberalism, produced a thriving capitalist industry that made Sacks and the rest of the PayPal Mafia fabulously rich. But somewhere along the way, Sacks became repulsed by what he saw in San Francisco. An occasional financial supporter of Democratic politicians, he emerged during Trump's first term as a leading prophet of urban decline, describing a formerly thriving city undone by crime- and drug-loving Democrats. With his sizable following on X, his friendship with Elon Musk, and his popular podcast *All-In*, which he hosted with fellow tech investors Jason Calacanis, Chamath Palihapitiya, and David Friedberg, Sacks became a tech celebrity.

Giving millions of dollars to potential Republican presidential candidates like Florida governor Ron DeSantis, Sacks became a political power broker in Thiel's image. With Thiel promising to sit out the 2024 election, Sacks became his putative replacement in the conservative tech hierarchy. On social media, he fashioned himself as an outraged wonk issuing dissenting takes on Biden's Ukraine policy and pushing several inept politicians he auditioned before eventually settling on Trump. His preoccupations were like those of other figures in his rolodex: experts were wrong about everything; Covid-19 restrictions were an assault on freedom; the Biden administration was failing on whichever policy was in the news that week; big government wanted to censor you and control your life.

Sacks specialized in the politics of outrage. In every bit of news to come across the transom, he saw the failures of liberal politicians. Slamming his fist on the social-media podium about each offending incident was enough to generate attention that boosted his profile. It made Sacks a perfect representation of the new techno-reactionary. Anything he didn't like could somehow be blamed on Democrats. It was only a matter of drawing the proper connections.

After Elon Musk bought Twitter, it became increasingly clear that he shared many of Sacks' views. Musk saw San Francisco as a petri dish for his bête noire. "The disaster that is downtown SF, once bea[u]tiful and thriving, now a derelict zombie apocalypse, is due to the woke mind virus," he wrote to right-wing Malaysian influencer Ian Miles Cheong.[5] "This is where San Francisco politics leads and Twitter was exporting this self-destructive mind virus to the world,"[6] Musk wrote to Ashlee Vance, one of his biographers.

With Sacks serving as his advisor, Musk was positioned to be the one tech mogul with the fortune and public profile to lead the public out of this mess—to lead a counter-revolution to purge government and society of the woke mind virus. Sacks, who had his own ample bankroll, had formed political connections with leading Republicans, including Donald Trump and Donald Trump Jr., that would help bring Musk firmly into the MAGA fold.

Sacks was a self-described "libertarian conservative" who had donated to many Republicans, but he'd also donated to Democrats when it might have been in his interest. Like many of his tech industry peers, including avowed libertarians like Peter Thiel, Sacks gave money to Representative Ro Khanna, a progressive whose district included Silicon Valley. (Khanna, for his part, made a point of engaging with conservatives and appearing on conservative media.) For a centi-millionaire or billionaire, a $2,900 annual donation—the maximum allowed to a congressional candidate—was simply covering one's bases, and the amount was trivial. In 2016, when he wasn't yet an open Trump supporter, Sacks gave $5,000 to Hillary Clinton's presidential campaign and $28,000 to the Democratic National Committee. In 2017, Sacks donated $58,400 to Democrat Gavin Newsom's campaign for California governor.

Just a few years later, Sacks changed his mind about the man he had helped elect. Sacks became a leading financial supporter of a campaign to recall Newsom, donating a total of $180,000 to two pro-recall groups. Chamath Palihapitiya, a venture capitalist and one of Sacks' *All-In* co-hosts, donated $100,000 to the recall effort and floated himself as a potential Newsom replacement. After a few weeks of stoking hype, Palihapitiya bowed out. "Let's be really honest," Palihapitiya said on *All-In*. "I'm not ready to do any of that."[7]

The public wasn't either. The Newsom recall failed, but the effort itself was instructive. It would help inform future efforts to remove Democratic politicians from office. It also spoke to a new era of politics in which elections were contested at every turn—at the ballot box, within the bureaucracy conducting elections and counting votes, in courts, in the media, and after a winner had taken office. With his attempt to overturn the 2020 election results, Donald Trump may have taken this strategy to its outer bounds. The politics of obstruction had long been a force in US governance, from Strom Thurmond's hours-long filibusters to Senator Mitch McConnell's legislative gridlock. Now, it was being applied to elections.

In 2022, Sacks joined other San Francisco elites in pouring money into a recall targeting three liberal members of the San Francisco Board of Education. No one had ever tried to remove a sitting member of the city's school board, who serve staggered four-year terms so that a few board spots are contested every two years. The city hadn't seen any kind of recall election in almost 30 years. The pro-recall side would raise more than $1.9 million—an extraordinary amount for a school board election. Sacks donated about $75,000.

The school board conflict was in some ways complex, reflecting the political realignment then underway. Some parents and city leaders thought that the school board was taking too long to reopen schools during the still-ongoing Covid-19 pandemic. Some thought that the school board had been captured by woke politics and was too focused on the fate of a controversial mural and the renaming of schools titled after racist historical figures. Citing racism and economic disparities, the board also voted to end merit-based testing for admission to Lowell High School, one of the city's top public high schools.

These decisions provoked fierce backlash and lawsuits. Together, they catalyzed the political anger of centrist and conservative San Franciscans who thought that city officials had lost sight of what was important. And they offered San Francisco's ultra-rich a chance to road-test their growing political influence.

On February 15, 2022, about 70 percent of voters elected to remove three school board members, whose replacements would be selected by Mayor London Breed. San Francisco's liberal Democrats received a bruising lesson in complacency and the new politics of resentment. The election helped spawn some of the political organizations and fundraising networks that would prove important in dragging San Francisco's Democratic establishment to the right in the next few years. The school board recall was a successful proof of concept: elite anger, properly channeled, could decide elections.

Having vanquished the woke officials apparently corrupting the city's school board, Sacks became a leading supporter of the effort to recall San Francisco district attorney Chesa Boudin, a progressive prosecutor who achieved supervillain status in Sacks' political cosmology as a representative of George Soros-funded reformist prosecutors who were allegedly endangering their constituents. The wealthy venture capitalist also became a vocal supporter and major financial backer of Florida governor Ron DeSantis, who was drawing support from tech leaders who had made the pandemic-era move to Miami.

Sacks had been writing and talking about politics in public for decades. In a 1998 C-SPAN appearance, Sacks advocated for the bombing of Iraq. He later claimed that he opposed George W. Bush's invasion. Sacks seemed to find his public voice as a political firebrand in the year leading up to the June 2022 recall of Boudin, who received overwhelming blame for the city's crime and social ills. Sacks branded Boudin "the Killer DA," arguing that his policies had caused innocent people to die.[8] He told former Fox News personality Megyn Kelly that there was "chaos and lawlessness in San Francisco," a product of "Soros DAs" with their "progressive agenda of decarceration."[9] He challenged Boudin to a public debate—"if you have the huevos," Sacks said—and then accused him of backing out of an agreed-upon appearance on *All-In*.[10]

Sacks became one of the Boudin recall's biggest donors. At one point in 2021, nearly one-third of all donations against Boudin had come from Sacks. The campaign succeeded. On June 8, 2022, months after recalling the three school board members, San Franciscans voted to recall Boudin in what was described as a setback for the progressive prosecutor movement, which sought to undo the social, economic, and political damage wrought by decades of mass incarceration.

The day after the Chesa Boudin[11] recall, Sacks went on Tucker Carlson's Fox News show to celebrate his victory and denounce the Democrats' radical agenda of "decarcerationism." Carlson credited Sacks with funding the recall and allowing "democracy to take place." Sacks explained that Democrats and their "woke billionaire" supporters—George Soros, Netflix CEO Reed Hastings—were deeply committed to the decarceral program, so it would be necessary to take the fight elsewhere. "This sort of playbook here is going to have to be replicated across the country," said Sacks.

Boudin's removal didn't do much to ameliorate the city's issues. In the first year under district attorney Brooke Jenkins, Boudin's successor, violent crime actually increased while her office hemorrhaged staff. And it turned out that Jenkins was on the payroll of billionaire William Oberndorf, who helped bankroll the Boudin recall and was on the board of two anti-Boudin nonprofits, one of which paid Jenkins $153,000.

With the Boudin recall victory in his pocket, while not yet a household name like his pal Musk, Sacks became a regular across conservative media and on X. He started to exert a growing influence in the political battles playing out in the tech industry. Sacks was part of the Tesla CEO's "shadow crew" of friends and allies, according to the *Wall Street Journal*. Text messages disclosed as part of Musk's legal battle with Twitter show that Musk sent his friend Sacks a tweet by conservative commentator Dinesh D'Souza expressing support for Musk's takeover of Twitter. Sacks said that he'd retweeted it. In other messages, the two discussed a potential investment from Sacks for the Twitter acquisition.

In early October 2022, Musk publicly proposed a negotiated settlement to Russia's war in Ukraine that mirrored arguments Sacks had made in a piece a week earlier for the *American Conservative*. Political consultant Ian Bremmer wrote that Musk had told him he had spoken with Russian president Vladimir Putin, who had influenced Musk's peace offer.[12] Musk denied Bremmer's report.[13] On Twitter, Sacks backed Musk's proposal and argued that the backlash generated—for example, against Musk's suggestion that Russia should be given the Ukrainian region of Crimea—was the product of a "woke mob" that, Sacks later wrote in *Newsweek*, would cause the next world war. In a tweet, Musk praised Sacks' *Newsweek* article as "exceptionally well-said." The *Wall Street Journal* would later report that Musk maintained regular contact with Putin, who had pressed Musk for favors.

At first quietly, Sacks became the leading practitioner of a new right-wing sensibility that emerged in the political realignments provoked by Trumpism and the pandemic. At times it seemed like a series of angry poses, much of it playing out on X, podcasts, YouTube, Rumble, Substack, and the occasional cable news hit. On foreign policy, it offered a blend of isolationism, Trumpist nationalism, suspicion of the deep state, and the anti-empire realism of John Mearsheimer. Domestically, it was mostly a rehash of corporate-friendly Reaganomics with a pungent disdain for the lower classes. In amplifying every instance of perceived wokeness run amok, it offered a welcome embrace to people who might have once counted themselves as liberals but now couldn't countenance the sight of homeless encampments.

For a brief period in 2021, the audio chat app Clubhouse was the locus of these reactionary political currents—the hangout spot for internet-famous venture capitalists and techies chafing against Silicon Valley's traditionally liberal culture. Though the app didn't sustain its early momentum, it inspired imitators and it helped propagate a culture of political complaint. It suggested that there was an audience for tech-driven, conservative-friendly media. With its audio-only format, Clubhouse also affirmed how much these guys loved talking—Sacks and Marc Andreessen, a Clubhouse investor, became regular podcasters.

In the fall of 2021, Sacks launched Callin, a podcast platform, with $12 million in series A funding. Building on its predecessors, Callin offered both live and recorded audio discussions, podcast hosting, and ways for users to interact with hosts. The company made deals to bring aboard established journalists and podcasters, and the site's sensibility quickly became defined by post-left, contrarian, or otherwise reactionary libertarian types. While it never achieved escape velocity as a business, it was eventually rescued in the form of an acquisition by Rumble, a MAGA-aligned video platform and an important entry in the parallel conservative tech-media ecosystem. Sacks, a Rumble shareholder, got a seat on the video-sharing site's board.

Sacks declined requests for an interview, both directly and through a representative. But his writings, media appearances, political donations, and professional network say a great deal both about his political rise and the way in which tech elites have come to exercise power.

Steeped in the inflammatory milieus of social media, Sacks and his fellow travelers often seemed less to stand for anything than simply against the evolving status quo—against criminal legal reform; against the public presence of homelessness; against a tradition of Democratic urban governance that, by indulging in identity politics, had failed to solve economic and social ills. They were angry, and they wanted the government to work for them again, while simultaneously seeing it as incapable of doing much good.

The Sacksian vision was evolving into coherence, finding increasing purchase in right-wing circles. This nascent movement's talking points had the kind of blunt simplicity that, if not convincing to everybody, at least racked up shares. In this corner of the political imagination, crime, drug addiction, and homelessness were outrageous horrors—but mostly for how they threatened the daily peace of responsible, economically productive citizens. For them, the defining feature of Covid-19 was not the death toll or the government's failure to provide adequate healthcare for all its people. The pandemic experience was about their personal disregard for quarantines and other mitigation measures, along with the supposed betrayal by government experts like Dr. Anthony Fauci. It was about their suffering. And it was about their inability to control their employees, who didn't want to return full-time to their old offices.

Occasionally, this fresh political breeze carried with it the stench of conspiracism. In an interview with Megyn Kelly on the day of the Boudin recall vote, Sacks said that the influx of fentanyl into the United States was China's "payback" for the nineteenth-century Opium Wars, calling Democratic politicians "useful idiots for the Chinese Communist Party."[14] On social media, videos of public drug use or homeless people were rendered not as social tragedy but as the perfidious, inevitable outcome of progressive policies, which were a kind of plot against America.

This ethos was perhaps best described by Vice's Edward Ongweso Jr. and Jason Koebler when they called the 2022 mayoral race in Los Angeles the "Nextdoor Election," referring to the social app that became an epicenter for racist and classist complaints about crime and homelessness. It was a draconian version of call-the-manager politics—time to let the police, the custodians of capitalist order, clear out the riffraff. If they had to crush some skulls, so be it. The same attitude could be seen in how many people, of varying political persuasions, supported university administrators who called in militarized police to crush Gaza solidarity protest encampments at American universities in 2024.

The symbolic epicenter of this movement was San Francisco, but really it was the entire curdled utopian dream of California. In the eyes of rich techies who saw their beloved metropolis falling into decay, vast inequality, and social misery, the state was dead. Their disappointment and alienation melded with traditional Republican disgust toward liberal cities (and their non-white residents) to paint a picture of irredeemable urban squalor. These frightened urbanites were echoing the Trumpist drumbeat that cities—particularly in California—were dangerous, dark places that needed to be tamed. But despite California's violent crime rate increasing by 6 percent in 2021, the state's violent crime rate (466 per 100,000 residents) was far lower than its 1992 peak (1,115 per 100,000 residents). That did not matter to people who saw danger and outrage at every turn.

A low point of this hand-wringing came in August 2022, when Boudin recall backer Michelle Tandler issued warnings about San Francisco dogs becoming addicted to meth by eating feces.[15] It was the kind of off-the-wall tale that became ripe for social-media mockery and suggested that perhaps this urban panic had veered off course.

Tandler worked at social networking service Yammer when Sacks was its CEO, and she praised him on Twitter, where she accumulated a large following as a blistering "anti-San Francisco influencer," according to the *San Francisco Examiner*, even though she had moved to New York City. In 2020, Sacks' Craft Ventures made a seed round investment in a Tandler-led startup called Life School, which later closed after releasing a few episodes of a self-help-style podcast. Both Tandler and Sacks made donations on August 6, 2021, to the campaign to recall three members of the San Francisco school board.

Other San Franciscans were getting paid to fearmonger about San Francisco's problems—some more openly than others. In January 2021, Jason Calacanis created a GoFundMe to raise $75,000 to "hold the DA of SF accountable to the people of SF" by hiring a journalist to write about Boudin.[16] "We must [hold] the 'Killer DA' accountable," Calacanis wrote on X.[17] The effort ultimately raised more than $59,000 from Calacanis, Marc Andreessen, and other venture capitalists, which Calacanis gave to Susan Dyer Reynolds as she launched a publication called *Gotham* that portrayed the city as a fallen hellscape. Reynolds' Gotham By the Bay LLC, which is incorporated in Wyoming, also received $100,000 from Neighbors for a Better San Francisco, which was the biggest donor to the campaign to recall progressive DA Chesa Boudin. After Boudin was recalled, Calacanis, speaking to the viciously anti-progressive Democrat tech exec Garry Tan, said, "This really helped."[18]

Calacanis recommended that his peers follow the same strategy of paid-for media.

Despite David Sacks' efforts to speak for San Francisco's disenchanted Democrats, his record of campaign finance donations told the story of a die-hard Republican. Sacks helped power the political ambitions of traditional Republican politicians as well as Blake Masters and JD Vance, both of them Thiel protégés. In 2016, he donated to Kyrsten Sinema—a Democrat who was known for bucking her party's priorities—"once again sticking a thorn in the side of progressives," according to the *San Francisco Chronicle*. In 2021, he gave $70,223 to Florida governor Ron DeSantis. He donated $60,000 to Republican Miami mayor Francis Suarez's Miami for Everyone PAC, whose lead donor was Sacks' podcast co-host Chamath Palihapitiya.

In summer 2022, an organization called Purple Good Government PAC filed its first donor report. The PAC's existence wasn't reported on at the time, and Sacks' representative declined to answer questions about its plans, but the organization's filings included people from Sacks' network. The PAC's treasurer was James Kull, a financial advisor who signed a mortgage for a Miami mansion purchased by an LLC whose address matched one used by Sacks. The PAC raised about $280,000 in the first six months of 2022, including $125,000 from David and Jacqueline Sacks. Three donors—EarthLink founder Sky Dayton, e-commerce entrepreneur Diego Berdakin, and the Dohring Family Trust—gave $50,000, with each entity giving separate payments of $5,000 and $45,000.

In its first year, the PAC dispensed about $135,000, most of it in the form of a $100,000 donation to Friends of Ron DeSantis leadership. In October 2021, Sacks hosted a fundraiser for the Florida governor. He tweeted his hopes for a Newsom–DeSantis matchup in 2024.

In April 2022, according to the court-disclosed Musk texts, Palantir co-founder and venture capitalist Joe Lonsdale told Sacks that Governor DeSantis had called him to offer help in sealing Musk's Twitter bid. DeSantis would later go on to officially announce his presidential campaign in that buggy audio-only Twitter Spaces event hosted by Musk and Sacks.

Under Thiel's guiding example, Sacks was forming his own political donor network. He hosted a fundraiser for Vance during his senatorial campaign. In April 2022, Sacks donated $1 million to Protect Ohio Values PAC, which supported Vance. Around the same time, Trump endorsed the *Hillbilly Elegy* author. Both the donation and the endorsement were reportedly brokered by Thiel. On September 15, Sacks co-hosted a Republican fundraiser with fellow PayPal Mafia member Keith Rabois. Guests included serving Republican senators Rick Scott, Marco Rubio, and Chuck Grassley, and Republican candidates Masters, Vance, and Mehmet Oz.

There were no reliable estimates of Sacks' net worth. He had mansions in San Francisco, Los Angeles, and Miami. In addition to a fortune made as an executive, he had access to the fruits of investing in successful startups under the aegis of Craft Ventures, his VC firm. In an episode of *All-In*, Sacks and his co-hosts suggested—somewhat tongue in cheek, but not entirely—that he had $1 billion worth of Solana, a popular crypto token that he had invested in through his interest in Multicoin Capital, a crypto-trading firm. (Donald Trump would later release his $TRUMP crypto meme coin on the Solana blockchain.)

Sacks said that his political views had "evolved" from libertarian to "populist." In a podcast interview with Bitcoin influencer Anthony "Pomp" Pompliano, Sacks said that he had "working-class views" in line with a transforming Republican Party. He cited the work of Ruy Teixeira, a liberal political scientist who co-authored the influential book *The Emerging Democratic Majority* with John B. Judis. Arguing that Democrats' "professional class hegemony" had made the party out of touch with working people's concerns, Teixeira defected from his political peers to join the right-wing American Enterprise Institute.

Sacks had his own version of Teixeira's critique: everything was run by Democrats with college degrees, who enacted "the tyranny of woke progressivism."[19] Even big corporations, Sacks tweeted, were run by Marxists, echoing the long-held belief of DeSantis that companies like Disney promoted a "woke ideology."

Musk, too, would become a prominent Disney critic, accusing the company of "mandatory, institutionalized racism and sexism" and funding a fired actor's lawsuit against the company.[20] "Disney has almost certainly broken the law thousands of times (no exaggeration)," wrote Musk.[21] In response to a report that Facebook was sued for allegedly facilitating child trafficking, Musk wrote of Disney's CEO, who had pulled his company's ads from X but not from rival platforms, "Bob Eiger thinks it's cool to advertise next to child exploitation material."[22]

Like others in his tech orbit, Sacks also became deeply concerned about perceived threats to online speech. In supporting Musk's Twitter takeover, he argued for a less-moderated platform, free from the censoriousness that conservatives accused tech companies of cultivating. In an April 2022 interview with Fox News, Sacks said that we were living in a McCarthyist period of "un-American movements" to stymie free speech. Comparing Musk's proposed Twitter purchase with the fall of the Berlin Wall, Sacks said, "It was the first time that you saw somebody stand up to this galloping wave of censorship that we've been seeing."

But while Sacks' project and carceral sensibility scored victories, including Boudin's recall, it later encountered significant headwinds. Los Angeles district attorney George Gascón, a progressive prosecutor in the Boudin mold, survived two recall attempts. Trumpist reactionaries like Masters, Oz, and Doug Mastriano, running for Pennsylvania governor, lost their races. Vance limped over the finish line, only for his sponsor Thiel to announce that he and his money would sit out the 2024 election. (That turned out not to be a problem for Vance.)

Thiel, at least, seemed to be shifting his focus to this question of political pragmatism—and perhaps a rejection of Sacksian doomerism. Speaking before the National Conservatism Conference on September 11, 2022, Thiel called for Republicans to find a "positive agenda" to present to the public, one that could "scale" beyond their own cloistered group of similarly aggrieved conservatives. "The temptation on our side is always going to be that all we have to do is say that we're not California," Thiel said. "It's such an ugly picture, it's the homeless poop people pooping all over the place, it's the ridiculous rat-infested apartments that don't work anymore, the woke insanities, there's so much about it that it feels like ... shooting fish in a barrel. It's so easy, so ridiculous to denounce."

Thiel was mocking this kind of rhetoric, but he also perhaps believed it. He just didn't think airing it repeatedly was politically useful. These complaints happened to be the stock-in-trade of Sacks, Calacanis, and the San Francisco crime hysterics they supported. Instead of addressing these issues, Republicans were performing their congenital form of what Thiel called "nihilistic negation"—that is, the kind of reactionary obstructionism that had helped bring us to this point.[23] In an age of widespread political cynicism, it played well on social media, which privileged conflict and sensationalism. But it didn't accomplish much in the way of policy or constructive political change.

Still, Sacks, Calacanis, and the San Francisco VC class had prominent fellow travelers. There were some loud, rich, and very online players espousing these ideas—with support from some corners of the GOP and self-declared political refugees like Tulsi Gabbard, who announced her departure from the Democratic Party by denouncing its supporters for their "cowardly wokeness," "anti-white racism," and their tendency to "demonize the police but protect criminals at the expense of law abiding Americans."[24]

The positive, Sunshine State-style program promised by Thiel in his September 2022 speech did not materialize. DeSantis failed in the presidential primary because his culture-warring obsession went beyond obnoxious rhetoric to encouraging the state to interfere in people's personal lives, from banning books to limiting their rights to healthcare and bodily autonomy. DeSantis chased right-wing political trends, ranting one week against Disney and another against lab-grown meat. Twitchy and sneering, DeSantis may have shared the same hatreds as people like his texting pal Joe Lonsdale, but he lacked all conviction. If you're going to be a bitter right-wing demagogue, you have to say it with your chest. DeSantis said it with a wet smirk.

One politician's failure—even one that he'd supported with millions of dollars and featured placement on Elon Musk's X—didn't matter to a tech oligarch with broader political ambitions. Sacks moved on from DeSantis, forming relationships with Robert F. Kennedy Jr., Vivek Ramaswamy, and other political aspirants before ultimately siding with Trump. Ideologically, Sacks remained in thrall to urban pessimism, a stance popular in San Francisco where Mayor London Breed lamented—to applause from a crowd—that drug dealers had more rights than "people who try to get up and go to work every day and take their children to school."[25] And he had company: a growing number of San Francisco elites refused to countenance what their city had become.

8

Billionaires v. The People of San Francisco

With 881,000 people living in less than 47 square miles, San Francisco packs a tremendous amount of wealth and cultural influence into a fiercely unequal city. San Francisco is far smaller than Los Angeles, New York, London, or any of the Chinese metropolises where technological devices are manufactured. It's smaller than Charlotte, North Carolina and Jacksonville, Florida. Its politics tend to be a battle between center-left and progressive factions, subsidized by the stratospheric wealth of policy-shaping tech and real-estate billionaires.

Although San Francisco was the inheritor of a distinctly American brand of social liberalism, tech elites were countercultural (in the sense that the more conservative ones cast their politics as a rebellion against the woke mainstream). Under this pretense, wearing a MAGA hat in a Google office or entertaining eugenicist ideas about race and intelligence was a way of daring to go where liberals feared to tread. "The most rebellious thing you can be in San Francisco is a Republican," wrote Elon Musk.[1]

A venture capitalist who ran the prized startup incubator Y Combinator, Garry Tan had used his wealth and professional network to become a San Francisco political power broker, helping to drag the local Democratic party to the right, pouring hundreds of thousands of dollars into the recall of school board members, the recall of district attorney Chesa Boudin, and campaigns benefiting conservative Democrats. On social media, Tan was pugilistic to the point of belligerence, casting his political enemies as corrupt malefactors responsible for the despoliation of his beloved city. He sat on the board of GrowSF, a tech-funded advocacy group with an associated PAC that could make it rain for like-minded politicians.

Late one night in January 2024, Tan had some drinks and went on a tirade on X against seven city supervisors, calling them out by name, writing, "Die slow motherfuckers."[2,3] It turned out that Tan was quoting a Tupac Shakur line, but the sentiment was clear. Tan apologized the next day and asked to be held accountable.[4] Five of the supervisors received death threats in the mail at their home addresses.[5] The mailed threats read, "Garry Tan is right! I wish a slow and painful death for you and your loved ones."[6] The mailer included an image of Tan's post. The supervisors filed police reports. Tan's supporters said that he couldn't possibly be blamed for the threats. Tan hired a new spokesperson and was profiled in the *New York Times* as a local political influencer whose civic passions sometimes got the best of him. In short order, he returned to posting with pretty much the same fury as before, without the semi-explicit death threats.[7]

One spring day, Tan's critical gaze landed on the work of freelance journalist Gil Duran, a tech-industry muckraker with a background in Democratic politics who was starting to take very seriously the right-wing political ambitions of San Francisco tech moguls. Duran had published articles on Tan and his wealthy colleagues, like Balaji Srinivasan, a tech investor who was promoting an esoteric but stubbornly influential concept called the Network State. Drawing on the anti-state and corporate charter city ideas then coming into vogue, the Network State described a potential "tech Zionism" in which right-wing techies ("Grays") would buy property, take over local institutions, and cleanse neighborhoods of their ideological opponents ("Blues"). Grays were generally intellectual tech elites who would reap the fruits of technological progress. Blues, who included woke Luddites and other political enemies, would be shut out of the bounty—forced out, in fact. It sounded like an intentionally dystopian mash-up of corporatist and colonialist ideas. Srinivasan's Network State—and its core idea of capturing or creating parallel, anti-democratic institutions—was attracting adherents on the tech right.

As Duran's work began to circulate more, Tan, writing on X, asked: who was paying this guy? The writer Susan Dyer Reynolds suggested—through a circuitous series of connections that defied space and time—that Duran was being paid by George Soros. "Interesting," replied Tan, who had called Duran a "parasite," "pathetic," and "an unserious clickbait blogger."[8,9,10,11]

On X and his blog, Srinivasan speculated about who must be funding a freelance journalist who had the temerity to question the political program being promoted by powerful tech leaders. The chart he devised was covered in slashing arrows that created an impression of a vast web of influence and money underwriting Duran.

The suggestion that someone was secretly paying Duran was hilarious to anyone with a cursory familiarity with the attenuated state of the journalism industry. Duran had provoked the VC class's ire for good reason, but he was not exactly splashing features on the front page of the *New York Times*. His work appeared in the *New Republic* (to which I have also contributed), the *San Francisco Chronicle*, and his own newsletter, which he had cheekily named *The Nerd Reich*. There was little money in this kind of work, only the satisfaction of uncovering information that powerful people didn't want the public to know. And maybe pricking their egos in the process. As Duran admitted to me at the time, his newsletter had three paid subscribers. (His fortunes have since improved.)

We do live in a culture where little escapes the cold logic of the market. For the ultra-wealthy, pretty much anything could be acquired for a price; their worlds were anointed to their specifications. If a relatively unknown freelance journalist was suddenly intruding on their good time, perhaps someone had put him up to it. Yet suspicious as it might have been to some, Duran was publishing articles about the authoritarian designs of tech VCs just because he thought it was information the public should know.

The irony was that someone in this situation *was* getting paid to spread skewed political narratives. As mentioned previously, Susan Dyer Reynolds, the journalist who had posted about a misconceived connection between Duran and George Soros (there was none), was being paid by some of Tan's political allies via a GoFundMe launched by venture capitalist Jason Calacanis while also receiving funds from Neighbors for a Better San Francisco.[12]

Duran had bigger concerns than who might be paying a local blogger. He was focused on Srinivasan and his role as the promulgator of the Network State ideology, which dovetailed with other right-wing libertarian tech movements that sought to claim land and political sovereignty for tech elites. "It is very much a right-wing ideology, but not exactly Republican," said Duran.[13]

The ideology was corporatist, with the startup as the platonic economic-political formation, which made startup founders herculean figures. It was dismissive of a political culture that seemed obsessed with wokeness and against tech's unrepentant pursuit of innovation and profit. It had a sense of religiosity, but God had been dethroned by AI—or at least by the promise of creating Artificial General Intelligence, also known as AGI, a greater-than-human intelligence that many seemed to think was only months or years away from emerging. AGI would change everything—many industry leaders openly talked about it somehow saving humanity or bringing about the end of the world. If an all-powerful AGI saw humans as an impediment to its own flourishing, it might kill us all. Whether any of this was even possible didn't matter. Venture capitalists and AI company executives controlling billions of dollars and vast, resource-guzzling data centers had convinced themselves of it. Some called AGI "the last invention," which would fix all problems facing humanity.

Duran described this belief system as a logical terminus for a group of coddled men possessing limitless money mixed with limitless self-regard. "They've kind of reached a point where they have so much wealth, and so much egomania—and, in some cases, so much drug-addled thinking—that they decide they're going to rule the world, and that democracy is an outdated form of software," he said.[14]

"They think that because they have an algorithm and an app, they can be the rulers of the world," San Francisco supervisor Aaron Peskin told the *New York Times*. "Good luck with that."[15] Peskin would become a top electoral target for San Francisco's tech elites in the 2024 election cycle.

For Duran, this rising tech authoritarianism wasn't a passing political fad but the culmination of shifts in wealth distribution, political power, and the computerization of society that had been decades in the making.

"These people have enough money to be dumb and dangerous for a very long time," he said. "They have to start finding ways to seize territory and power and create a different world that doesn't look anything like the United States we have today. I think what we're seeing here in San Francisco politics is like the emergence of that strategy."[16]

In the 2024 election, Silicon Valley's boutique tech-fascist ideologies found themselves in convenient alignment with Donald Trump and the Republican Party. They shared the politics of resentment, a sense of elitism masquerading as populism, and disgust for the Democratic Party. They didn't like taxes or the government interfering in their corporate affairs. As Trump surrounded himself with VCs and tech executives, he began preaching the virtues of Bitcoin and echoing their talking points on AI policy. He gave the keynote speech at the country's biggest Bitcoin event, promising to fire SEC chair Gary Gensler and to establish a national strategic Bitcoin stockpile. He had dinner at the palatial San Francisco home of David Sacks and, impressed by Sacks' portfolio, listened as a roomful of centi-millionaires and billionaires urged him to name JD Vance, a venture capitalist and Peter Thiel disciple, to be his vice presidential running mate. North Dakota governor Doug Burgum, a software mogul and VP contender who was also in attendance, could only look on as his name went unmentioned.

As the home of the tech industry and the battleground over the perceived failures of Democratic urban governance, San Francisco became a hotbed of elite resentment and an unlikely source of cash for the Trump campaign. The city's dwindling middle and working classes blamed tech millionaires and billionaires for pricing them out of a once-vibrant city and promoting regressive policies on homelessness and criminal justice. Millionaires and billionaires in turn blamed progressives for making it difficult to build housing and turning the city into a supposedly lawless zone of violent crime, public drug use, and social disorder. Tech elites proposed tried-and-failed punitive strategies to address homelessness (bans on outdoor camping) and drug use (arrests, incarceration, forced treatment). The left tended to emphasize a housing-first policy that prioritized finding shelter for homeless people. Tech elites thought this rewarded drug use and irresponsible personal behavior.

The two sides were not quite irreconcilable. Garry Tan told a reporter that he'd had a rewarding meeting with one of the supervisors whom he threatened in his infamous X post.[17] But that gesture toward detente seemed unlikely to stem the very real anger expressed by Tan and his colleagues. Tan and his political opponents were at odds for good reason. They had vastly different ideas about the causes and solutions to San Francisco's problems. They disagreed about who should wield power and the management of the city's limited resources. These were classic political differences, but they had been amplified on the social-media stage. As a wealthy, well-connected political player with a large audience, Garry Tan was key to this new dynamic.

"There's a deep polarization taking place, and the tech people with all their money are throwing a lot of gasoline on the fire, to try to move everybody's politics toward the right," said Duran. "And to pretend that they have solutions to the problems."[18]

Some of the tech leaders presented themselves as moderates, but they politicked and spoke like right-wing reactionaries, especially on social media. Tan referred to himself as a moderate or centrist.

Elon Musk adopted the same label. In March 2024, Musk posted on X what sounded like a declaration of war.

> This is a battle to the death with the anti-civilizational woke mind virus.
>   My positions are centrist:
>
> – Secure borders
> – Safe & clean cities
> – Don't bankrupt America with spending
> – Racism against any race is wrong
> – No sterilization below age of consent
>
> Is this right-wing?[19]

Musk also seemed to refuse to interrogate his own political positions. In another post, he seemed baffled that people might have problems with Alternative for Germany, or AfD, the far-right, deeply anti-immigrant German political party that was the closest thing the country had had to a Nazi party since 1945.

"Why is there such a negative reaction from some about AfD?" Musk asked Naomi Seibt, a right-wing German activist and influencer in her early twenties. "They keep saying 'far right', but the policies of AfD that I've read about don't sound extremist. Maybe I'm missing something."[20] (Seibt worked as a paid spokesperson for an anti-climate science campaign launched by the libertarian Heartland Institute.[21])

Musk would become a vocal supporter of the AfD—to the point where he was denounced for electoral interference by Chancellor Olaf Scholz. In the run-up to the February 2025 national elections, Musk appeared via video at an AfD rally and urged Germans to move beyond "past guilt" and to vote AfD to protect their civilization from outside invaders.[22,23] AfD finished second, the best result for a far-right German political party since the Nazis came to power.

When France's right-wing political parties ran strongly in a June 2024 election, Jacob Helberg, the Palantir advisor who'd emerged as an influential hawkish voice against China and TikTok, asked why Marine Le Pen's National Rally (NR) party was considered right-wing. This was the party that was forced to expel its founder—Marine Le Pen's father, Jean-Marie Le Pen—for his racism and dismissal of the Holocaust as a "detail of history."[24,25] The party had long promoted mass deportations of immigrants, xenophobia, and nativism. Helberg either wasn't aware of this history, or perhaps he wanted to gild it as something it was not.

"They want borders, they want law enforcement, they want deregulation, they want lower taxes, they want nuclear energy, they want to choose what cars they drive," said Helberg, before repeating his first point. "And most importantly they want borders. That's not 'far right.'"[26]

People with highly partisan beliefs can think they are acting more rationally and morally than those they oppose. Presenting oneself as the face of moderation is both a common political strategy by extremists and central to the supposedly logic- and reason-based politics of tech reactionaries. In a world devoured by woke extremism, they represent innovation, merit, and American excellence (a phrase favored by Vivek Ramaswamy). Political billionaires stand atop the pile of their wealth and promise that the smart thinking that got them there is now being made available to you, the citizen. They are reasonable. The other side is not.

It turned out that they were not moderate. It's possible that billionaires seeking to impose their political whims on a city or a nation could never be considered "moderate." They command too much power, too many resources, and have too much self-interest on the line to be considered anything but prime examples of what has increasingly been described—by academics and former president Joe Biden alike—as America's slide into oligarchy.[27] In practice, many of these professed moderates gave money to Republican candidates and organizations. They typically put their political weight toward familiar conservative shibboleths: lower taxes, anti-union efforts, charter schools, recalls of Democratic politicians, police funding, criticism of progressives as obsessed with identity politics. In San Francisco, they donated to organizations that promised on the surface to represent a forgotten middle.

A number of these self-designated moderates donated to various Republican presidential primary candidates before ultimately settling on Donald Trump. Billionaire hedge fund manager William Oberndorf—a conservative who gave to "moderate" groups supporting the recall of DA Chesa Boudin—was a major donor to establishment Republicans like Jeb Bush and former Senate majority leader Mitch McConnell. North Dakota governor Doug Burgum, who ran a blink-and-you'll-miss-it campaign for the Republican nomination, owed whatever flicker of notoriety he received to his nine-figure fortune as a software mogul and the support of other plutocrats like Oberndorf.

In a supposedly ultra-blue political climate, it was these self-proclaimed moderates of the top 0.1 percent who were trying to steer city policy in their preferred direction. Their goals included taking over the Democratic County Central Committee (DCCC), defeating leftist supervisor Dean Preston, and denying Aaron Peskin the mayor's office.

In the lead-up to the 2024 election, a constellation of interlocking political 501c(3) organizations—which must report their contributors—and 501c(4)s—which don't—flooded San Francisco with money, political advertising, and the mixed motives of its backers. Their names were easily confused, which, given that some of them shared money and personnel, might have been intentional: GrowSF, TogetherSF, AbundantSF, Neighbors for a Better San Francisco, and so on. Like many political-influence operations, these organizations tended to introduce themselves as humble grassroots affairs, only to later be unmasked as billionaire-funded astroturf operations that wished to appeal to disaffected moderates and Democrats. Promising common-sense solutions, they tried to move the Overton window of political possibility to the right, toward the interests of big business.

They were helped by a pliant media poorly resourced to investigate the city's billionaires. As in every American metropolis, San Francisco's media was hollowed out by the advent of digital advertising and the rise of the Google–Facebook ad duopoly. Private equity firms bought and siphoned resources from the regional newspaper chains that were once vital parts of a healthier news ecosystem. In San Francisco, an attenuated *San Francisco Chronicle* competed against upstarts like *Mission Local* and the *San Francisco Standard*, which was owned by Michael Moritz, a billionaire venture capitalist who was in the thick of many of the political battles described here.

I found several efforts, formal and informal, to chart the flows of dark money in San Francisco politics. One was led by a group of middle-class, left-wing San Franciscans, longtime residents troubled by the indomitable rise of a small group of moguls who seemed to think the solutions to the city's overlapping crises—housing, drugs, healthcare, inequality—could be found in their bankrolls. One of them described herself as part of an "incredibly online group of moms and dads" who had come together in opposition to the school board recall. They were not anti-tech—some of them worked in the industry, or adjacent to it. They were anti-plutocracy.

The Phoenix Project was one of the more concerted efforts to map the money. Employing former journalists and political professionals, the Phoenix Project had the feel of a progressive lobbying and research outfit. A two-person operation with undisclosed backers—it was another 501c(4)—the Phoenix Project sought to warn San Francisco's voters of how the ultra-rich were trying to capture the city's politics. "They're seeking to transform San Francisco into a city that prioritizes the needs and desires of developers, corporations and the wealthy," went one dispatch.[28]

It wasn't just about the money pouring in. The Phoenix Project charged that major political players were trying to mask their donations and the relationships between various interest groups. The Phoenix Project found at least ten organizations "sharing an agenda, funding sources, and leadership." The executive directors of two groups—Neighbors for a Better San Francisco and TogetherSF—were married to one another. The journalist Ali Winston, writing in the *Guardian*, described the setup as a "network of interlocking nonprofits, dark money groups, and political action committees," with 501c(4) PACs being contained within similarly named 501c(3) nonprofits.[29]

These organizations were raising tens of millions of dollars. The Phoenix Project counted more than $33 million in donations between 2020 and early 2024, and that may not have represented the whole sum when dark money was taken into account. 501c(4) organizations are allowed to engage in political campaigns as long as it's not their "primary activity." If you need to farm out political work to avoid one 501c(4) making it their "primary activity," then it helps to have a network of such organizations doing it piecemeal. Many of the institutions discussed here had relationships with 501c(4) groups.

The group of influential businessmen called out by the Phoenix Project was small. Of the donations that the Phoenix Project was able to link to specific donors, three-quarters of them came from "23 extremely wealthy, mostly right-wing and conservative donors and corporations." Jeremy Mack, one of the Phoenix Project's employees, described what was going on as a "billionaire takeover" of the city's politics.[30]

The fingerprints of these organizations could be seen all over San Francisco politics and media in the run-up to the 2024 election. Neighbors for a Better San Francisco paid Brooke Jenkins, who replaced Chesa Boudin as district attorney, as did two nonprofits that received grants from Neighbors for a Better San Francisco. Michael Moritz funded TogetherSF, the *San Francisco Standard* news outlet, and proposition-specific campaigns. Chris Larsen and Garry Tan gave money to GrowSF, which was targeting Connie Chan and Dean Preston in the fall 2024 election.[31]

By March 2024, San Francisco's wealthy moderates seemed well on their way to capturing the city's political institutions. That month, a slate of candidates supported by Tan won election to the DCCC. At a party, Mayor London Breed celebrated what she called the "new" DCCC, clearly aligning herself with the tech elites who had barnstormed city government.

The politics of San Francisco's ascendant wealthy tech class tended to mix tepid social liberalism and soft authoritarianism.

The cryptocurrency billionaire Chris Larsen was one prominent example. Larsen was a successful entrepreneur and e-commerce executive who, in 1997, co-founded E-Loan, an early online lender and credit score provider. Larsen later became an important backer of a California financial privacy law. In 2011, he raised money for Occupy protesters in San Francisco.

Embracing cryptocurrency as a tool for financial freedom, Larsen co-founded Ripple Inc, which distributed the XRP crypto token. The company became involved in a major lawsuit with the SEC, but Larsen became a billionaire many times over and emerged as a major Democratic donor. When pro-Kamala Harris PACs accepted cryptocurrency, Larsen donated millions of dollars' worth of XRP.

At the same time, Larsen was paying millions of dollars to develop a privately owned camera system that surveilled public places in San Francisco. San Francisco police would have easy access to the systems, which were controlled by nonprofit groups involved with different business districts.[32] The camera network grew to more than 1,500 cameras across six neighborhoods. Larsen said that his goal was to provide "communitywide camera coverage," which he thought would enable police to do less while responding more effectively to property crimes.[33] Amidst heavy debate about the efficacy and legality of mass surveillance, the Electronic Frontier Foundation, a civil liberties group, obtained records showing that San Francisco police used the privately funded surveillance system to surveil activists protesting against police violence. The documents showed that the SFPD had requested and received live access to the feeds for at least a week—something that Larsen had previously described as illegal.[34]

In the run-up to San Francisco's election in March 2024, Larsen donated $1 million to advance two ballot measures supported by Mayor London Breed. Both of them, as described by the *San Francisco Standard*, seemed to exemplify the authoritarian turn in Democratic politics: "one to force welfare recipients suspected of drug addiction into treatment; and another to bolster public safety, which included giving cops greater access to surveillance tools like drones and license-plate readers."[35] More surveillance tools for cops potentially meant more surveillance cameras in Larsen's network.[36] Both ballot measures passed.

For the fall 2024 mayoral election, in which San Francisco's voters would order several candidates as part of a ranked-choice voting system, tech leaders were divided. The ranked-choice system seemed to encourage disagreement, though it could also prove effective at neutering leftist mayoral candidates like Aaron Peskin. Garry Tan endorsed both Mark Farrell and London Breed, with Daniel Lurie, an heir to the Levi Strauss fortune who received a $1 million donation from his billionaire mother, as his third-ranked choice.[37,38] Billionaire venture capitalist Michael Moritz put $3.5 million into the race, much of it via TogetherSF, which was run in part by former Farrell staffers.[39] Moritz's money went to support Farrell and Proposition D, which would reduce the number of commissions helping govern the city to 65.[40]

Chris Larsen supported Mayor London Breed, who he thought had shepherded the city through rough times. "The social justice protests, riots—whatever you want to call them—she held the city together," Larsen told the *San Francisco Standard* in an interview in which he criticized the political left as making impossible demands of city officials.

"I get mad at the progressives," said Larsen. "They want to label everybody 'right-wing' that opposes them. But with a Mark Farrell, that is what you're going to get. He's basically a Republican running for mayor."[41]

Every major mayoral candidate was a Democrat, including Farrell. Accusing someone of being a Republican—much less a Donald Trump supporter—was a grave charge. Farrell's campaign manager said that Larsen should be "ashamed of himself" for such a comparison.[42]

While donations to individual candidates were capped at $5,500, there were no such limits on donations to PACs and other organizations supporting a candidate, ballot measure, or cause. Larsen gave $600,000 to PACs supporting Mayor Breed. Like many of his peers, Larsen supported tech executive Bilal Mahmood over incumbent Dean Preston for the District 5 supervisor race.

Between the Board of Supervisors, the mayor's office, and a raft of ballot measures designed to reshape city governance to empower the mayor and undermine the city's many interest groups and commissions, there was a lot at stake for San Franciscans in the fall 2024 election. The city's issues—a housing shortage, a drug epidemic, homelessness and gaping inequality—were the same being faced by cities across the country. But San Francisco had become not just a political testing ground for Silicon Valley tech billionaires. It had become part of a broader national struggle over how the country would be governed and what values it would pursue.

"I thought I was covering how this billionaire/millionaire group was going to try to take over San Francisco and use that as a template for the rest of the country. And that's kind of what Garry Tan had spelled out in his speech at the Network State Conference in 2023," said Gil Duran. "I figured it's going to be important in the future. Well, the future is now."[43]

9

A Working Model

The political battles playing out in San Francisco would mirror ones playing out in Miami, Austin, and nationally during the 2024 presidential election. Elon Musk's ruthless purge of Twitter's staff and David Sacks' reactionary campaigns against liberal Democrats would be replicated in various political arenas—including, eventually, the federal bureaucracy, which Musk would seek to gut with his DOGE project. In the meantime, tech leaders searched for places that could replace San Francisco, cities where their budding authoritarian politics might be better welcomed. Miami and Austin—socially liberal blue redoubts in otherwise red states with no income tax—became Covid-era refuges for technological innovators and the people who funded them. Miami, a financial center a stone's throw from the Caribbean in a solidly Republican state prone to corrupt governance, offered a flashy beachside siesta far from San Francisco's upmarket squalor. While Miami was already suffering the ravages of climate change, tech moguls plunked down eight-figure sums for waterfront mansions in the city's exclusive island districts. Miami also became home to financial firms like Citadel Securities, headed by Republican mega-donor Ken Griffin, who moved his company from Chicago.

With Dell and Texas Instruments, along with a number of companies serving the military and energy sectors, Austin already had an established tech industry and pockets of quirk amidst a booming events scene that saw spectacles like SXSW and Formula 1 attracting tens of thousands of visitors. As its population neared one million people, the city may have outgrown its "keep Austin weird" mantra, but with its huge public university, state capitol, cultural offerings, solid housing stock, and Texan strain of hippiedom, it had matured into one of the country's more desirable places to live.

Venture capitalist Joe Lonsdale, another disciple of Thiel, with whom he co-founded the surveillance and data analytics contractor Palantir, was one of the Silicon Valley executives who left San Francisco for safer climes in Austin. Lonsdale announced his move in November 2020. Palantir, which was based in Denver, had an office in Austin. Lonsdale said he moved because California was too expensive, "not a good place for middle class living standards." There were, he said, "a lot of billionaires and a lot of people who are just getting along," perhaps not recognizing which category he belonged in.[1] Describing himself as "socially liberal and fiscally conservative"—he had once called transportation secretary Pete Buttigieg a "loser" for taking paternity leave to care for his newly adopted baby—Lonsdale thought that San Francisco had gone too far, slipping into a "decadent society," as he told the *New Yorker*.[2]

California's legal environment had become oppressive in a way Lonsdale didn't like. "If you get sued you're probably guilty until proven innocent," he said.[3]

When Lonsdale was 29 and already a successful entrepreneur, he became romantically involved with a Stanford undergraduate whom he was mentoring through a university program. The relationship was tumultuous, its power imbalance described by the young woman as confusing and difficult, and ended badly.[4] In a complaint to campus authorities, the woman accused Lonsdale of rape. No charges were filed. Stanford banned him from campus, then later welcomed him back. Lonsdale and his accuser sued one another, before settling all claims.

In Austin, Lonsdale put his wealth to work. He bought a mansion on a plot of land northwest of the city. According to one person who visited Lonsdale's property several times, the tech entrepreneur required visitors—even delivery drivers—to sign a six-page nondisclosure agreement, sign a "surveillance consent form," have their face photographed, and submit their phone number. After completing the process, visitors received a text message with a link to a set of "guest instructions" and copies of the signed surveillance consent form and the signed NDA.

Nondisclosure agreements tend to be restrictive for a reason. They're a favored tool of the powerful to shape their public image, maintain advantages in business, keep privileged information secret, or to exercise control over others. The *Wall Street Journal* reported that Elon Musk required partygoers to sign NDAs at events where he allegedly consumed drugs like LSD and ketamine.[5] Similar stories abound for entertainment-industry celebrities engaging in one-night stands or simply welcoming people into their homes.

But not many rich and powerful people make delivery guys sign NDA agreements for the honor of being allowed past their security gatehouse. And even fewer probably craft the kind of draconian document that was shared with me. According to the Lonsdale NDA, visitors were banned from saying anything about pretty much anything or anyone they met, learned, encountered, or otherwise stumbled upon while at chez Lonsdale. Visitors were forbidden from sharing anyone's name, taking photographs, or describing a person's "characteristics, customs, patterns, views, opinions, ideas, conduct, habits, purchases, shopping preferences/habits, personal database/contacts …"—the list went on. Visitors were forbidden from responding to requests from the media and "shall report to the Company any such media inquiries."

Should someone violate the NDA's terms, the document offered the usual promises of civil litigation and even criminal charges. "Any breach of this agreement would cause irreparable harm to the Company and/or the Lonsdale Family for which damages are not an adequate remedy," the NDA read.

The NDA also applied in perpetuity—and beyond. "This Agreement shall inure to the beneficiaries or the legal representatives of the Company and the heirs of Tayler and Joe Lonsdale and shall be binding upon your heirs and legal representatives." Make sure to tell your grandchildren about their future legal obligations to the grandchildren of Joe Lonsdale.

After securing his Austin fiefdom, Lonsdale established a nonprofit organization called Cicero Research, also known as the Cicero Institute, which would quickly grow into an influential policy and lobbying shop with an annual budget of almost $10 million. Cicero had an associated 501c(4), Cicero Action, which didn't have to disclose its donors. The Cicero Institute was a registered 501c(3), but its 990 forms from 2021 and 2022 stated that its contributors were "restricted," which entities registered as "public charities" are allowed to do. As of 2022, Cicero didn't satisfy the requirement that at least a third of a public charity's contributions come from the public, with no individual supplying more than 2 percent of the total. Most, if not all, of the Cicero Institute's financing appeared to come in the form of large gifts from people connected to the organization, likely Lonsdale himself. Tax filings from 2022 listed an "interest in limited liability company" that was worth $5.5 million (down about $800,000 from the prior year). The organization mentioned multimillion-dollar stock holdings in financial software firm Anduin, co-founded by Lonsdale, and biotech startup National Resilience. Lonsdale's venture capital firm, 8VC, was an investor in both companies.

The Cicero Institute's directors were Lonsdale's family members and close associates. The directors were chosen by Lonsdale, who was "the sole member of the corporation." In 2021, Cicero gave $2.5 million to the University of Austin, a new school of higher education appealing to anti-woke sensibilities and a tolerance for "dangerous ideas" that had allegedly been snuffed out at today's risk-averse colleges. In 2022, Cicero gave the school $6.7 million as Lonsdale promoted the venture in appearances with University of Austin co-founder Bari Weiss and other like-minded supporters.

In 2021, the Cicero Institute began using a company called Arpinum to process payroll, taxes, and other financial services. In 2022, Cicero paid Arpinum $2,242,721—"an amount equal to the direct costs incurred" by Cicero that year. In other words, Arpinum wasn't taking a fee. Arpinum—which is named after the real Cicero's hometown in ancient Rome—was 35 percent owned by Lonsdale and Cicero Institute treasurer Whitney Munro. Lonsdale was Arpinum's president and Munro its chief operating officer (although she didn't list Arpinum in any of her public bios or on her LinkedIn profile). It was registered in Virginia and Texas, where it shared an address with the Cicero Institute. That same address was also home to Anchor & Arrow Strategies, a lobbying firm that, according to the political tracking site LegiStorm, had four clients in 2024: Palantir, Epirus, Saronic Technologies, and American Phalanx. Joe Lonsdale co-founded Palantir and his firm 8VC invested in the second two. According to state corporate records, Anchor & Arrow was the trade name for Arpinum; the company has done business under that moniker since January 2024. The same day, Cicero Action, Lonsdale's 501c(4), registered a new trade name: American Phalanx. Later it paid $20,000 to Anchor & Arrow. Maybe someone from Cicero Action/American Phalanx walked down the hall to drop off a check.

This kind of dizzying, circular integration—of big-time tech and military investments, Heritage Foundation-style policy advocacy, educational activism, nonprofit payroll processing, and old-fashioned influence peddling, much of it taking place under the same roof, all of it reinforcing shared concerns and ownership interests—is not necessarily illegal or even unusual. But it's revealing of how wealthy entrepreneurs operated in multiple related domains at once, sometimes with a great deal of self-promotion, sometimes more quietly. Their interests tended to converge, if not share office space, with the fortunes of one raising the fortunes of others. And without much notice, a company that was a payroll and accounting firm for a billionaire's nonprofit foundation could become a lobbying firm representing his other investments.

Ensconced in Austin, Lonsdale began pouring money into local and state politics, with a particular focus on public homelessness, which he said was being worsened by the "homeless-industrial complex." In public writings, Lonsdale and the Cicero Institute derided homeless groups' "housing first" policy, which prioritized finding stable housing for the person (without imposing conditions). Lonsdale said that housing first was "lucrative for many activists" but ineffective, despite a raft of research that found that housing-first policies can help reduce long-term homelessness, providing people with a stable place from which to address drug abuse, health, employment, and other issues. New York City, for example, had a "right to shelter" policy—one that Mayor Eric Adams attempted to revoke—guaranteeing every homeless person a shelter bed. Many policy experts have cited the essential need to build more housing—thereby making it more affordable for all—to help address homelessness and the overall cost-of-living crisis.

The Cicero Institute disagreed. "Permanent supportive housing doesn't address homelessness," the Institute wrote on its website.[6] "It creates demand for more homelessness and supports cronyism."

The Cicero Institute seemed to be shading toward conspiracism, arguing that corrupt nonprofits were promoting homelessness in order to line their pockets.

In an April 2021 piece titled "Banning Street Camping Gets People the Help They Need," which was published by the Cicero Institute and on his own blog, Lonsdale claimed that "the explosion of homelessness" in Austin had nothing to do with rising housing costs or other economic stresses. Instead, "permissive camping laws lure needy individuals away from services and back out on the streets." He seemed to operate from a perspective that some people were homeless by choice or that homelessness might be cleaned up by simply forcing people out of public view.[7]

In 2021, Lonsdale donated $40,000 to Save Austin Now, a super PAC that pushed Proposition B, a measure to reintroduce a ban on camping on public property. The proposition passed with 57 percent of the vote. That year, Texas passed an anti-camping bill based on Cicero's work. Similar bills were passed in Georgia, Kentucky, Missouri, Oklahoma, and Utah, where, Lonsdale later wrote triumphantly, "we made civil commitment—aka involuntary commitment—easier."[8] He denied that these laws were criminalizing homelessness.

Not long ago, so-called model legislation—proposed bills written by corporate interest groups and lobbyists—was distributed a bit more discreetly. It could be a scandal that ideologically motivated outsiders were writing bills for state legislators. But the practice has only grown and become more accepted over time, especially as legislators barely take time to read some of the bills they pass. The most powerful of these organizations is probably the American Legislative Exchange Council, or ALEC. *USA Today* once called it "the nation's best-known 'model-bill factory,'" and it's also a lobbying and influence-peddling operation with a vast network of connections in Republican politics.[9] Founded in 1973, ALEC starts courting conservative legislators as soon as they're elected, inviting them to conferences and developing the kind of lobbying relationship that might endure throughout a politician's career.

ALEC provides legislators with so-called fill-in-the-blank legislation, pre-crafted bills that between 2010 and 2018 were introduced 2,900 times in state houses and in the United States Congress. More than 600 of these bills were passed into law, according to *USA Today*'s investigation. The bills that ALEC helped pass tended to be pro-corporate, reducing regulations, chiseling away at consumer rights, eliminating "sanctuary cities," and pushing other conservative priorities. In 2012, ALEC became briefly infamous after vigilante George Zimmerman shot and killed Trayvon Martin, a 17-year-old Black child who was out walking and eating a snack. ALEC had helped pass "Stand Your Ground" laws in a number of states, which gave ordinary citizens broad legal cover to shoot people whom they found threatening. These laws were cited to defend the shooting of Martin and other Black people. ALEC disbanded the committee that had created a Stand Your Ground model bill, which was one of more than 1,000 pieces of model legislation that ALEC had disseminated.

ALEC wasn't a secret operation and had touted its success in the mainstream press. It had many corporate members, who could pay for seats on the ALEC committees that drew up model legislation. Still, these kinds of relationships used to play out with a certain sub-rosa discretion. Not so anymore. Influence peddling and crafting cut-and-paste bills for state legislators now were the subject of boastful press releases and moralizing tabloid op-eds.

For Joe Lonsdale and the Cicero Institute, the adoption of its model legislation, with its draconian approach toward homelessness, was talked about as a point of pride. In Florida, Lonsdale donated hundreds of thousands of dollars to Republican politicians and organizations, becoming a vocal public supporter of Governor Ron DeSantis, and the Cicero Institute helped shape the bill that passed through Florida's Republican-led legislature.[10] When Governor DeSantis signed HB 1365 into law in March 2024, Lonsdale praised it on X as "the toughest homelessness law in the nation."[11] On his own blog, Lonsdale proclaimed that "Florida's homelessness revolution" was at hand.[12]

"When we started working on homelessness, many people considered these ideas fringe," wrote Lonsdale after Florida banned street camping. "Activists have vociferously opposed us at every turn. It takes guts to stand up to the homeless-industrial complex."[13]

Fringe ideas can be revolutionary, part of an intellectual vanguard staking out a claim for progress, or they can be regressive, consigned to society's margins for understandable reasons. It's clear how Lonsdale viewed his homelessness policy.

The United States' conservative-dominated Supreme Court agreed with Lonsdale. On June 28, the Supreme Court ruled 6–3 in *City of Grants Pass v. Johnson* that a town in Oregon could maintain an ordinance banning "people who are homeless from using blankets, pillows, or cardboard boxes for protection from the elements while sleeping within the city limits." Supreme Court justice Elena Kagan, arguing in dissent, said that the decision "leaves the most vulnerable in our society with an impossible choice: Either stay awake or be arrested."[14]

Even with dissent from prominent liberals like Justice Kagan, criminalizing public homelessness had a troubling degree of bipartisan support. Politicians from both major parties welcomed the Grants Pass ruling. The Cicero Institute was one of dozens of conservative groups that filed an amicus brief in the case. California governor Gavin Newsom and San Francisco mayor London Breed—both Democrats—filed amicus briefs arguing that politicians needed more powers to clear encampments. On the other side of the case, at least 40 amicus briefs were filed by "223 experts on unhoused youth, 57 published social scientists studying homelessness, leading members of the Congressional Progressive Caucus, six Democratic state AGs, and the Southern Poverty Law Center."[15]

With the Grants Pass decision, Lonsdale proclaimed another victory against "the homeless-industrial complex." Addressing Cicero Institute supporters, he wrote, "Data and phrasing from these briefs made an impact on the opinion of the court, written by Justice Gorsuch. We want to thank Leonard Leo, a legal giant whose advice and support of our brief was essential."[16]

Cities could now expect more latitude when implementing anti-camping bans and clearing homeless encampments. In some places, it wasn't just illegal to pitch a tent in public; it had become illegal to even sleep with a blanket—or a piece of cardboard—anywhere outside. Like other initiatives to seize homeless people's possessions and bus them out of town, it was part of an effort to clear the homeless from public view. That was the priority. As being homeless became increasingly criminalized, municipalities would continue to use the police to address a social and economic problem. Less than two months after the Supreme Court ruling, the town of Grants Pass officially banned camping on public property while establishing four designated sites where homeless people could camp for several days before being asked to leave.[17] (That ban was followed by another legal challenge.)

"I wouldn't look at this decision as a question of jailing homeless people," said Devon Kurtz, Cicero's public safety policy director. "I would look at it as authorizing law enforcement to engage with homeless people with the threat of punishment."[18]

That threat of punishment, of course, included jail.

Social workers, activists, and homeless people themselves emphasized that the precondition for addressing homelessness was providing people with stable, safe, permanent shelter—hence the importance placed on housing-first policy. Existing homeless shelters could be dangerous, overcrowded, or impose conditions—ranging from religious worship to sobriety—that didn't work for people struggling on the margins. Indeed, people were much more likely to get off drugs after they had a place of their own to call home, rather than bouncing between the streets and unsafe shelters.

The VC push against homelessness seemed to go beyond clearing away the unhoused masses. It was part of a classist, authoritarian vision for how cities should be run and for whom.

After Sachin Agarwal, a co-founder of GrowSF, posted about a wild incident in which a joyriding driver crashed into a bike shop at 3 a.m., Lonsdale chimed in on X to thank Agarwal for "speaking up." The article about the bike shop accident cited a reckless street-racing culture as the cause of the accident while portraying it as one of many accumulating frustrations—including lower foot traffic, lack of economic development, and theft—that might lead the bike business owner to close his shop for good.[19] The article mentioned homelessness once as a concern in the area but didn't connect the issue to the store's troubles.

But Lonsdale seemed to see it differently, leavening his anti-homeless policy with a dash of conspiracy. "Grants Pass lets us clean this up," he wrote to Agarwal, referring to the Supreme Court case. "I'm told a high % of homeless criminals they pay to come to SF are also sex offenders; it's a mess."[20] Replying to someone else, Lonsdale wrote, "SF tax dollars pay thousands to come in and take advantage of the drug markets and harm themselves and the city."[21]

Lonsdale may have been speaking figuratively about economic inducements, because San Francisco did not have a program to pay homeless people, or homeless sex offenders, to come to the city.

It wasn't just Joe Lonsdale and his colleagues at the Cicero Institute who were enthused about the Grants Pass decision. Some Democratic politicians saw an opportunity to excise a problem. A month after the Supreme Court ruling, California governor Gavin Newsom issued an executive order decreeing that state agencies should start clearing encampments from state land.[22] Municipalities now had political cover to exercise the power recently granted to them by the Supreme Court. San Francisco mayor London Breed attended an encampment clearing in her city. She stood across the street as city employees took away the shelter and possessions of a handful of homeless people and pressed them to move on—anywhere else. Breed refused to be interviewed by reporters.

Governor Newsom offered a more hands-on approach. On August 8, Newsom was filmed helping clear an encampment in the San Fernando Valley. Wearing work gloves, a baseball hat, and aviator sunglasses, he pushed a shopping cart apparently filled with someone's stuff and lugged around garbage bags. Speaking to a journalist, his attitude was practically triumphant. "A lot of stuff we do you don't [physically] see the results," said Newsom, who threatened local officials with cutting off state funding if they didn't do more to clear encampments. "It's nice to see the before and after. You feel like at least you accomplished something at the end of the day."[23]

It was for many a nauseating scene: a millionaire politician throwing away the few possessions owned by someone who had no home and nowhere to go. This was somehow considered good policy and good PR.

Even with all of the problems posed by addressing homelessness and building more housing in this country, it seemed like a cruel, regressive measure—a sure step backwards that would further destabilize the lives of homeless people. I found it unconscionable that politicians were proud of forcing vulnerable people deeper into destitution, into invisibility.

Yet for Joe Lonsdale and the conservative legal and business organizations that had poured millions of dollars and thousands of billable legal hours into this effort, it was exactly what they wanted to see.

10

Finding The Exit

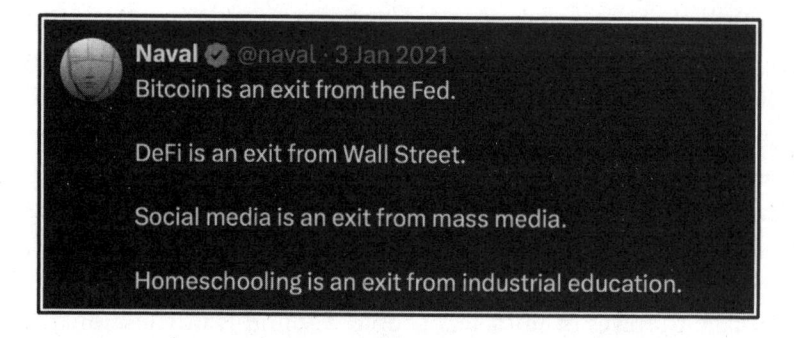

> **Naval** ✓ @naval · 3 Jan 2021
> Bitcoin is an exit from the Fed.
>
> DeFi is an exit from Wall Street.
>
> Social media is an exit from mass media.
>
> Homeschooling is an exit from industrial education.

For some billionaires, America's urban centers couldn't be reformed or rescued. Maybe the people didn't deserve it. *Noblesse oblige* had been rendered a relic of a previous gilded age. People like Elon Musk seemed to have progressed from the 1980s Wall Street mantra of "greed is good" to something even more profoundly solipsistic. Their wealth was deserved and virtuous not because of some specious notion of hard work or innovation but because they were leading humanity to a brighter future. "Elon Musk is projected to become world's first trillionaire," posted Doge Designer, one of the Musk-centered accounts that the billionaire frequently quoted. "He said 'My plan is to use the money to get humanity to Mars & preserve the light of consciousness.'"

"That's the goal," Musk responded.[1]

While they celebrated their Napoleonic accumulation of power and resources, these moguls dreamed of leaving society and wielding their influence from a protected remove. Since William Randolph Hearst built his castle in the hills of San Simeon, America's moneyed elite have sought to create their own Xanadus. Howard Hughes attempted to disappear from public view entirely—a product partly of his obsessive-compulsive disorder, but also of his desire to avoid the intrusions of lawmakers and process servers.

Tech moguls began using the term "exit" to describe their desire to leave existing institutions behind. While enjoying incredible wealth and wielding power of their own, the political system was constricting in a way that they found intolerable. It couldn't be fixed. It had to be escaped—exited.

"I think it's hard to even have an illegal Swiss bank account, and that's a really modest way," said Peter Thiel in April 2024. "It's hard to exit. It's much harder to exit the United States than it was 20, 30 years ago."[2]

Land and luxury had long been requirements for billionaire redoubts, but in this search for an exit, sovereignty became equally important, as tech leaders espoused American nationalism while collecting foreign passports. Thiel reportedly owned passports for the US, New Zealand, and Malta. Eric Schmidt sought citizenship in Cyprus. Members of the tech leadership class combined far-right libertarian ideology, a belief in an inevitable near-term apocalypse, and Darwinian survivalist beliefs to create their own bunkers against the end of the world. Peter Thiel in New Zealand, Mark Zuckerberg in Hawaii, Sam Altman in the green hills of California—all maintained fortified homes in fairly remote locations, with an emphasis on survival.

"I have guns, gold, potassium iodide, antibiotics, batteries, water, gas masks from the Israeli Defense Force, and a big patch of land in Big Sur I can fly to," Altman reportedly told colleagues at a party for Y Combinator, the influential startup accelerator he ran.[3]

Trae Stephens, the Anduril co-founder credited with helping launch the defense tech boom, said at a conference that he had a survival bunker. He recommended to the audience that they supply theirs with nonperishable food, water, and perhaps a shotgun.[4]

Some Silicon Valley leaders began to look for a more novel kind of exit: places where they could create new countries—new polities beyond the reach of politicians, regulators, and the ungrateful mob. Giving up on politics and society, they sought to create their own fiefdoms, personal dictatorships built on their desire for a certain kind of freedom that, in practice, meant immunity from consequence. Lawlessness for the ultra-rich.

At Google's annual I/O conference in 2013, company co-founder Larry Page talked about how US laws seemed practically antique by virtue of their age. "The laws when we went public were 50 years old," said Page. "A law can't be right if it's 50 years old."

There's no inherent property of democratic governance that means laws somehow molder and break down with time. They're not people—or computers for that matter. Laws can be elastic and resilient, able to accommodate changes in how we live, work, and communicate. And some—like prohibitions on theft, murder, and fraud—reflect universal values.

Page wasn't the first to think that technological innovation was outstripping democratic governance. For some, this might seem like a potentially existential problem, a reason to refurbish our governing institutions and patch gaps in the law and devise regulations for the digital age. Let's ensure that new technologies underwrite, rather than inhibit, human flourishing. But for Page and other tech leaders, democracy's supposed lagging behind capitalist technological innovation was a reason to privilege the latter.

Some were explicitly ideological in their assessments. "I no longer believe that freedom and democracy are compatible," wrote Peter Thiel in his 2009 essay "The Education of a Libertarian."[5] He and Page shared a belief that tech industry leaders were part of a select class who could see beyond the political horizon imposed by democratic governance.

In short, if the government couldn't keep up, it should get out of the way. Invoking the example of Burning Man and its weeklong state of exception, when wealthy techies could party and escape the staid social trappings of civilian life, Page said that the tech industry should have places removed from everyday governance where it could experiment at will.

"I think as technologists we should have some safe places where we can try out some new things and figure out what is the effect on society, what's the effect on people, without having to deploy kind of into the normal world," said Page, describing something like a test server for humanity. "And people [who] like those kind of things can go there and experience that and we don't have mechanisms for that."[6]

In the years that followed, Page and fellow Google co-founder Sergey Brin bought their own islands in the South Pacific and the Caribbean. Larry Ellison, the Oracle billionaire and longtime government contractor, snapped up 98 percent of the Hawaiian island of Lanai. Marc Benioff, Pierre Omidyar, Jeff Bezos, and Mark Zuckerberg also bought up tracts of Hawaiian land. After Benioff's large land purchases—which were conducted through anonymous shell corporations[7]—generated discontent among locals worried about rising housing prices, the Salesforce founder donated $150 million to two Hawaiian hospitals.[8]

Investing in charter city startups, promoting cryptocurrency and borderless digital money transfers, and agitating for the end of the democratic nation-state, Peter Thiel became the movement's presiding spirit. In 2020, he published an introduction to a new edition of *The Sovereign Individual*, a 1997 book by James Dale Davidson and William Rees-Mogg, which had become influential on the libertarian right. Describing a coming "winner-take-all" battle between the US and China, Thiel wrote:

> On the dimension of technology, the conflict has two poles: AI and crypto. Artificial Intelligence holds out the prospect of finally solving what economists call the "calculation problem": AI could theoretically make it possible to centrally control an entire economy. It is no coincidence that AI is the favorite technology of the Communist Party of China. Strong cryptography, at

the other pole, holds out the prospect of a decentralized and individualized world. If AI is communist, crypto is libertarian.

In practice, Thiel's work had often drifted away from libertarianism, but it was still his intellectual guiding star. He was convinced that technology was the only path toward the sort of essential freedom that he sought. As he wrote in "The Education of a Libertarian": "The fate of our world may depend on the effort of a single person who builds or propagates the machinery of freedom that makes the world safe for capitalism."[9]

As an idea, it was Manichean and austere, fearful of the rabble, worshipful of wealth because it was a proxy for freedom. As a political program, it had some success. In an effort to attract capital, countries around the world ceded aspects of their sovereignty to foreign corporations, establishing tax-free special economic zones, allowing oil companies to maintain private militaries, privatizing public resources like water and electricity grids, overlooking bribery and money laundering, or affording other special rights to companies that would normally be the province of the state.

In Honduras, the project went a touch further. In 2013, after years of political lobbying by US tech moguls and anti-tax ideologues, the Honduran government passed a law that allowed for the creation of what were called Zones for Employment and Economic Development, or ZEDEs. More than a free-trade zone, a ZEDE was a place where a corporate entity could create its own governance platform on a piece of Honduran land. The land deals lasted 50 years and gave buyers a free hand, although they were still bound by some basic Honduran laws. You couldn't create a ZEDE where murder was legal. But ZEDE operators could do a lot in their little corporate city-states—for example, conducting medical experiments that would be illegal in the United States. As biotech investing, biohacking, transhumanism, and longevity research took off in Silicon Valley, that kind of experimental freedom was enticing.

Having waited for this kind of opportunity to capture foreign land for private entrepreneurial ends, several venture-capital-backed

ZEDEs soon appeared. The most prominent was on the island of Roatan. It was called Próspera and it had accrued $120 million in venture capital support from Sam Altman, Marc Andreessen, Balaji Srinivasan, Peter Thiel, and other prominent investors.[10] They also obtained funding from Pronomos, a financial firm headed by Patri Friedman, the grandson of conservative economist Milton Friedman, whose ideas helped underwrite the economic policies of various right-wing Latin American dictatorships.

The same men invested in other charter-city-style ventures. Praxis, which aimed to build a 10,000-person "cryptostate" in the Mediterranean,[11] raised more than $544 million in investment capital from investors including Srinivasan, Joe Lonsdale, the Winklevoss twins, and Pronomos.[12] Thiel's line about "the machinery of freedom" was written in support of Patri Friedman, the Pronomos chief whose seasteading project—building floating city-states on the open ocean—counted Thiel as an investor.

By 2022, Honduran politics had shifted and the new government wasn't keen on the deal its illiberal predecessor had made a decade earlier to sacrifice political autonomy for foreign investment. Honduran president Xiomara Castro signed a bill to repeal the ZEDE law. Próspera responded by suing the Honduran government for $10.7 billion. Fourteen other ZEDE operators also sued the Honduran government.[13] Their demands for damages, if fulfilled, would bankrupt the country.

"The ZEDEs were broadly unpopular, and viewed by some as a vector for corruption," the US State Department wrote in a 2022 report about foreign investment in Honduras. "But their elimination raised concerns in the business community about the government's commitment to commercial stability and the rule of law."[14]

In the US government, the concern was bipartisan. "Any direct or indirect expropriation of U.S. investments in Honduran Economic Development and Employment Zones would be regarded as a direct assault on the guarantees of CAFTA-DR [a regional free-trade agreement] and surely trigger a devastating loss of private sector confidence," wrote Senator Bill Hagerty (R-TN) and Senator Ben Cardin (D-MD) in a letter to Secretary of State Antony Blinken.[15]

When I asked a Próspera official on X how many people lived there, I got two very different answers. "Several hundred full time residents today," said J. Robertson, VP of Development at Próspera. Seconds later, Nick Dranias, General Counsel of Honduras Próspera, wrote that there were "around 10" full-time residents, with 50 more expected in the next month when new housing opened. Both officials said that there were at least 1,300 "e-residents," mostly Hondurans "who work in the zone."

However many people actually lived there day to day, Próspera was very much a real entity, creating unavoidable facts on the ground. It owned land and real estate, was constructing new buildings and refurbishing a run-down old beach resort, and had capital to deploy to defend its position. This kind of digital neocolonial project wouldn't be easily uprooted.

In fall 2023, I attended an evening of sales pitches on charter cities like Próspera. The event was held at a Lower Manhattan venue called Sovereign House that had become a clubhouse for young reactionaries, especially those with ties to the tech industry. Not exactly monetized—there was no entrance fee and an open bar—the book-lined basement venue was rumored to be financially backed by Peter Thiel, or by monarchist writer Curtis Yarvin. For some, the event space had acquired an air of right-wing radical chic—a place where one could drink, network, and embrace reactionary ideas without fear of social opprobrium. While there I was briefly buttonholed by a tall blonde man who was eager to talk about his belief in something called esoteric Hitlerism.

A few dozen people shuffled in and listened to proposals to found new cities and countries abroad—to conduct risky medical or biological experiments; to strike some blow against the liberal nation-state; to mine crypto; or, in the vision of one presenter, to be a place where guys could get together, study ancient Greek, and lift weights. No women allowed. There was a lot of that coursing through this world: masculine insecurity manifesting as homoerotic body worship. Tucker Carlson had just aired a special about the rejuvenating powers of tanning one's balls.

Most of the proposed charter cities were online communities offering virtual citizenship. They didn't have much of a life beyond their Discord servers. Some said they preferred the governance-as-a-platform idea and didn't aspire to hold and build on physical territory. A Próspera representative offered a brief presentation on the company's latest construction and land acquisitions in Honduras while eliding the fact that the state was in the process of trying to take it all back. Still, it was by far the most developed of the political entities presented there.

However much they were dressed up with transgressive philosophical ideas or appeals to personal freedom in an age of ideological conformity, the appeal of charter cities was clear. There were no taxes, no impediments to the movement of money. They were places where people like Thiel, who had expressed an aversion both to women voting and democracy itself, would get to play dictator. It was pure corporatism—the company as state, the founder as commander-in-chief. Only within this kind of purified polity could the heroic work of technological innovation fulfill its practitioners' wildest ambitions. At some point, the state, and all of its meddlesome regulations, had to step aside for men to pursue what they insisted on calling destiny—which here seemed to amount to running dubious medical-testing operations and establishing a weight-lifting commune in crypto-friendly El Salvador. These projects could only succeed abroad, in boutique nations and experimental island zones. No matter how much the US, and Silicon Valley in particular, had helped them achieve their wealth and power, the future lay in escaping its strictures.

The presentations at Sovereign House were half-baked and uninspiring—at least for those who preferred the comforts and relative peace of a socially cohesive democratic society. But these novices were following a path that was being tilled by people with far more power and money. And some of them were pretty far along.

In 2023, reports emerged that Elon Musk was building what was essentially a company town called Snailbrook, Texas. He was believed to own thousands of acres around Austin,[16] where he had also developed a compound housing some of his 14-plus children and their mothers. The new town, named after The Boring Company's mascot, would provide housing for employees of Musk's companies and other facilities. Musk had also talked about building a town called Starbase near SpaceX's launch facility in Boca Chica Village, Texas.[17] Already, for some of the 190,000 residents of nearby Brownsville, where SpaceX and its employees also had a large presence, the area felt like a Musk company town—especially when SpaceX rocket launches shook their homes.[18]

Company towns and charter cities promised something that, according to a certain worldview, had been sadly lost: a return to the frontier and a chance for heroic conquest. The story of the United States' founding and expansion was one of colonists, motivated by the promise of free real estate, settling, killing, and tilling their way from one distant coast to another. They tamed the land and removed or killed most of its indigenous people. Eventually, the continent's frontier was exhausted, causing the American empire to look to the Caribbean, the Philippines, Hawaii, and other Pacific Ocean islands that made for good naval refueling stations.

After World War II, as the US and its allies lived under the nuclear umbrella of a Pax Americana, we found new frontiers to explore in computers, drugs, psychotherapy, space, and the planet-annihilating potential of nuclear weapons. All roads led to California, the country's imaginarium. Silicon Valley's ruthless pursuit of technological innovation became a new sort of undiscovered country, a dark continent whose interior would be lit by enterprising technologists, venture capitalists, and startup founders. The internet became the ultimate site of frontier exploration—until it was colonized by the private sector, where they paved over paradise and put up an intensely surveilled shopping mall. Later technologies like virtual reality and the metaverse tried to reanimate the frontier concept, promising to immerse the user in three-dimensional digital worlds that never managed to fulfill their developers' fanciful promises.

There's a problem with the frontier, at least the kind represented in American folklore: it's a dangerous place. It's riven by battles over land and sovereignty. People grab what they want with no regard for who was there first. Not everyone wants to live or do business there.

Charter cities had the same aura of lurking danger—a sense that, say, if you violated the laws of an ultra-libertarian nation-state carved out of a sliver of Honduras and financially sponsored by American venture capitalists, the prosecution might resemble something out of seventeenth-century Salem or the nineteenth-century American West.

Silicon Valley luminaries who became daily social-media campaigners against San Francisco, American cities, Democrats, and the woke mind virus may eventually realize that they need the societies they resent. They need San Francisco—the place, the people, the resources. They need the financial markets of New York and the rotten-as-old-Swiss-cheese governing institutions of Washington, DC. They need the US dollar—the world doesn't run on Bitcoin yet. And they know it: that's why tech elites tend to keep multiple homes in San Francisco, New York, Los Angeles, Miami, and other centers of global capital. Peter Thiel is not yet living on the open ocean. Elon Musk hasn't left Planet Earth.

Some tech leaders have proposed a kind of colonization from within, reclaiming the city—legally, financially, politically—by buying up real estate, forming new political alignments, and taking over existing political institutions at the local level. With his Network State concept, the tech investor Balaji Srinivasan espoused such a program, giving it an almost proudly neocolonialist gloss. His proposed "tech Zionism" project would divide San Francisco between luddite "blues" and pro-tech "grays" who would compete for power.[19] Grays would receive special privileges, Srinivasan said in a lecture, and would cultivate relationships with power centers like law enforcement. As Gil Duran noted, Srinivasan explicitly likened the project to ethnic cleansing.[20] And he said that his friend Elon Musk's post-purchase purge of Twitter employees represented a model for what was to come.

"Elon, in sort of classic Gray fashion ... captures Twitter and then, at one stroke, wipes out millions of Blues' status by wiping out the Blue Checks," Srinivasan said. "Another stroke ... [he] renames Twitter as X, showing that he has true control, and it's his vehicle, and that the old regime isn't going to be restored."[21]

Some in tech didn't explicitly embrace Srinivasan's patchwork ideology or the charter cities concept, but they often shared a similar desire for total control, to create a society master-planned according to their whims. And it turned out that they didn't need to go to El Salvador or Honduras or the open ocean to execute their plan. It turned out there was a perfect spot right across the San Francisco Bay. On his podcast, Srinivasan would praise it as an example of the Network State ideology put into action.[22]

11

The Great Solano County Land Grab

Sometime in 2017, a mysterious group of companies with names like Flannery Associates, Kingstree, and Arran began buying up land in Solano County, California, which sits alongside the California Delta, northeast of the Bay Area. The parcels were mostly agricultural, though the purchasing companies would later claim the land was "non-prime farmland" and could be put to better use. The buyers were offering well above market price—sometimes two or three times more. A real-estate agent offered one farmer $20 million for 3,700 acres that his family had lived on since the 1880s; when he declined, the offer was increased to $30 million. Again, he said no. "It's like asking the Pope if he would give up being a priest for $2 billion," he told a reporter.[1]

Some of the plots contained windmills or natural gas storage facilities, and as an inducement, the buyers offered to allow landowners to continue earning income from the windmills even after they sold their properties. The purchases happened in relative secrecy, with Flannery et al. represented by brokers. By the end of 2018, nearly every landowner in the area had received an offer to sell their land to this unknown buyer.[2]

According to state corporate registries, the companies involved two men, Jan Sramek and Thomas Mather, though the latter's name would eventually disappear from corporate records. The companies had no real address—some were registered to PO boxes at a mail shop in a Folsom strip mall. Another was in Delaware, America's center of corporate anonymity. The companies occasionally changed names or merged with one another. But it was all one massive land-buying operation.

The land purchases started to pile up, provoking questions and community conflict. About 450,000 people lived in Solano County—mostly in towns like Vacaville, Fairfield, and Vallejo—and the land purchases were happening in a relatively small area in the eastern part of the county, not far from Travis Air Force Base, a major military facility. Locals started to talk, learning who was selling, who wasn't, and who wanted to hold out for more. Some farmers, whose families had been growing wheat and raising sheep there for generations, traded information with one another.

Journalists started sniffing around, and in August 2023, the *New York Times* broke the story that the giant parcel was being put together by tech moguls in order to build an entirely new city on Solano County farmland.[3] Funded by some of the biggest names in venture capital—Marc Andreessen, Michael Moritz, Reid Hoffman, Laurene Powell Jobs—Flannery Associates had already spent at least $800 million acquiring some 60,000 acres of land, making it Solano County's biggest landowner.

Perhaps sensing the exposure coming its way, Flannery began contacting local officials for the first time,[4] years after it had begun purchasing land, and presenting information about its project. It conducted phone polls with locals asking whether they would support a ballot initiative that would allow for the creation of a new town—a walkable bedroom community serving as a cozy suburb with kid- and bike-friendly streets, solar panels and windmills, and access to nearby tech employers. Initially envisioned to host around 50,000 people,[5] its promoters said that it could scale to 400,000 people, virtually doubling the county's population.

The main selling point was housing—an undeniably scarce and expensive necessity in any state, but especially California. Solano County's largely working-class residents paid high prices for housing and often commuted long distances to work in Sacramento and the San Francisco Bay Area. Flannery's development was meant to, if not alleviate the housing shortage, take one step toward a solution: an entirely new community built for homeowners, with the company providing financing toward home buying. They called it California Forever.

While Flannery Associates was finally talking about its plans in public, the situation between the company and locals had deteriorated into open conflict. Mistrust bloomed, as people with century-old connections to the area wondered why a bunch of tech billionaires wanted a piece of their county. People worried about water rights, vehicle traffic, promises of jobs, and the unknown designs of tech billionaires. Residents of nearby towns demanded answers of California Forever officials at local town halls. The US government wanted answers, too. Members of Congress asked the FBI to investigate the proposed city. The Committee on Foreign Investment in the United States, or CFIUS, which monitors foreign investments with national-security implications, took a look.

"We got the FBI and Treasury involved," John Garamendi, who represented the area in Congress, told the *New York Times*.[6] Garamendi called the project a "scam" to enrich investors by rezoning the properties and flipping them to developers.[7] "These folks have used strong-arm mobster techniques to try to force landowners to sell generational family farms. Farmers have been sued for their unwillingness to sell because they don't want to sell their family farm."[8]

In May 2023, Flannery Associates sued a number of Solano County landowners, claiming that they were engaging in an "illegal price-fixing conspiracy"—even as Flannery's own buying spree, paying millions above going rates, helped froth the market. Flannery pointed to text messages between landowners—co-conspirators, they were called—as evidence that the farmers were working in concert to gouge the billionaire-backed utopian-city project. They accused a local lawyer of being "one of the conduits to coordinate their price-fixing conspiracy," named him in the suit, and pledged to challenge claims of attorney–client privilege "regarding communications in furtherance of the conspiracy." Flannery asked for $510 million in damages.

The initial civil complaint was a remarkable document, stunning in its sense of corporate entitlement. It accused ranchers of having "manipulated" Flannery, demanding "outrageous concessions" and displaying "endless greed" in setting "extortionate" prices. But it wasn't the first time Flannery had engaged in these tactics: its Arran LLC entity had already sued "the Hamilton conspirators"—the Hamiltons, a landholding family ensconced in the area for generations—before reaching a settlement, resulting in Flannery purchasing some Hamilton-owned properties.

The text messages quoted in the civil complaint suggested regular communication among locals and even some "we're all in this together"-style strategizing against an incredibly wealthy adversary. But they were largely innocuous: for example, one landowner was quoted as emailing her neighbor, "I wanted to share with you that we are proceeding to sell a 278 acre parcel to the Flannery LLC 'mystery guy' we spoke about." The email recipient then emailed his father and said they should ask a friend of theirs what was going on. It was the kind of routine communication that one might expect—this was a community after all, that numinous quality that Flannery said it wanted to cultivate. As Flannery mentioned in its suit, many of the landowners knew one another; some leased land from each other or otherwise had business and social ties. But Flannery treated the messages as evidence that "the Conspirators started working together against Flannery in or around late 2018—shortly after Flannery began acquiring properties in this area."

Any evidence of a finely coordinated plan to extort Flannery was underwhelming. The messages suggested that the landowners were looking to protect themselves against a powerful interloper and, yes, to get premium prices for land they were reluctant to sell. In some instances, the landowners, or their representatives, told Flannery that they were not interested at the current offer price, which Flannery seemed to take not as a simple refusal or bargaining tactic, but as evidence of a more sinister conspiracy.

Flannery's decision to pay double the assessed value (or more) of certain parcels appeared to be the real cause of spiking land prices in the area, naturally leading landowners to believe that they could get even more for their properties. The market had been distorted by Flannery's actions and its enormous bankroll, along with its secrecy. Flannery seemed to operate as if it had the inherent right to buy the land it wanted at the price it wanted. When it couldn't do so, the company turned to lawfare—an aggressive action likely designed to force a legal settlement and the sale of the desired properties.

And it worked: less than two months after filing the lawsuit, Flannery began settling with some of the dozens of named defendants. The land sales continued. And for the remaining defendants, so did the lawsuit. As the months ticked by, more settlements were announced: more landowners, worn down by litigation, cutting a deal with Flannery.

"I cannot tell you how much hatred I have for these people," said one farmer.

"They've destroyed families," said Catherine Moy, who was mayor of the nearby town of Fairfield. "They don't care."[9]

At a public event in Rio Vista, a nearby town partially surrounded by Flannery's land purchases, residents heckled Flannery representatives. "Good neighbors don't sue their neighbors," one person shouted.

The anger seemed to be felt throughout the county, across political and class lines. "I will never trust anything that they bring forward on anything," said Monica Brown, a member of the Solano County Board of Supervisors, at a public hearing. "You broke the public trust. You operated in bad faith. You went after our farmers."

The project's secrecy hurt them, said Nick McConnell, a journalist for the *Vacaville Reporter* who covered California Forever. "If they had just come out and said, 'Hey, this is what we want to do. We're interested in working with you. What does Solano County want?', rather than trying to get Solano County to want what they did, I think people would feel very differently about that."[10]

Flannery seemed unconcerned about the reputational cost from suing people who had lived there for generations. But the company did need the goodwill and cooperation of locals. While Flannery claimed to have most of the land it required, it needed to pass a ballot measure that would allow it to rezone part of its 60,000 or so acres from agricultural land to mixed-use residential and commercial. After that, California Forever could start building. But first, Flannery needed to get the measure on the ballot, which required canvassing locals for their signatures, convincing them of the potential economic benefits coming their way at some future date.

In April 2024, California Forever began promoting what it called the East Solano Plan, which promised "15,000 local jobs paying over $88,000/year, a $200 million commitment to invest in revitalizing downtowns in existing Solano cities, and $500 million in community benefits for down payment assistance, scholarships, and small business grants for Solano residents."[11] It said it had formed a community working group to "solicit input and inform the design of a Solano Sports Complex," showed off a digital rendering of an artificial swimming lagoon, and offered grants for job training and local nonprofits. Notably, the media rollout included a video about how California Forever would "increase the resilience of Travis AFB," for instance by providing housing for military families. The company offered a statement from Travis AFB officials, who thanked California Forever for modifying some of its plans to address their concerns.

The East Solano Plan website presented dozens of short video testimonials from Solano County residents, some of them clearly reading from scripts, touting the potential of California Forever to provide housing, jobs, and an alternative to traffic-ridden commutes. It had an endorsement from an architect—a post he had written on X saying he was impressed with the plan. Company officials began giving interviews to major newspapers and appearing on their investors' podcasts. There were blogs and X posts and assurances that innovative tech companies would do business in the future city. Community organizations in adjacent towns received hundreds of thousands of dollars in grants. Nearby UC Davis received $50,000 for agricultural research.[12] California Forever released a list of a dozen companies, some of them backed by its own investors, which "expressed intent" to create jobs there.[13] They commissioned studies on the area's income gap, water usage, and the economic prospects of a planned multibillion-dollar solar project.[14]

California Forever hired dozens of people from the community for outreach and canvassing jobs. According to LinkedIn profiles, many of them retained their day jobs, meaning that they were probably working for California Forever part-time. Their hiring helped to provide a local face on a project led by San Francisco financiers. The company filled out its upper ranks with urban planners, policy specialists, Democratic political operatives, and communications professionals from big tech companies like Slack. They paid millions of dollars to contractors, canvassing firms, and political consultants with connections to local and state politicians.[15]

THE MYSTERIOUS FOUNDER STEPS FORWARD

As it was pressed into the limelight, California Forever introduced its CEO: Jan Sramek, a fresh-faced former banker and entrepreneur who seemed to have been hustling since he was born in a rural Czech town in 1987. One of the earliest English-language news clippings about him was from when he was still at a British boarding school, which he received a Soros Foundation fellowship to attend. Sramek had just taken British A-level exams and aced them, earning ten A grades, compared to three or four for a typical top student. "Although I was more attracted by the challenge of taking so many exams in a short period of time than the results themselves, I am, of course, delighted," the 19-year-old Sramek told the *Guardian*.[16] He later called the marathon exam-taking "not that difficult."[17]

From there he was off to the University of Cambridge, where he studied mathematics, was vice president of the investment club, and did some ballroom dancing. He founded oxbridgeadmissions.com, a site that advised prospective applicants to Cambridge and Oxford. He enrolled in spring-break programs at Deutsche Bank and UBS, developing an interest in finance that motivated him to transfer to the London School of Economics. Later he would intern at Barclays and Goldman Sachs. In July 2009, at age 22, Sramek got a job at Goldman Sachs, where he worked as a trader on the emerging market credit and emerging market currency desks.

Lots of 22-year-olds from elite institutions end up at Goldman, but Sramek seemed to have the gift of the gab, of charming interviewers and securing press coverage depicting himself as a brilliant young man on the make. Sramek accumulated mentions in the more gossipy rungs of the financial press. He was added to lists of future moguls among the young finance set.

The *Gateway*, a now-defunct financial paper that catered to students, ran an interview (conducted by one of Sramek's associates) anointing the young financial professional as one of the "tycoons of tomorrow." Asked to identify a role model, Sramek said, "Peter Thiel. Lateral thinker, hedge fund manager, entrepreneur, venture capitalist, intellectual, philanthropist. He seems to combine everything extremely well."[18]

The *Standard* called him a teetotaling "party boy."[19] Another publication placed him on its list of 100 "rising stars" in finance.[20]

What exactly Sramek did to earn this relative notoriety was less clear. Having spent some of my early media career laboring in the seamier corners of the content industry, I can tell you that the coverage of young Sramek had the whiff of PR placement. Some of the most flowery articles about Sramek's career movements appeared on a jobs site called efinancialcareers.com, where the young banker was called a "wunderkind extraordinaire," a "prodigy," and a "trading guru."[21] The site's correspondent claimed that Sramek slept five hours a night, ran marathons, and had co-authored a business advice book (where he quoted a popular line inspired by Ayn Rand's *The Fountainhead*: "The question isn't who is going to let me; it's who is going to stop me"). Even his LinkedIn page came in for praise. Sramek was also mentioned in the comments sections of some efinancialcareers.com articles that had nothing to do with him.

Across the ocean, American publications, always in need of content and willing to draft off their British colleagues, wrote the kind of "here's who they're talking about in London financial circles" pieces that established a reputation of intrigue and ambition for someone like Jan Sramek. *New York Magazine* noted that

CNN had glommed onto his "cocksure arrogance combined with youth."[22] Most importantly, all of this appeared in a Google search and could be promoted on social media to give the impression of professional activity and growing renown.

Sramek's rise was helped by his social life, itself an exercise in entrepreneurship. The scene in the City of London for young, well-compensated financial professionals from elite schools was a constant party—if you wanted it to be. Along with a young Deutsche Bank trader named Anjool Malde, Sramek was a partner in an events company called Alpha Parties, which threw swanky parties at nightclubs, bars, and concerts. Malde was also a musician and photographer and he documented Alpha Parties' events on Facebook—expensive, dimly lit affairs filled with beautiful, stylishly dressed young people.[23] A former BBC journalist, Malde was described as the kind of knows-everyone nightlife promoter who made an events company go. He was also ambitious in his work and, at only 24, was considered on the fast-track to being named a vice president at Deutsche Bank.

In July 2009, Malde learned that he was being investigated by his employer. Someone pretending to be an employee of Brevan Howard, a hedge fund that was a Deutsche Bank client, had written "I'm hot, I'm hot" on a finance discussion forum.[24] The relatively obscure incident spawned a complaint to Deutsche Bank. According to reporting from the time, Deutsche Bank believed the comments had come from Malde's work computer. Malde denied that he had written anything and was forced to turn over said computer for inspection.[25] On July 5, Malde put on a Hugo Boss suit and went to Coq d'Argent, a luxury London restaurant. He ordered a glass of champagne. He then walked off the roof of the six-story building, falling to his death.

Malde's suicide was a shock to the glittering young social scene in which he was a center of gravity. It seemed that an attempt at a prank—by whom was unknown—had spawned a disastrous, irrevocable chain of events that caused Malde to believe that his career was in jeopardy. Online forums and Facebook groups filled with photos and eulogies. Academic awards were established in his name.

"I would have loved to have had the chance to explain to you in two minutes that Sunday was the worst deal you ever made," wrote Sramek in a group dedicated to Malde that accumulated hundreds of tributes (and continued to do so on the anniversary of Malde's death). Sometime later, Sramek deleted his post.

Ownership of Alpha Parties, the company that Malde ran, was transferred to Jan Sramek. According to British corporate filings, Alpha Parties' original directors included Jan Sramek and his father Karel. The company had one other shareholder, a friend of Malde who didn't respond to a request for comment. By November 2010, the party was over: Sramek filed to have Alpha Parties struck off the UK corporate registry, and in March 2011, the company was officially dissolved.[26]

The next month, Sramek announced he was leaving Goldman Sachs to build his own company. On finance message boards and in blog comments, some speculated that the inveterate self-promoter had fallen foul of the annual culling of the bottom 5 percent of Goldman employees. Sramek himself sometimes appeared in comment sections to argue with his detractors.

Sramek moved to Zurich and founded an edtech company called Erudify, later changed to Better. It was soon sold to GRC Solutions, a compliance training company. Sramek became known as a serial entrepreneur—a badge of distinction in the tech industry. He had also founded an Oxbridge dating site and a social network called Nicube, which acquired a company from his friend Malde. None seemed to last more than a couple of years.

With some laudatory news coverage, a brand-heavy CV, and "startup founder" permanently etched before his name, Sramek moved to San Francisco. He founded a company called Memo; it folded about 14 months later, though Marc Andreessen, a future California Forever investor, praised the software on Twitter. Sramek got a fellowship at Y Combinator, a prestigious startup incubator that can allow founders to establish powerful connections, tinker with business plans, and pitch VCs for precious funding. Sramek blogged on Medium about climate change (worse than most people think); Bitcoin (a bright future); Neil Postman's *Amusing Ourselves to Death* ("a classic that stood the test of time"); and Apple's encryption battle against the FBI ("Are Apple and Tim Cook the new Thomas Jefferson?").[27]

He read *Sapiens*, Yuval Harari's enormously popular history of the human species. On Medium, Sramek quoted a passage from the end of the book, where Harari expressed regret that humans were powerful "self-made gods" who turned out to be irresponsible brutes, unaccountable and dangerous, selfish and insatiable. *Sapiens* ended with a sincere lament that still managed to flatter its reader: "Is there anything more dangerous than dissatisfied and irresponsible gods who don't know what they want?"

Sramek spent a brief time as a consultant for Stripe, the payments processor. He met Stripe CEO Patrick Collison, who, along with his brother John, became the first investors in California Forever. Stripe, an enormously successful, privately owned fintech company, made both of the Collison brothers billionaires. They helped introduce Sramek to other potential investors.

California Forever was a putative return to the American frontier—a back-to-the-land effort of a kind rarely attempted at this proposed scale, certainly not in the United States. Other resource-rich countries built cities—China, Saudi Arabia, South Korea—and following the wave of postwar decolonization, many freshly independent nations constructed new capitals. But California Forever was a pure product of private investment capital, although it would require the build-out of water, electrical, and other infrastructure in cooperation with county officials—a fact that spurred some local opposition. It was also that most traditional of American business schemes: a real-estate play.

The ironies presented themselves almost immediately. Top venture capitalists—some of whom aligned themselves with NIMBY organizations and lobbied against changing zoning laws in their own neighborhoods—wanted to build a bedroom community. Their main point seemed to be that we needed more housing—no argument there—but that the only way to do it was through an entirely new, multigenerational undertaking. Cities couldn't be redeveloped, but they could be built from scratch if a single corporation had total control over master-planning. Why not focus on pouring all of this money into building up existing cities that needed more resources for housing and urban development? Catherine Moy, the mayor of Fairfield, told journalists from More Perfect Union that she had offered Sramek a full city block to redevelop. He declined.[28]

It was a bit discordant. These venture capitalists were people who, judging by their frequent remarks on X, at conferences, and in the media, didn't typically exhibit much interest in urbanism or walkable cities or cultivating community. Their vision of walking through a city was navigating a hellscape of zombie addicts encircling them like something out of *The Walking Dead*. "San Francisco is the inverse Soviet Union. There are goods on the shelf, but the goods are locked up, and the criminals are free," wrote Marc Andreessen in 2022.[29]

How did a moderately accomplished tech and finance professional manage to convince some of the biggest names in tech financing to pour nearly a billion dollars into this quixotic project? Notably, they had invested their own money from personal fortunes and family offices, not their VC firms.

"We've been working on this for seven years quietly, and so, it's nice to be able to tell it," said Sramek in an interview with Andreessen Horowitz, whose co-founder Marc Andreessen was a California Forever investor.

Sramek lamented the "limited engagement between the defense community and at least some of the venture firms." Now things were different, he explained. "I think our project has an opportunity to be a nightmare for our enemies where it is an opportunity for the leading venture capital investment funds and individuals in the valley to come together with the military in a location that can accommodate growth for the next 30 years."[30]

Sramek was beginning to echo the bombastic martial register favored by tough-guy venture capitalists and executives who bragged about their "defense tech" holdings. It was the argot of Palantir's Alex Karp and a gaggle of tech bros who belonged to the "effective accelerationist" subculture, which *Forbes* described as "a philosophy that calls for technology to advance no matter the cost."[31] For this group, software was boring; as Marc Andreessen exhorted his faithful, it was time to build cool stuff.

Sramek, who was supposed to be building a large planned community, was talking about allying with the nearby military base to be a "nightmare for our enemies"—as if the Chinese leadership might sweat at the thought of a new subdivision being built in the East Bay when they had built new cities for millions of people. It may have all been a way of signaling that California Forever's proximity to Travis Air Force Base should be a mutual opportunity, not a problem. It was also a way of acknowledging his venture capitalist interviewer, who invested in military startups.

California Forever described its mission as building more affordable housing so that more people could come and work lucrative tech jobs in the center of American innovation.

"It's really simple: We just aren't building enough houses," Sramek told an audience during his charm offensive.[32]

Quite reasonably, Sramek thought that $5 million for a family home in Palo Alto was insane. He said that he thought that $1 million would be a good deal for a nice home in his future city.

It was hard to find any evidence of Sramek expressing an interest in housing or real estate earlier in his career. His past work was mostly in finance and edtech startups. He had spent a year thinking about how to build more in existing cities but decided it was too difficult. He seemed to have little interest in lobbying for fairer housing laws or a government home-building program or investing in urban real estate.

There were so many questions still unanswered. What kind of government would California Forever have? How would the community pay for the hundreds of millions of dollars in infrastructure (electricity lines, water, sanitation, etc.) that needed to be built out and connected to county services? For that matter, how would they pay for the whole project? It could cost hundreds of billions of dollars to build a city from scratch. Were VCs who usually operated on time horizons of only a few years really committed to a generational project?

It remained baffling to me that someone with Sramek's CV could somehow charm the Valley's biggest venture capitalists into buying so much land. That was one of the things I planned to ask Sramek about when I finally got a chance to speak with him.

The project to spend almost a billion dollars to buy up land to build a city started quietly and humbly, Sramek explained to me in an interview. He had found the spot while fishing in the area and decided its geography and landscape made it ideal for development.

"I borrowed money from multiple sources myself, personally, and went into pretty serious personal debt to get the project off the ground," said Sramek, "and then used that money to pay for some initial studies, and used that money to tie up the first few properties that were listed on the market at the time."[33]

Asked to explain the role of Thomas Mather, whose name appeared on early corporate documents, Sramek said:

> Tom is an old friend from London, who I've known for 20 years. He was an early investor, and then he agreed to serve as a nominee manager of the LLC that was doing the purchases, because he was someone that I trusted, and he had a fairly common name. For any land assemblage, confidentiality is important, and my name is not very common, and his is. He agreed to serve as the nominee manager, so he would basically sign the paperwork when we had negotiated a deal. And then eventually, I think a couple of years, I think it was about 18 months ago, we found someone else who was an actual nominee manager, and he took over. And then Tom remains an investor in the company.

After bringing aboard the Collison brothers, he continued fundraising, describing the process as "very incremental"—raise some money, buy land, raise more money, buy more land. "Over eight years, [we] ended up raising close to a billion dollars," said Sramek.

The A-list investors brought different interests to the project, he explained. "We have people who really care about economic mobility and economic opportunity and education, like Laurene Powell Jobs," said Sramek. "We have people who really care about climate change and sustainability, like John Doerr. We have people who really care about building stuff again, in the physical world and advanced manufacturing, like Marc Andreessen and Chris Dixon."

Sramek wouldn't disclose the size of investors' stakes. He said that Mather's was "small" and that his own was "very significant." The company's backers were operating on a different time scale than usual. "The investors would most likely realize profit by selling their stake," he said but added that that might not be for decades. This was more like a real-estate investment than a venture investment.

What puzzled me most was that Sramek talked about building a family-friendly, walkable community, but he was acquiring his land partly by suing its owners. "You don't want to be displacing anyone," he told me, but in challenging longtime landowners to sell their land and suing others in court for alleged criminal conduct, he was pushing pretty hard. In the name of building a new community, he was breaking up an existing one.

And while Flannery had settled with some landowners, it was still in litigation with others. I asked how his company would get past the anger and resentment felt by locals. "I think the tone of most of those discussions really changed," said Sramek. He said that a federal judge did find evidence of price-fixing and that that revelation had changed public perception. "In the county, there was a real watershed moment, and I received a number of phone calls from politicians, community leaders, or even people, just residents, saying, 'I'd like to apologize for how we talked about the litigation, because we've seen the articles about what the federal judge wrote, and it looks like there was actual misconduct. And so I apologize. We would still ask you to be reasonable when settling these cases, even if people did something that wasn't legal.'"

It seemed terribly unlikely that locals had been suddenly converted by a judge's claim that their neighbors may have colluded to raise land prices. While many people in the region saw economic opportunity, the opposition was widespread. So was the sense that there was something incredible about billionaire venture capitalists and their corporate representative being deemed the victims of a price-fixing conspiracy.

"You can't make this shit up. I've never seen anything like this," said Princess Washington, the vice mayor of nearby Suisun City. "This is setting a precedent for the future trajectory of what our society looks like."[34]

By the time Sramek and I spoke, it seemed that the East Solano Plan was failing to convince county residents. On July 22, 2024, California Forever announced that it was pulling the East Solano Plan ballot measure from the fall election.[35] The company would try again in a couple of years, after more environmental studies, more engagement with Solano residents, and more promises about the livable future that could be built there. It was a remarkable admission of failure, but Sramek spun it as a strategically prudent move. "We pulled a ballot measure because we found a better way to run the process," he said, explaining that it would allow more time for an environmental review and other preparatory work. The ballot measure would be back in front of voters in 2026. In the meantime, his team could continue making inroads locally and perhaps sponsor challenges to the supervisors and other elected officials who criticized the project.

If Jan Sramek and California Forever were serious about building something enduring, two years wouldn't matter much. He had already moved his family to Solano County and intended this to be his life's work. "We'll move into the first house," said Sramek. "We can't wait."

While his path to becoming the biggest landowner in Solano County may have seemed hazy, Sramek's commitment was clear. Nick McConnell, the local reporter, told me about attending a public listening event where audience members heckled Sramek for suing their neighbors. The opposition seemed heated, emotional, and in the open. It would probably not be solved by some question-and-answer sessions. McConnell asked Sramek what he would do if he couldn't win over recalcitrant locals.

Sramek looked at McConnell and said, "I will make this happen no matter what."[36]

"That's stuck with me," said McConnell. "Where does that confidence come from? Your guess is as good as mine."

12

It's Free Money

Faced with public backlash, Jan Sramek learned that building a new city takes a different kind of vision and timeline than a startup. It requires local buy-in, consent of the governed. While the project itself was deeply ambitious, it required a kind of humility—a willingness to admit that you are coming bearing disruption as much as potential economic opportunity. Starting an aggressive legal campaign against local landowners helped Sramek secure the parcels he needed, but the reputational cost will take a while to pay down. Sramek treated Solano County as a frontier to be settled, but it was something far more solid: a society.

That we live in a society seemed lost on some evangelists of exit—the people talking about the need to start new cities or new currencies. They wanted an à la carte approach to the social contract, to enjoy the benefits they preferred with few of the compromises or responsibilities toward others. For that reason, however much they may have wanted to overthrow or destroy existing political institutions—or simply bypass them—these ideological entrepreneurs tended to crop up in city halls and legislatures, looking to make a deal. For now, that's where the money and power were. That's why it somehow made sense that, even in the financial capital of the world, the heart of US dollar dominance, a crypto executive would try to convince New York City's new mayor to allow a company to start issuing digital money to city residents.

In December 2021, during the height of the Covid-19 pandemic, a dozen-plus members of a technology advisory group for New York City mayor-elect Eric Adams met on Zoom to discuss plans for the new administration. The group had a wide range of city tech issues to potentially discuss—municipal WiFi, 5G services, the 911 system, the subway.

The day's agenda included a single outside presenter: Patrick Stanley, the founder of a cryptocurrency company called CityCoins. The company's pitch was that it would develop crypto tokens for America's metropolises as a method of raising revenues for cities. Token holders would be able to support their communities, vote on budgeting and governance issues, and, this being crypto, earn some passive income. The plan included a healthy amount of gambling and speculation, as everyday people could trade in the tokens and try to buy and sell according to their price fluctuation. Miami's crypto-happy mayor Francis Suarez, who took his salary in Bitcoin, had already embraced the scheme, supporting the launch of MiamiCoin. The CityCoins team hoped they could do the same with Eric Adams, who had promised to receive at least a few paychecks in crypto.

Stanley's very presence in the meeting—the only outsider—was puzzling to some attendees. It wasn't clear how he had found his way onto the agenda. It wasn't supposed to be a sales call, and the pitch wasn't warmly received. Few people wanted to let a private company establish a convoluted crypto scheme to channel revenue to the city while ensnaring residents in a dubious market. It seemed risky and potentially illegal. Some of the advisory team members present vowed to prevent the mayor from getting involved in the program.

There was a hitch: it was the height of the cryptocurrency bubble, and Eric Adams had embraced the industry wholeheartedly. In addition to being paid in crypto, he attended conferences and said blockchains should be used to record birth certificates and property deeds.[1] He flew to Puerto Rico, a crypto tax haven, on the private jet of crypto entrepreneur and former child actor Brock Pierce. Less than a week after his election, Adams tweeted approvingly about CityCoins: "We're glad to welcome you to the global home of Web 3! We're counting on tech and innovation to help drive our city forward."[2]

CityCoins aimed to create a set of crypto incentives that would encourage residents of a city to mine crypto tokens and receive rewards in the form of small amounts of Bitcoin and STX, another token operated by the company. City governments would have their own crypto wallets tied to the scheme. As tokens accumulated, the tokens could be spent on governance and city projects. The plan attracted some understandable skepticism from crypto watchers, who wondered about its sustainability and whether a municipality should be deriving some of its funding from a crypto scheme devised by a private corporation.

One of those skeptics was Mike Bloomberg—not the billionaire former NYC mayor—who advises municipalities on technology issues and, among his past jobs, worked for the mayor of Holyoke, Massachusetts. Bloomberg was part of Eric Adams' transition team, leading the agency review process for the technology subcommittee. He was alarmed by NYCCoin and its possible entanglement in city politics. Among other issues, it was not legal to buy NYCCoin in New York. It could only be mined or purchased on OKCoin, a Chinese exchange that US residents would have to use a VPN to access.

Eric Adams had said that he wanted to "promote crypto literacy" in public schools, and NYCCoin had some potential inducements that would tempt an elected politician like Adams. Bloomberg decided to speak out about his concerns, going on podcasts to discuss what he saw as a morally dubious pyramid-shaped enterprise that could be a legal disaster for city governments.

Appearing on *The FinReg Pod*, hosted by law scholar and regulatory expert Lee Reiners, Bloomberg talked about the "innovation" obsession that had consumed mayors nationwide—a competitive interest in being more tech-forward than other municipalities. Some of that innovation had taken the form of more policing tech and mass surveillance, proving that, as an economic paradigm, innovation wasn't necessarily a good unto itself.

"Innovation usually costs them money," said Bloomberg, a structural limitation that can prevent disruptive mayors from "being too destructively innovative." But this was different. "Not only can you claim to be an innovative mayor if you adopt this, but instead of costing you money, we're going to give you money," said Bloomberg. "You're going to get to grab the bag."[3]

Still, free money was free money, so why not? Well, the money wasn't quite *money*. The cost to buy NYCCoin on OKCoin was lower than the cost to mine it. That meant there was no incentive to mine and participate in the project. And there was very little liquidity on the one exchange that did list CityCoins' projects. No one wanted to trade in them.

"The tokenomics of this are terrible," said Bloomberg. "It doesn't work as a local currency."

Receiving free money from a company in return for touting it was "tantamount to a bribe," said Bloomberg. In Florida, meanwhile, when it came time to gain access to the MiamiCoin wallet, Miami couldn't accept crypto as a gift, so the city council had to get involved and negotiate terms with the company.

Embracing MiamiCoin enmeshed the city in an economically and legally dubious project. The city, which had no way to verify that token owners lived in Miami, now had an incentive to work to boost the coin's value. In the process, it might find itself guilty of promoting an unregistered security—or, depending on the promises a crypto-happy city official might make, perhaps even fraud.

Suarez was the chair of the US Conference of Mayors and his example might have carried influence with some of his colleagues. Like executive headhunters, mayors were competing for talent and private investment, and Suarez had spent the last few years and a not inconsiderable amount of city resources to promote Miami as a center of technological and financial innovation. Bloomberg said that he was worried about what Suarez was doing. "He's investing city headcount in how do we create value out of cryptocurrency," Bloomberg told Reiners. "Is that a good thing?"[4]

Miami was a matter for concern, but NYC was the heart of global finance. CityCoins was also knocking on politicians' doors in Philly, Austin, and other cities. The token still had no use case—it wasn't yet a vehicle for voting on city governance—except for speculating on the volatile price of a token that was difficult to trade. Like many crypto projects, CityCoins was mostly about hype, promises of future utility, and betting on price fluctuations. Like a classic pyramid scheme, the risk would fall mostly on those coin holders who could least afford to lose their money. It was a prime example of what the economist Tonantzin Carmona called "predatory inclusion": "marginalized communities gaining access to goods, services, or opportunities that they were historically excluded from—but this access comes with conditions that undermine its long-term benefits and may reproduce insecurity for these same communities."[5] Crypto claimed to offer financial liberation, but it came with a price tag, including, Carmona wrote, "high risks and insufficient consumer protections."

The dissident work of Mike Bloomberg, other tech advisors, and city officials to fend off CityCoins' encroachments must have worked. When CityCoins finally launched NYCCoin, the mayor was nowhere to be found. "New York never accepted the bag, so to speak," said Bloomberg. In retrospect, given the scale of the corruption revealed within the Adams administration—which led to a spate of criminal investigations from which Adams was saved by what the *New York Times* called a quid pro quo deal to help the Trump administration deport migrants—it's remarkable that this potentially free-money grab escaped his sustained attention.[6]

As the country's appetite for digital baubles and cryptocurrencies faded, CityCoins failed to secure the lucrative civic pact it hoped for in New York. But there was still one place where this fantasy economy was thriving; the only place, perhaps, where a scheme like CityCoins could succeed: Miami.

SELLING MIAMI

Miami has been variously mythologized in the popular imagination as the "magic city," the northernmost tip of Latin America, the sultry dream capital of America's twenty-first-century hustle-and-grind culture of drop-shipping grifters and compulsively streaming influencers. Where else was a tech innovator supposed to go when they'd exhausted all frontiers? Vegas was too hot, too gauche, a traffic-choked theme park. Los Angeles was beset by the San Franciscan social ills histrionically demonized in conservative media—homelessness, crime, the looming specter of wokeness.

Denver had potential as a place for outdoorsy folks who wore fleece vests and could code-switch between blue and red political registers. It had a decent airport, as close to New York as to DC, offering access to the defense industry that was quickly becoming a Silicon Valley priority. In 2020, Alex Karp announced that Palantir was moving to Denver. "I was fleeing Silicon Valley because of what I viewed as the regressive side of progressive politics," he told the journalist Maureen Dowd.[7] Another billionaire facing a vaguely defined form of persecution, he and his peers had exiled themselves from San Francisco, Chicago, New York, and Boston for Denver, Austin, and Miami. Some of them made a big show of it, stomping their feet as they swapped mansions.

Presided over by business-friendly Republican politicians like Governor Ron DeSantis and Mayor Francis Suarez, Miami offered elites an almost ideal blend of social liberalism and plutocratic governance. It was LA without Hollywood or income tax. Or capital gains tax. Or wealth tax. Or estate tax. It was a good deal, especially for a network of billionaires who considered themselves above California's self-regarding progressivism. They could enjoy the libertine culture of Miami and with their eight-figure budgets, there was plenty of premium real estate to be had, picturesque ocean-side manses from which financiers and venture capitalists could ride out the Zoom years in luxury.

At a conference in November 2020, Keith Rabois, the pugnacious Founders Fund venture capitalist who was married to Palantir advisor Jacob Helberg, announced his own move from San Francisco to South Florida, where he spent $28.9 million on a mansion on the Venetian Islands, a small artificial archipelago in Miami's Biscayne Bay. "I think San Francisco is just so massively improperly run and managed that it's impossible to stay here," said Rabois, who during this period tweeted about the efficacy of hydroxychloroquine as a Covid-19 treatment—a popular, if discredited, meme on the MAGA right.[8,9] A year later Rabois wrote, "Miami is paradise. SF is miserable on every dimension."[10] By 2024, he had left his position at Founders Fund and moved back to San Francisco.

In April 2021, an LLC connected to David Sacks bought a home on the Venetian Islands for $17.1 million.[11] Less than three years later, the LLC sold the property for $22.5 million to a Bulgarian fintech entrepreneur.[12] Peter Thiel spent $18 million on two homes that also were on the Venetian Islands. Former Sequoia Capital partner Jim Goetz, who made a fortune investing in WhatsApp, plunked down about $30 million for two homes, one of them a pricey tear-down.

In interviews, Ken Griffin, the founder of hedge fund titan and market maker Citadel, telegraphed his intent to leave Chicago, where his $28 billion-plus fortune made him Illinois' wealthiest resident. "If people aren't safe here, they're not going to live here," he told the *Wall Street Journal* in April 2022.[13] "I've had multiple colleagues mugged at gunpoint. I've had a colleague stabbed on the way to work. Countless issues of burglary. I mean, that's a really difficult backdrop with which to draw talent to your city from." Three months later, he announced his intention to move his business to Miami, calling it "a vibrant growing metropolis that embodies the American dream."[14]

Jeff Bezos bought three mansions on Indian Creek Island, a patch of Miami land sometimes called Billionaire Bunker. By making Florida his primary residence as he continued to sell massive amounts of Amazon stock, Bezos would be able to avoid at least $600 million in potential capital gains taxes.[15]

Some companies opened offices in the Sunshine State or, like JPMorgan Chase, announced major expansions to existing outposts. Microsoft, Amazon, and Apple poured millions into beefing up their South Florida operations. Crypto companies like Blockchain booked office space in up-and-coming areas of the city. Industry darling FTX, which already had a small office in Miami's financial district where many of its big-money celebrity endorsements were arranged, agreed to a 19-year, $135 million sponsorship deal for the Miami Heat's basketball arena. In September 2022, five months after opening a 9,000-square-foot US headquarters in Chicago, FTX announced that it would be moving its HQ to a 35-floor building in Miami's Brickell district.[16] Miami mayor Francis Suarez celebrated the announcement: "Very honored to have your new US headquarters moving to the MIA. @FTX_Official is one of the most innovative companies on the planet and you @SBF_FTX are one of the most innovative technologists. Welcome HOME!"[17]

FTX filed for bankruptcy less than two months later.[18]

The mayor of Miami was practically a figurehead executive, with most governance responsibility lying with a board of commissioners. That left Suarez with the time—and the legal right—to continue working as a lawyer and lobbyist for undisclosed real-estate interests and to mix the role of mayor and entrepreneurial showman in a way few had done before. Suarez seemed like a full-time tech and crypto booster, with Miami playing the role of the city of the future, open for business.

Suarez promised to accept his mayoral salary in Bitcoin. He created a new city position of Venture Capitalist in Residence.[19] He seemed to show up at practically any event where the word "blockchain" might be uttered. Suarez tweeted at venture capitalists and tech executives, telling them to bring their businesses to Miami. One post read simply, "Thinking about moving to Miami? DM me."[20] Later, a supersized version of the tweet was printed on two billboards in San Francisco. The billboard project had Suarez's knowledge and blessing, but it was paid for by Reddit co-founder Alexis Ohanian and venture capitalist Shervin Pishevar, both of whom lived in Miami. Ohanian was an investor in the adtech company that rented the billboard.

The shamelessly flamboyant mayor made the most of his growing media profile, blasting his tech boosterism across social media on his way to becoming a nationally known figure, if electorally doomed as a Republican presidential candidate. His representation of local real-estate developers led to concerns about potential corruption. The FBI and SEC opened investigations into a developer's company that paid Suarez $10,000 per month. The Miami-Dade Commission on Ethics and Public Trust investigated Suarez for his role in helping a developer obtain permits for a $70 million real-estate project.[21] The state attorney also took a look at his lucrative private-sector work. Most of the investigations into Suarez were eventually closed or seemed to sputter out without charges being filed.

Along with San Francisco and New York, Miami became the country's third major center of crypto hype—and perhaps its most delusional one. At the April 2022 Bitcoin Conference, the crypto industry's biggest annual confab, which I attended while writing a book about crypto and fraud, Suarez stood in front of a statue that resembled a laser-eyed version of the famous Wall Street bull wearing some kind of high-tech mech skinsuit (laser eyes signaled devotion to Bitcoin). This was supposed to be the future of finance: a titanium-plated cyberpunk bull, rampaging through the markets. Francis Suarez presided over the bull's ribbon-cutting, promoting it as an emblem of Miami's status as a new crypto powerhouse. Six months later, the crypto industry cratered amidst the multibillion-dollar frauds perpetrated by FTX, Celsius, Terra, and other once-vaunted crypto companies. The bull itself was quietly moved to the campus of a local community college.

Unlike Mayor Adams in New York, Miami mayor Francis Suarez had embraced CityCoins, telling Fox News that it might "revolutionize the way governments are funded."[22] CityCoins personnel and officials from Suarez's office were in close contact. On October 6, 2021, Kara Miley, an outside press representative for CityCoins, emailed Suarez's chief of staff asking for an hour of "comms training" to instruct the mayor how to better sell MiamiCoin to the public. There were legal concerns, too. "There are a few regulatory wires the Mayor has tripped in recent interviews and it's really important for the sustainability of the project that he is better prepared," wrote Miley in the email, which was obtained by *Quartz* through a records request. "We really care about the Mayor and his role in making MiamiCoin a success—it's critical that we get time with him as soon as possible."[23]

The token did manage to produce some revenue for Miami—$5.25 million, which was put toward a rental assistance program.[24] It was a bit short of Suarez's suggestion that MiamiCoin revenue could replace all tax revenue. MiamiCoin's value never rose above about 5.5 cents; by May 2022, it sputtered to near zero. The following year, the only cryptocurrency exchange where MiamiCoin and NYCCoin could be traded decided to delist the tokens, citing low liquidity.[25] Suarez, who had acknowledged that MiamiCoin might not survive, immediately distanced himself from the project. "It wasn't a city-sponsored or city-promoted initiative," he said on Fox Business. "This was something the city benefited from."[26]

Francis Suarez's political career followed a similar decline. He ran a dismal campaign for the Republican presidential nomination that mostly succeeded in drawing attention to the investigations surrounding him. On August 29, 2023, Suarez dropped out of the race and duly endorsed Donald Trump.

Miami's crypto golden age was over, having barely begun.

13

The Crypto Swamp

Beyond the idealism, a dark political culture was forming in Miami's crypto scene. It wasn't just about hyping silly tokens or perpetrating the kind of petty scams that seemed endemic to the crypto space. In South Florida, some coiners were embracing extreme libertarian and anti-state ideas that would bring them to the Capitol steps on January 6, 2021. Some wanted to deploy crypto on behalf of its most radical potential use case: overthrowing the government.

On May 24, 2023, Florida governor Ron DeSantis officially announced his entry into the race for the Republican presidential nomination in that disastrous appearance on Elon Musk's Twitter Spaces discussed earlier. Spaces is an audio chat space where masses of people could listen to speakers and digitally raise their hands to chime in.[1] The Spaces feature was unable to handle tens or hundreds of thousands of potential listeners, and the event became a drawn-out farrago of technical snafus as Musk and David Sacks struggled to fix the site whose infrastructure they had gutted. After the stream was finally underway, Sacks, Musk, and some friendly questions from the audience prompted DeSantis to tick off his list of culture war grievances, from Disney to DEI. When Sacks teed the governor up with a question about crypto, DeSantis, perhaps conscious of speaking to a very online, Musk-loving audience, offered the kind of tribute to digital currencies that had become standard on the Republican right.

"You have every right to do Bitcoin," said DeSantis. "The only reason these people in Washington don't like it is because they don't control it."

In DeSantis's telling, crypto represented a challenge to bureaucratic master-planning and government control over the economy. Adopting coiner rhetoric, he emphasized Bitcoin's subversive potential.

"Bitcoin represents a threat to them," said DeSantis. "As president we'll protect the ability to do things like Bitcoin."

As suggested by his "do Bitcoin" phrasing, DeSantis probably didn't have much direct experience with crypto. But like a growing number of his colleagues, he took it up as a political cause, leveraging its popularity among right-wing voters who were either coiners themselves or sympathetic to its libertarian, anti-government ideological underpinnings. Touting Bitcoin as a tool for freedom—as presidential candidates Robert F. Kennedy Jr. and Vivek Ramaswamy also did—was a sure way to activate a very online Republican base and to pull in donations from a clutch of voters who had made crypto their singular issue.

By then, CBDCs—or central bank digital currencies—had come to occupy a similar political role. Essentially a digital dollar (or euro or renminbi), a CBDC is a digital currency issued directly from a government's central bank, potentially enabling fast settlement of transactions, easy distribution of social benefits, and more flexible monetary policy. It was also, critics feared, a tool of social control, and the right-wing narrative described CBDCs as an ominous step toward a Chinese-style social-credit system. The US may already have had many of the elements of a social-credit system in place—credit scores, consumer surveillance, manipulative algorithms, a multibillion-dollar trade in personal data—but for coiners, a CBDC was a step too far. (Dozens of countries, including China, have experimented with CBDCs, but they haven't been adopted yet by any major economies.)

That's why DeSantis became one of the leading US politicians speaking out against a CBDC, even though a governor had practically no influence over the issuance of currency or monetary policy.

DeSantis signed a bill banning CBDCs, a move with tenuous legal standing but one that cemented his profile with crypto enthusiasts. Several other states announced plans to do the same. Using his typical political rhetoric, DeSantis called CBDCs a product of "government overreach and woke corporate monitoring."[2]

Samuel Armes, a Florida-based crypto lobbyist, took credit for the bill's passage, which was broadly celebrated on the political right. On social media, Armes repeatedly referred to the legislation as "our bill" and touted his meetings with Florida state officials in the lead-up to the bill's passage. "To understand the Anti-CBDC Bill, you must first understand that [it] is a political play first, and a policy play second," Armes wrote on his Substack. "Desantis' Anti-CBDC bill put him on the forefront of 'Freedom & Liberty' based policies, showing that he does not support an authoritarian surveillance state."[3]

DeSantis's freedom-and-liberty mantra seemed like empty rhetoric to some. This was the obsessively anti-woke governor who promoted initiatives to allow cops to check people's genitals in bathrooms and to investigate teachers for showing Disney movies. DeSantis was devoting his political energies to culture war issues that invariably required the state to interfere in family life, classroom education, and people's most personal health matters. His version of freedom was ideological and circumscribed, enforced by local police and state bureaucrats. DeSantis's defense of free speech meant banning children's books.

These contradictions didn't seem to matter to Armes and other coiners in Florida, who gravitated toward DeSantis and Francis Suarez as like-minded defenders of economic freedom. Together, DeSantis and Suarez made Florida a crypto redoubt.

Armes' profile rose through his involvement in South Florida's crypto scene. Some of his crypto colleagues had ties to the January 6 riot at the US Capitol. Among crypto diehards, right-wing extremists settled in comfortably as ideological fellow travelers. And with gangs like the Proud Boys cut off from many mainstream banks and finance apps, crypto became an ad hoc substitute for Venmo and Visa.

> # 1776 Returns
>
> **Contents**
>
> **Storm the Winter Palace (INTERNAL ONLY)**
> Plan overview...................... Page 2-5
> Location Assignments.............Page 6
>
> **"Patriot Plan" (TO DISTRIBUTE EXTERNALLY)**
> "Patriot Plan" Logistics.....................7
> We the People Demand.................. 7
>
> **Read Directions Carefully**

Samuel Armes might be familiar to some readers from his strangely comic appearance in the January 6 Committee Report. Armes, who was in his mid-twenties at the time, was interviewed by committee investigators who were looking into "1776 Returns," a planning document that circulated among Proud Boys members, including its leader Enrique Tarrio, in the lead-up to the January 6 riot. The document contained logistics and battle plans for seizing control of government buildings and demanding a new presidential election. According to Eryka Gemma, the self-proclaimed "godmother" of Miami's crypto scene who was also interviewed by committee investigators, Armes wrote the document and sent it to Gemma, whom he asked to pass it along to Tarrio, her boyfriend at the time. On December 30, 2020, Gemma, who was also known as Erika Gemma Flores, sent Tarrio a document called "1776 Returns."

Armes disputed Gemma's account. "She's just blame-shifting," Armes said to congressional investigators. "I mean, she's just throwing me under the bus."

Armes' interview with the January 6 committee is a bizarre text—an evasive and at times hilarious conversation with a political operator who repeatedly claimed he had nothing to do with right-wing extremists, despite being surrounded by them in his professional and personal life. From the beginning of his questioning, Armes appeared to inflate his right-wing political credentials while also disavowing any influence he might have had on the Proud Boys and other rioters.

Armes studied at the University of South Florida, where he earned his undergraduate degree in 2018. "I was being groomed to work for the CIA and the FBI," he told investigators. He claimed that he did work for the State Department and Special Operations Command—which, upon further questioning, sounded like a college internship.

Q		Did you ever end up working for either of those agencies?
A		Not formally, but I've done work for the State Department and for United States Special Operations Command out of MacDill Air Force Base, which is in Tampa.
Q		And when you say "not formally," how did you end up doing the work for those agencies?
A		I was a -- I was not a government employee. I was a citizen. And they were both programs through USF, through the intel program that I was at.
Q		All right. So this was while you were at undergrad?
A		Yes.
Q		Okay.

In 2017, before he finished college, Armes decided to become a crypto lobbyist, founding the Florida Blockchain Business Association. He dedicated himself, in his words, to "passing crypto/blockchain-friendly legislation in the State of Florida."

Armes worked as a legislative affairs director for Joel Greenberg, who was the Seminole County tax collector. The two formed a company together called Government Blockchain Systems LLC. In 2022, Greenberg was sentenced to 11 years in prison after pleading guilty to half a dozen charges, including sex-trafficking minors and wire fraud.[4] Greenberg cooperated with a federal sex-trafficking investigation into Representative Matt Gaetz, who allegedly hosted sex parties with Greenberg, according to party participants who testified to Congress. Some underage girls were paid to participate. Two witnesses told the House Ethics Committee that they saw Gaetz have sex with a 17-year-old girl. Venmo records showed that Gaetz paid more than $10,000 to girls in transactions that he marked as for "school" or "tuition."

Part 4: Occupy

Present our list of demands – the "We The People" page of the patriot plan. Lead, Second or Hypeman to lead the following chants

- Free and fair elections
- Liberty or Death
- We are watching
- No Trump, No America
- No Justice, No Peace
- We the People

We the people require our representatives to represent us.

Part 5: Sit In

We have the ability to go into office
Target Specific Senators Offices

WHATS THE ENDING POINT FOR THIS?
Does everyone just leave at a certain time?
WHO DOES GOV RESPOND TO?

In his committee interview, Armes said that he first heard about the "1776 Returns" document from committee investigators. But "1776 Returns" could be traced back to Armes. In August 2020, Armes told the committee, he wrote up a memo and shared it with Gemma on Google Drive. Armes described his text as just a bit of war-gaming, the musings of a would-be defense intellectual.

"It was not specific to any group," he said. "It was just how I thought things might happen in a scenario where a certain President doesn't leave the White House or there is just mad chaos in the streets because no one knows who's in charge."

Some of the text and images from that document were copied and pasted into "1776 Returns." In the rest of his interview, Armes went through "1776 Returns" page-by-page with investigators, acknowledging some parts as his own and disclaiming others.

The document included Google Maps screenshots with pinpointed locations where rioters might gather. Armes repeatedly told investigators it was just a general exercise, not connected to any plan or party.

Eryka Gemma, the conduit between Armes and the Proud Boys for the "1776 Returns" plan, was deeply involved in Armes' other work. "Anything that I have done, cryptocurrency, blockchain, normally, if it's in Miami, she would be someone that I consulted with," he told the January 6 committee. "And as a board member, she was actively advertising my association and her people to join in the Miami region." At one point in the interview, Armes said, "Erika and I were business partners."

Armes met Proud Boys leader Enrique Tarrio through Gemma. Tarrio participated in a popular Telegram group chat for Miami crypto people that counted Armes as a participant. After investigators inquired about the Telegram group, and whether Armes could provide message logs, Anessa Santos, Armes' lawyer, chimed in to say that as a prominent crypto lawyer, she was a part of many crypto Telegram groups, including the one with Tarrio and Gemma. Santos said she could provide the chat logs.

That's when, during a sensitive point in his interview with government investigators, Armes suddenly fell to the ground with a leg cramp, in what appeared to be one of the most unsubtle guy-fakes-a-medical-incident scenes outside of a TV sitcom.

> Mr. Armes. Sorry, I'm cramping.
>
> Ms. Santos. Okay. Take a moment. Take a moment. Take a moment. Go ahead and -- that's all right. Take a moment.
>
> ████ Do you want a quick --
>
> Mr. Armes. No, no. I'm good. I just did a --
>
> Ms. Santos. Charley horse. Charley horse. Just --
>
> Mr. Armes. I'm good. I just did leg day today, and I maxed out my PR squats, and now it's hurting.

The show continued. While still on the floor, Armes, who on his Linktree account identified himself as a "bodybuilder," started bragging about his weight-lifting feats.

> Ms. Santos. Take a moment.
>
> He's on the floor.
>
> Mr. Armes. No, I'm good, I'm good. Man, this is embarrassing.
>
> ████ You're all right. I understand what you're feeling.
>
> Ms. Santos. It's okay. Take a moment.
>
> Mr. Armes. No, I'm good, we're good. I'm back.
>
> By the way, that PR was 425 pounds.
>
> ████ That will now be in the congressional Record, so that's good.
>
> Mr. Armes. Yeah, that's cool.
>
> Ms. Santos. So I can probably -- so since -- I can probably --
>
> Mr. Armes. So let's get -- do you want to go to the document?
>
> Ms. Santos. I will assist the -- just relax. Just exhale.
>
> Mr. Armes. No, I'm good, I'm good. Let's go.
>
> Ms. Santos. Pause. Pause.

Whether the interruption was planned or not, it didn't stop the questioning. Armes cooperated but frequently responded with vague answers and generalities—I don't know, I can't recall, I was just thinking about a scenario that other people might engage in. He described his war-gaming memo as both based on his expert training and government experience but also a fanciful act of "extrapolation," not an operational plan.

Armes denied having any association with the Proud Boys or other militia groups. But as his lawyer explained, Armes was once invited to join the Oath Keepers, a right-wing militia that played a prominent role in the January 6 riot.

> Ms. Santos. So, again, in the interest of being completely candid and transparent, ▓▓▓ you might recall that in our phone call, our brief phone call last week, I mentioned that Sam was recently questioned in regards to someone -- oh, yes, yes, I just remembered -- in regards to whether or not he was physically present at the January 6th event. And it was because -- it was an Oath Keeper?
>
> Mr. Armes. Yes.
>
> Ms. Santos. I get those confused. Pardon me. An Oath Keeper had a misunderstanding in the nature of his relationship with Mr. Armes and included his name on a hotel room. But Mr. Armes was not aware of this and had no such relationship with this gentleman, did not want the relationship with this gentleman. This gentleman did invite Mr. Armes and encouraged him to participate in the Oath Keepers, which Mr. Armes vehemently rejected.
>
> And Mr. Armes did provide substantial conclusive evidence that he was, in fact, at work that week of the Capitol riots in Tampa.
>
> Mr. Armes. And that association, once again, comes from a crypto-related --
>
> Ms. Santos. Yes.
>
> Mr. Armes. -- conversation. So --

Armes met one of the Oath Keepers, whom he identified as James Beeks, through the crypto world. Beeks invited Armes to join him in Washington, DC on January 6 and put his name on a hotel reservation. "He viewed me as a romantic potential," Armes told investigators. He said that he had no interest and tried to distance himself from Beeks' radical politics. But he admitted that he had met Beeks socially at blockchain events and that they had talked about the Oath Keepers' esoteric belief system, including that "our entire government was fake."

> A   We met in person because he lived in Orlando and would come to my crypto/blockchain meetups here in Orlando.
>
> Q   Okay.
>
> A   So, once again, it was another cryptocurrency/blockchain connection, which I feel like is making my community look very bad.
>
> Ms. Santos.   I have a feeling that --
>
> Mr. Armes.   I promise we're not all like that.
>
> Ms. Santos.   I feel like that, at the end of this conversation, we need to have a followup rehabilitative conversation about the joys of crypto.
>
> Mr. Armes.   There are plenty of law-abiding citizens who do not think like this within the crypto community.   But we do --
>
> Ms. Santos.   I echo --
>
> Mr. Armes.   -- I guess, attract crazies.
>
> Ms. Santos.   -- that.   We do attract crazies, but we're overwhelmingly governmental-friendly.

Beeks was one of a number of Oath Keepers charged with felonies related to the January 6 riot. Several were found guilty of seditious conspiracy, including group leader Stewart Rhodes, who was sentenced to 18 years in prison, and Kelly Meggs, who headed the Oath Keepers' Florida chapter. Two Oath Keepers, one of whom had acted as a bodyguard for infamous Republican political operative Roger Stone before joining the Capitol melee, were sentenced to prison terms of three years and four and a half years.

A musical theater actor, Beeks was arrested in November 2021 in Minneapolis, where he was on tour for *Jesus Christ Superstar*. He was playing Judas. During his arraignment, Beeks told the court that he had "divine authority" that made him ungovernable. "That's all gobbledygook," the judge said.

Beeks denied membership in the Sovereign Citizen movement—another right-wing belief system charging that the government's authority was illegitimate—but he repeatedly used its rhetoric and symbolism. After telling a judge that "I cannot represent myself because I am myself," he later changed his mind, firing his public defender and announcing that he would defend himself. Beeks, who wore a jacket from Michael Jackson's *Bad* tour while helping breach the Capitol, stamped legal filings with his own crest, which announced him as part of House of Edwards, Florida.

> An accompanying motion from Beeks appears to further reveal an apparent alignment with the so-called "sovereign citizen" movement.
>
> "Comes now :james beeks: (the Accused) by special appearance, an Aborigine Autochthon, 5/5ths realized **Free Qualified** Inhabitant, and **Private Citizen** of Turtle Island/Amaru-Inca (now known as America); who upholds the Great Law of Peace, a lawful de jure, jus sanguinis **Preamble Citizen** of the Florida Republic **(1861-1865)** in his own proper person sui juris pursuant to the **unpurviewed 6th Article of the Bill of Rights, the 9th Article of Amendment** to the **Constitution for the United States (1781-1791)** and other applicable provisions of law, knowingly and intelligently, with full awareness of the dangers of proceeding sui juris respectfully requesting a Faretta motion for the duration of this litigation process," the motion said (all emphasis in original).

The teetering pile of esoteric titles and apocryphal references was standard Sovereign Citizen signaling. Elaborate revisionist histories and conspiracy theories are a bonding agent for right-wing extremists, providing a common culture and a shared list of grievances. If the whole thing was an elaborate act of roleplay, then it needed its lore and world-building to sustain the game.

In an interview with an Orlando news station, Beeks, who was 49 at the time, denied having any extremist beliefs or really any political ideology. He hadn't known much about the Oath Keepers when he joined them and didn't associate with them after January 6.

"I wasn't there to overthrow the government or anything like that," said the person who joined a military-style "stack" of militia members breaching Capitol doors. "I'm just a man that was in the wrong place at the wrong time."

Beeks was eventually acquitted of "conspiracy to obstruct Congress' certification of the 2020 election and civil disorder," one of only six Capitol riot defendants—out of more than 1,000—to be acquitted at trial.[5] Beeks' co-defendant was convicted on both charges.

Armes was never charged with any crimes related to January 6.

After the 2020 presidential election, Eryka Gemma attended Stop the Steal events with members of the Proud Boys and shared plans to be in DC on January 6. "ill be in the District of Communism on the 6th with @ToneVays @thetruechannel1 and other friends who all were deleted from social media," she tweeted on January 4, 2021. "DM me if you're attending." Tone Vays was a popular crypto influencer who attended the January 6 Stop the Steal rally in DC, where he live-streamed from outside the Capitol. While there, Vays posted a celebratory tweet. Gemma responded with one word: "Amazing."[6]

"If you don't like my plan, let me know," Gemma wrote to Tarrio when she sent him the "1776 Returns" document. "I will pitch elsewhere. But I want you to be the executor and benefitor [sic] of my brilliance."[7]

After Eryka Gemma's role in the January 6 investigation became public, she locked her Twitter account, but she remained active on the crypto circuit, appearing as a panelist and speaker at public events. The former Ron Paul Republican presidential convention delegate described herself as a fan of Austrian economics and her Twitter profile included the hashtag "#sovereign."[8] She had a pilot's license and was credited with getting Mayor Suarez up to speed about Bitcoin. The right-wing coiner and the Bitcoin bro mayor were photographed together at public events, including at the 2019 opening of the Blockchain Center, a crypto incubator in downtown Miami.

Gemma scrubbed some of her political tweets, including about January 6. But her political affinities were reflected in "1776 Returns," which ended with a "special mention," a shoutout from the Capitol insurrectionists to the movement's enemies and heroes. First, there was a warning to Mitch McConnell, Kevin McCarthy, Mike Pence, and, naturally, Bill Gates: "we the people are watching you." That was followed by a note to Rand Paul and Ron DeSantis. It said, simply: "We the people love you."

> **Special Mention**
>
> Mitch McConnell, Kevin McCarthy, Mike Pence & Bill Gates
> We the people are watching you.
>
> Rand Paul & Ron DeSantis
> We the people love you

THE EMPTY PENTHOUSE AND THE FAKE CEO

The conspiracism and extremism emerging from the Florida crypto swamp were just as much a part of South Florida's brief crypto boom as the crypto startups, token hustlers, industry meetups, swanky conferences, and hammy pitches from Francis Suarez. Some high-end realtors and exclusive nightclubs offered to accept crypto as payment. There was always a new round of startup funding, a boozy conference, or deal to celebrate. And it wasn't a party without a few (rented-for-the-day) $250,000 sports cars sitting ostentatiously in front of that night's venue.

Sudden fortunes appeared overnight, some of them of dubious provenance. Huge transactions for seemingly useless NFTs and "digital collectibles" became the norm. People splashed out millions of dollars—or the equivalent in Bitcoin, Ethereum, or some other desired token—for apartments in zip codes doomed by climate change.

In late 2022, over the messaging app Telegram, I talked to one crypto entrepreneur whose murky history I was trying to pin down. His name was Deepak Thapliyal, and he was the CEO of a company called Chain.com. On paper, Chain resembled the crypto equivalent of a penny stock, not much more than a corporate facade. It had its own token that seemed to be barely traded, and the company offered just enough social-media posts, white papers, and promises of big plans ahead to make the business still seem like a going concern. Thapliyal had almost no web presence or verifiable work history. He was from India and, in the only company video I could find that featured him, looked barely out of his teens. Still, he somehow had enough crypto to spend tens of millions of dollars on NFTs. He was setting price records for JPEGs, which attracted a flutter of attention for his company, but crypto media seemed to only care about the big numbers, not where the money was coming from or who was spending it.

Once a well-funded Bay Area crypto startup, Chain's ownership and stated purpose had changed so many times that the documentary trail was muddied. Thapliyal's version of Chain appeared to be owned by a Chinese shell corporation. It was hard to tell if any of its employees were real. When a Chain press release announced the hiring of a new executive, I looked him up. I emailed his employer, an Irish cybersecurity company, and asked about their employee leaving. They hadn't heard about it.

Even Chain's transactions were semi-fictional. When the company coordinated an NFT sale with the jewelry company Tiffany's, Thapliyal personally bought most of the NFTs with a digital wallet he had used in the past. The evidence was right there, in publicly viewable blockchain transactions. What little reporting there was on the partnership ignored or missed that fact—self-dealing was common in crypto and NFTs—and it was chalked up as a success. Soon after, Chain announced a partnership with the Miami Heat.

In 2020, Chain bought a penthouse apartment in Miami for $22.5 million—about double its assessed value. On Telegram, I asked Thapliyal why the company had made the extravagant purchase. "An investment," he said. (I was unable to verify how Chain paid for the property.)

In spite of its mysterious finances, Chain didn't stand out as that unusual for the time and place. There were so many shady operators to investigate; so many inexplicable crypto transactions sitting there on public blockchains; billions of dollars, real and fake, being sunk into ventures that, to any reasonable outsider, seemed doomed to fail or like old-fashioned money laundering in a new digital format. Study after study found that, on many crypto exchanges, 80 percent or more of all trading activity was "wash trading"—fake trades between the same party to simulate activity and drive price action. It was classic market manipulation, but the market itself was largely fake.

On the inside of this industry, as Armes' testimony showed, the attitude was far different. Some were genuine believers, thinking that they were in the vanguard of forging new economic structures. The rest of the world just had yet to wake up—to be "orange-pilled" by the miracle of Bitcoin, to emerge converted. It had taken 15 years and still there was no mass adoption. The utility of this stuff wasn't clear, unless you were a ransomware hacker in the former Eastern Bloc. But for the true believers, Bitcoin's victory was foreordained. "Fix the money, fix the world," went one mantra. Enough purists believed it to keep the dream alive—and the money moving.

Some of the crypto industry's leaders, we soon found, were just crooks lining their pockets during a wild speculative bubble. The poorly regulated parallel financial system constructed around cryptocurrency proved perfect for fraudsters to move money—indeed, that was its main value proposition. And some people who willingly participated contributed the good money that helped launder the bad.

For a while, I wasn't sure which one Chain was. How to explain the tens of millions of dollars' worth of crypto—usually

Ethereum—that Thapliyal and his company were moving? Why dump $20 million on an NFT? (He told me it was part of a larger strategy betting on the long-term potential of Ethereum.) And why spend even more on an apartment where no one lived? Where had all the crypto come from, and where did it go?

Soon, the answers didn't seem to matter. In November 2022, FTX collapsed, revealing an $8 billion-plus crater where the crypto exchange's customer funds were supposed to be. I shelved the mystery of the $22 million penthouse apartment in favor of higher-stakes intrigue. The crypto industry and the media became obsessed with the subsequent arrest of Sam Bankman-Fried, the fintech wunderkind who once seemed to have it all figured out while his colleagues seethed about him behind their social-media avatars. His aggressive deal-making and political-influence campaign was supposed to make crypto safe for the American masses. Instead, his downfall became a canonical example of a crypto fraudster who briefly soared to unbelievable heights because rich, powerful people were personally invested in the myth of his genius. His vicious crash deflated the hype bubble surrounding an industry whose products could never succeed on their own relative merits. Token prices and trading volumes tumbled. The gamblers left the crypto casinos. The FTX name came down from the Miami Heat's arena. FTX's newly built Miami headquarters never opened for business. Blockchain.com, which had signed a deal for a 22,000-square-foot office in Miami's Wynwood neighborhood, backed out of its lease. The venture capital firm Andreessen Horowitz, one of the principal investors in the crypto boom, closed its Miami office.

As for Deepak Thapliyal, he and his company disappeared. Chain introduced a couple more tokens that went nowhere, pumped out press releases about projects that didn't come to fruition, and then basically ceased as a going concern. Its website continued to publish buzzword-laden content about cloud computing and blockchains that read as if it was written by a chatbot. There was no evidence that the company had any real employees or operations. The one video that Chain had released of Thapliyal—an obviously scripted Q&A session—was removed from YouTube. His crypto wallets, which had once held millions of dollars' worth of tokens and NFTs, were emptied. He ghosted from Telegram. The Miami penthouse apartment in Chain's name was sold—presumably for real fiat currency—to the wife of a billionaire Canadian property developer. The disclosed sale price was $16.5 million—$6 million less than the amount Chain had paid, in a real-estate market that had mostly appreciated in value. But in the murky world of crypto finance, sometimes you had to be prepared to take a loss to get out of a position.

Thapliyal became another figment of an increasingly hallucinatory economy, one that seemed to produce little beyond a few massive fortunes. As the crypto industry lapsed into winter, its failures offered an opportunity, in the great Silicon Valley tradition, for entrepreneurs to pivot. They had collectively prophesied the development of an overwhelmingly powerful artificial intelligence that would revolutionize life on Earth (and off it). Its development used some of the same technical infrastructure—massive data centers filled with Nvidia chips—left over from the crypto boom. (CoreWeave, a publicly traded company offering computing capacity to AI companies, began life as a crypto miner.)

It was time to build AGI, the god in the machine. It would take hundreds of billions of dollars, an unknown amount of time, some unpredictable technical breakthroughs, and a few high-level government favors. But just when the tech industry needed to raise more capital than ever to fund its moonshot ambitions, the free money began to run out.

14

The Tap Turns Off

The pandemic economy stayed afloat (barely) on a tide of quantitative easing, increased social spending, occasional stimulus checks, and the labor of essential workers braving the possibility of infection. For those stuck at home, typing away at "email jobs,"—I was one of them—the overall economy developed an air of unreality. People gorged on Zoom calls, streaming television, food delivery, and the other conveniences of the Amazon Prime era. On the internet, digital photos were rebranded as blockchain collectibles and sold for millions. People bought luxury apartments with crypto while the awkward, perpetually bed-headed Wall Street dropout named Sam Bankman-Fried was feted as a visionary and quickly became the richest person in the world under 30.

But how much of it was real? What could you hold in your hands? The decline of American manufacturing reflected the material side of what was also a metaphysical problem: what did America still make? Besides bombs and apps and Amazon fulfillment centers. And novel forms of gambling.

The United States was supposed to be a prosperous country—"the richest nation in the world," according to one moribund cliche—but its widespread inequality and injustices were obvious to anyone with a conscience or a decently tuned social-media feed. Miami's steamy glitz and gated mega-mansions didn't stop the high-tide floods that regularly clogged city streets. As tent encampments bloomed in the country's urban centers, public protest movements emerged to urge action on sexual assault, economic injustice, police violence, climate change, and US complicity in Israeli atrocities against Palestinians.

These movements largely struck Silicon Valley elites as intolerable disruptions to the social and economic order that they dominated. When these political currents swept through their companies, it became a veritable crisis. "The most privileged people in society, the most successful, send their kids to the most politically radical institutions, which teach them how to be America-hating communists," said Marc Andreessen. Their elite credentials helped these "America-hating communists" get in the doors of tech companies, only for their executives and investors to realize that these young hires were "professional activists in their own minds, first and foremost. And it just turns out the way to exercise professional activism right now, most effectively, is to go and destroy a company from the inside."

Andreessen described the phenomenon as a potentially deliberate conspiracy: "I had this moment with a senior executive, who I won't name, but he said to me with a sense of dawning horror, 'I think some of these kids are joining the company not with the intent of doing things for us but destroying us.'"[1] That was the paranoid view from the C-suite. "These companies became captured," as Andreessen described it, by anti-capitalist activists. "Captured" may have been hyperbole. Beyond some token statements in favor of Black Lives Matter or the proliferation of DEI programs, there was no real cultural revolution in Silicon Valley, no guillotines appearing on the Google campus. Even #MeToo barely made a dent in the industry power structure, as prominent accused sexual harassers, like Android creator Andy Rubin, received massive settlements to leave their positions and start new ventures.

What did change was the generous economic policy that had helped Andreessen and his colleagues build the companies and make the deals that made them fabulously wealthy.

For more than a decade after the 2008 financial crisis, the Federal Reserve kept interest rates near zero. That's what allowed your neighbor to cheaply refinance their mortgage but also allowed WeWork to raise $22 billion in investment capital to sublet office space to other well-funded startups that lacked viable business models. It's what allowed Sam Bankman-Fried to use a crypto token that he invented as collateral for multibillion-dollar loans. Borrowing money was cheap, especially if you asked for a lot of it. If you were canny, you might not even have to pay it back.

In exceedingly broad strokes, this was the financial engineering that underwrote the period's relative prosperity and its gaping inequality. It was only possible when big institutions could borrow practically endless amounts of cash and keep moving the bag around. The mega-rich kept getting richer, but most did it without doing much at all—through the miracle of passive income, capital gains, management fees, or inventing digital tokens.

Vivek Ramaswamy made a fortune by selling shares in biotech startups that had few finished products. His peers similarly cashed in on psychedelic drug startups whose therapies never made it to market. Elites could get friends-and-family discounts in startups that would be acquired down the road by their colleagues, as when David Sacks sold his podcast startup Callin to the MAGA-aligned video platform Rumble, in which he had invested alongside Ramaswamy, Peter Thiel, and JD Vance. Venture capitalists performed similar financial maneuvers with crypto tokens that would later be dumped on naive retail investors who had been pumped up by commercials featuring Tom Brady telling them that this was the future of finance. It was the era of casino capitalism, when everything began to resemble gambling—not least the newly legalized sports betting industry that was taking over people's smartphones.

After the country emerged from the worst of the pandemic, as the job losses of the Trump years were reversed under Biden, and as the specter of inflation loomed, the Federal Reserve decided it was time to raise interest rates. It would have profound effects on the technology industry, especially venture capitalists and their startup investments, which depended on easy access to large amounts of capital. ZIRP was coming to an end, the free-money spigot turned off. No more cash sloshing around to invest in ape JPEGs or the 24-year-old guys making them. The party was over. And the celebrants weren't happy about it.

In the fall of 2022, as interest rates increased and lenders began calling in debts, the crypto industry collapsed. Token prices plummeted, numerous startups went bankrupt or collapsed amidst allegations of fraud, and the industry's most famous persona, Sam Bankman-Fried, was arrested for crimes connected to his theft of more than $8 billion in customer funds from FTX, his crypto exchange. Yet even this colossal scandal was interpreted by tech and crypto leaders as an indictment of the US government, their perpetual antagonist. Why hadn't the SEC chair Gary Gensler stopped Sam Bankman-Fried? Why was Bankman-Fried compelled to go offshore, where his crimes were easier to conceal? (The answer to that one might be that a criminal goes where crime is easy to commit.)

This was about the level of self-examination that the tech industry allowed itself when Silicon Valley Bank (SVB), the home bank of numerous venture capitalists and startups, teetered toward collapse in March 2023. SVB was a mid-size bank with an outsized role in the tech industry, serving venture capitalists and the startups they funded. Its top depositor was Circle, which distributed a popular crypto stablecoin called USDC. That month, as rumors circulated about SVB's shaky finances, panic spread among its well-heeled customer base, who raced to withdraw their funds. The bank faced the possibility of running out of money. SVB's potential collapse would have caused economic damage for a lot of the people mentioned in this book, though none were likely to be left destitute.

There was no great malefactor at work, no epic fraud, no regulatory injustice inflicted upon SVB. The bank's financial downturn was the result of its own bad institutional-investment strategy amidst a changing interest rate market. SVB had planned for the ZIRP free-money train to keep running longer than it would in reality. And it had been bruised by the recent failures of other banks, like Silvergate, which serviced practically every crypto company and had collapsed alongside its customers' businesses.

By March 11, 2023, Silicon Valley Bank had gone from the crown jewel of tech industry finance to a deeply distressed asset. Its panicked depositors raced for the exits. It seemed like it could collapse entirely, causing calamity for the many startups and financiers who used the bank for everything from personal loans to company payroll. The bank had $150 billion in uninsured assets.[2]

VCs like David Sacks and his friend/podcast co-host Jason Calacanis spent several days screaming on social media and cable news that the sky was falling and that ordinary American consumers would find their bank accounts empty if this tech bank weren't saved.

"WE ARE DRIFTING INTO DERELICTION OF DUTY TERRITORY," Calacanis wrote in one of several all-caps posts. "SPEAK UP IMMEDIATELY #LEADERSHIP #NOW."[3] Late that night, he added: "YOU SHOULD BE ABSOLUTELY TERRIFIED RIGHT NOW,"[4] demanding that the president and Treasury secretary, whose accounts he tagged, appear on TV and "GUARANTEE ALL DEPOSITS UP TO $10M OR THIS WILL SPIRAL INTO CHAOS."

For most Americans, there was nothing to worry about. A regional bank failure—even one likely to get a lot of press—wouldn't affect them. Their checking accounts were FDIC insured, and they contained far less than the FDIC's $250,000 limit. The situation was more perilous for venture capitalists and startup executives, some of whom used SVB as a personal bank or otherwise had far more than a quarter of a million dollars in their accounts. As shown by a clip that circulated in which Calacanis talked about getting a sweetheart mortgage deal, SVB was operating for a different tier of clientele.

The knowledge that many of their peers might be exposed helped spread fear among tech leaders in back-channel group chats. Peter Thiel's Founders Fund had reportedly told its companies to move their money to another bank. On Twitter, Sacks claimed that his firm Craft Ventures had no money in SVB, but he didn't say when they had moved their funds, or whether their many portfolio companies still banked at SVB. Sacks emerged as one of the loudest voices agitating for the Biden administration—which he constantly railed against while financially backing its political rivals—to *do something*.

"Where is Powell? Where is Yellen?" wrote Sacks in a post. "Stop this crisis NOW. Announce that all depositors will be safe. Place SVB with a Top 4 bank. Do this before Monday open or there will be contagion and the crisis will spread."[5]

Soon enough, the VCs got what they wanted: a government takeover of a failing bank and FDIC backing beyond the typical $250,000 limit. It was a dramatic intervention, a bailout announced on a weekend overflowing with tension and elite hysteria. The tech industry's preferred bank had made some mistakes amidst changing interest rates, but Uncle Sam was here to limit the damage—and the need for anyone from the bank or its tech industry partners to take responsibility.

After the SVB crisis, a group of researchers published a paper finding that Twitter posts from frantic VCs and startup founders helped catalyze the bank run. Sacks and Calacanis's panicked tweets likely contributed to the crisis. They also added to the downward pressure on banking and tech stocks. Because Twitter was a public chat platform, and not just a one-way broadcasting tool, the fevered warnings, speculation, and desperate pleas for help from tech millionaires and billionaires built up a wave of panic that anyone could see and participate in. As the topic trended, it became algorithmically amplified.

Several publications reported on the role of group chats and private messages between Silicon Valley mandarins in spreading SVB panic. Rumors about the bank's poor health traveled from billionaire CEOs' group chats to startup founders' Signal groups to Slack messages among the Valley's rank and file. These neurotic back-channel discussions spread concern more than facts among SVB clients. "It was like we were all locked inside when the fire alarm went off," one entrepreneur told *Fortune*. "And nobody knew where the exit was."[6]

The Silicon Valley Bank crisis ended up being like many in recent American economic history: created by politically influential elites, who would soon be saved by the politicians they influenced but still resented, with their losses socialized among the American people. Yet for some SVB customers, the exceedingly generous government intervention wasn't enough.

"And just like that, crisis averted," Sacks wrote after the FDIC swept in to offer unprecedented guarantees to some of the country's wealthiest people. "So easy to do and so unnecessary to ever have this outcome in doubt."[7]

The reactionary strain exemplified by Sacks and company would always, at the end of the day, be opposed to any action by Democrats, progressives, Biden, Yellen, et al.—whomever they saw as their oppressors. Graciousness was not one of this crowd's virtues. They had done very well without it.

The ZIRP era produced a tech economy dominated more than ever by a few monopolies and some incredibly well-capitalized startups pumped full of cash from Amazon, Microsoft, and Middle Eastern sovereign wealth funds. A few new brands entered the cultural lexicon, and gig work, built on the backs of precarious laborers summoned by app, introduced new conveniences for the consumer class. Beyond that, little endured except a sense of wasted opportunity. So much money was raised, borrowed, spent, lost, and wasted. As the country reeled from the ongoing effects of the Covid-19 pandemic, the office buildings sat empty, the tokens worthless and discontinued, the grand prophecies of financial abundance unrealized. Billionaires added to their fortunes and politicians padded their campaign treasuries while most people got poorer and the country suffered from a worsening housing shortage and decaying infrastructure. The oceans continued to rise, and the waterfront mansions would still disappear one day, no matter who owned them.

15

The Companies Suck

By 2024 the easy money was gone and inflation had been tamed, but the tech industry managed to create another bubble for itself. It was far bigger—and should it pop, more sweeping in its implications—than anything having to do with cryptocurrency. Tech leaders were obsessed with the possibilities of artificial intelligence—a capacious category that seemed to encompass everything from chatbots to autonomous vehicles to image generation tools, all of them imbued with totemic power. AI fever spread to practically every business leader, university administrator, and politician. California governor Gavin Newsom, who in his zeal had personally pitched in to clear out a tent encampment, said that he wanted to use AI to tackle homelessness. The 2024 Super Bowl was festooned with expensively produced AI ads from Google, OpenAI, Salesforce, Meta, GoDaddy, and even water bottle company Cirkul, recalling the 2022 Super Bowl's half-dozen crypto ads.[1] (After the 2022 crypto bubble popped, the 2023 Super Bowl featured precisely zero crypto ads.)

With AI, the potential gains were supposed to be self-evident—newfound efficiencies and productivity improvements that we couldn't imagine. Indeed, we literally couldn't conceive of them; they could only be dreamed up through the magic of AI.

For some in the tech industry, everything that had been developed in the AI field was just a preamble to the sole pursuit that mattered:

the creation of artificial general intelligence, or AGI. The so-called "last invention," AGI would be a revolutionary leap forward in computing that would produce a greater-than-human intelligence. AGI would be a universal solvent, fixing every problem facing humanity. Unless, in some act of apocalyptic misunderstanding, this new life-form decided to wipe us out first.

It wasn't clear how AGI would come into existence, but some treated it as an inevitability, one to be feared or embraced depending on your alignment in the AI community. It was all but assumed that companies like OpenAI were close to such a breakthrough, that if only they could bring together enough engineers and computational power, AGI would emerge from this substrate, a computer god willing itself into being. Any attempt to stop or slow this pursuit—to argue for a focus on the ethics of AI and automation; to curtail the massive resource consumption of AI data centers—was immoral. Public skepticism and government regulation were delaying humanity's enjoyment of the guaranteed future benefits of AI, which would extend across every industry and discipline. AI would save lives—already, some AI systems showed themselves to be useful at parsing CT scans and X-rays. If we tempered this technological progress through more regulation, people would die.

"Any government that slows down the development of spacecraft, medicine, robots, and intelligence is an impediment to civilization," wrote the investor Naval Ravikant.[2]

Musk quoted the post, adding "True."[3]

With its faith in a utopian salvation, the AI industry sounded a lot like religion, and it had the wealth of the Catholic Church to match. Hundreds of billions of dollars were poured into AI startups, data centers, and hardware, as chipmaker Nvidia rose from being a niche provider of video cards for computer gamers to the most valuable publicly traded company in the world. Practically every public database, movie, text, website, Reddit post—every fragment of available culture and media—was ingested by AI models operated by dozens of companies, who decided that it would be easier to one day ask for forgiveness (or a legal settlement) than pause and ask for permission. While some AI companies made content deals for copyrighted materials, it was largely a free-for-all.

AI helped enforce a culture in which intellectual property was disposable, all chaff for the training mill, to be consumed in unbelievable quantities. Startups were interchangeable until one of them achieved a major breakthrough.[4] Speaking to college students, former Google CEO Eric Schmidt described a way to get beyond a potential TikTok ban:

> If TikTok is banned, here's what I propose each and every one of you do: Say to your LLM the following: "Make me a copy of TikTok, steal all the users, steal all the music, put my preferences in it, produce this program in the next 30 seconds, release it, and in one hour, if it's not viral, do something different along the same lines."

He later added an important qualifier:

> So, in the example that I gave of the TikTok competitor—and by the way, I was not arguing that you should illegally steal everybody's music—what you would do if you're a Silicon Valley entrepreneur, which hopefully all of you will be, is if it took off, then you'd hire a whole bunch of lawyers to go clean the mess up, right? But if nobody uses your product, it doesn't matter that you stole all the content.[5]

That was the Silicon Valley way. Do what you want to do, and then "hire a whole bunch of lawyers to go clean the mess up."

Guided by the philosophy espoused by Schmidt, the AI revolution was supposedly underway, but few Americans seemed to be enjoying its glories. Software engineers reported leaps forward in productivity, as AI began to write code. The tools of generative AI and video manipulation were initially novel but became less interesting the more one interacted with them. They felt like parlor tricks, modern-day player pianos simulating creative ability. For some workers, AI apps—which frequently "hallucinated," inventing information, articles, and historical facts—were less a useful partner than a drunk colleague barking incoherent orders.

As with so many past technological innovations, the early use cases for AI seemed to lie with waging warfare. In military research labs in the US, China, Turkey, and Ukraine, AI-controlled drone swarms were becoming the present and future of military conflict.

At public appearances and in op-eds in *Time* magazine and the *Wall Street Journal*, Eric Schmidt lobbied for more technological innovation in warfare, with a special focus on Ukraine and drones. Schmidt met with government officials in Ukraine, and White Stork, his drone startup whose existence he didn't publicly discuss, developed suicide drones for Ukraine's armed forces. Discussing Russia's own innovations in drones, air defense, and electronic warfare, Schmidt argued that Ukraine needed to respond with "faster-evolving software that 'internetizes' the battlefield with autonomy, AI, and ad hoc networking"—technologies that Schmidt, of course, was invested in developing.[6]

At the 2024 Future Investment Initiative conference in Saudi Arabia, Schmidt recommended that the US military get rid of its tanks. "Give them away," said Schmidt. "Buy a drone instead."[7]

The world's conflicts became zones where military powers could experiment with new AI-assisted technologies that could then be commercialized and sold to partners abroad. The Israeli military described a 2021 military operation in Gaza as the "world's first AI war."[8] Two years later, the IDF used AI programs called Gospel and Lavender to generate bombing targets as part of its genocidal war against Palestinians in Gaza. "During the first weeks of the war," reported *+972 Magazine*, the AI system designated "37,000 Palestinians as suspected militants—and their homes—for possible air strikes." Another automated AI system called "Where's Daddy?" tracked men selected for assassination and alerted commanders when they returned home. It made for easier targeting and higher body counts: "The result, as the sources testified, is that thousands of Palestinians—most of them women and children or people who were not involved in the fighting—were wiped out by Israeli airstrikes, especially during the first weeks of the war, because of the AI program's decisions."[9]

In the civilian world, the hype seemed unsustainable. The tech industry was finding little success in monetizing its new innovation, and some analysts wondered if the promised gains would ever arrive. Some observers thought that large language models—the technology behind generative AI—had inherent limitations that would limit AI's potential to go beyond inference and prediction to actual thinking and reasoning.

"AI technology is exceptionally expensive, and to justify those costs, the technology must be able to solve complex problems, which it isn't designed to do," said Jim Covello, Goldman Sachs' Head of Global Equity Research. Beyond its cost, Covello noted that AI often failed at basic tasks like summarizing a document, which meant that it was far from ready for mass adoption. "And I struggle to believe that the technology will ever achieve the cognitive reasoning required to substantially augment or replace human interactions," he said.[10]

The resource expenditures were massive, as Amazon, Microsoft, and Google each spent tens of billions of dollars on data center construction. Desperate for as much energy as they could acquire, they invested in moonshot fusion startups and paid to reboot old nuclear reactors, like at Three Mile Island, whose undamaged reactor Microsoft agreed to pay Constellation Energy to bring back online.[11]

AI was widely accepted as a bubble, but that didn't necessarily concern the investors who hoped to cash out before it all fell apart. Some still considered its ascension to be inevitable. Just as we'd all been told to learn to code a decade earlier, we were all now expected to learn to work with AI—or to be replaced by it.

But as startup darlings like OpenAI soared to a $150 billion-plus valuation, the lucrative exits—the liquidity events—failed to materialize. The costs were piling up as billions had to be poured into the money funnel just to keep up. Oracle CEO Larry Ellison said that the cost of entry for a cutting-edge AI model was at least $100 billion. Some of the VCs felt the coming squeeze. Despite the huge capital raises by AI startups like Musk's xAI, which raised $12 billion in venture investment from Middle Eastern sovereign wealth funds and VCs in 2024 alone, overall technology investments were down significantly compared to their ZIRP-era highs. In 2021, US venture capitalists announced about $345 billion in investments; the number dropped to $242 billion in 2022 and $170.6 billion in 2023.[12]

VCs made fewer investments but participated in more "megarounds," with huge financial outlays that put even more pressure on AI startups to fulfill their lofty goals. In the last quarter of 2024, four AI companies raised $26.6 billion. (According to the *Wall Street Journal*, xAI sent "hundreds of millions of dollars" to X to help Musk's social network, which was deep in the red, cover its bills.)[13]

Big deals—splashy IPOs, multibillion-dollar acquisitions—were drying up. A few were struck down by regulators like FTC chair Lina Khan, Biden's most effective appointee, who reached supervillain status on the Valley's Sand Hill Road. The inability to cash out seemed to amplify VCs' ire toward the Biden administration.

"Kind of amusing to hear VCs complain that a future tax policy would stop them from taking their companies public," wrote Dan Primack, Axios's business editor. "Really? What's stopping you RIGHT NOW?"[14]

"The companies suck," responded the venture capitalist Chamath Palihapitiya.[15]

It was a glib, brazen comment from the former "SPAC king" who had taken a number of companies public via the briefly trendy, and risky, method of special purpose acquisition companies. These publicly traded shell companies merged with startups to provide quicker access to capital markets—without much of the usual Wall Street due diligence. The SPAC craze ended as interest rates rose and as it became clear that many SPACs were not fundamentally sound businesses. Many companies that Palihapitiya took public tanked, like Opendoor, Virgin Galactic, Clover, and SoFi. Some of his planned SPAC mergers never happened and eventually Palihapitiya gave up on the SPAC concept entirely. His reputation was bruised, but he'd done very well, with his company Social Capital taking in $750 million from SPAC deals.[16]

"The companies suck" seemed like a startling, if deliberately provocative, admission. But it felt honest, at least as a reflection of the point of view of a class of VCs who were struggling with rising interest rates and unprofitable startups that couldn't be sold or dumped on public markets. Having recently survived the near-implosion of their industry's essential bank, their reputations as technological and financial seers were at stake.

"Never thought I would see SPAC Jesus—the man who would take a bag of shit public if there was a profit—claim no one is going public cause the companies suck," said the tech critic Edward Ongweso Jr., pungently summing up the amazement of industry watchers.[17]

The truth was written in weakening profit-and-loss statements, declining startup valuations, and the plain fact that the deals weren't being signed. The 10x and 100x exits just weren't there. There was also an international technological race that the United States seemed at risk of losing. While Silicon Valley was floundering, their competitors in China shocked the world with the release of DeepSeek, an AI model reportedly as strong or better than its Western counterparts, made at a fraction of the cost. China's BYD was also producing cheap, high-quality electric cars—which was eating into Tesla's sales in Asia. As the US tried to limit Chinese access to high-end microchips, Chinese companies either found ways around export restrictions, or, in the case of telecom giant Huawei, began creating advanced chips in-house. When Huawei debuted its Mate 60 Pro phone, its sophistication shocked the Biden administration, which prompted the Commerce Department to start an investigation.[18] Commerce secretary Gina Raimondo called reports about the Mate 60's capabilities "incredibly disturbing."[19]

Rather than compete on innovation and appeal to customers, tech VCs decided that, if they wanted to salvage their investments, they would have to bend government economic policy to serve them even more generously than it already had. And there was only one presidential candidate who could do that, someone whose resentments aligned with theirs and who, for a fee, would give them virtually anything they wanted. Donald Trump's transactional approach to politics—his willingness to follow the priorities of his donors—had been on full display in 2024, especially when he suddenly changed his mind about a certain controversial Chinese app, which happened to be backed by some influential American investors. Trump's about-face on TikTok would become a model for how tech elites could use him as a vehicle for achieving greater power.

16

TikTok, China, and the Moneyman of the Moment

You may remember that, during his first term in office, President Donald Trump claimed that one of the grave problems facing the country came in the form of TikTok, the social video app that counted an estimated 150 million users in the United States and nearly 2 billion globally. He wasn't alone: a bipartisan swath of US politicians and national-security officials issued warnings about the short-form video app, from sensible concerns about foreign data collection to those who felt that TikTok was bewitching America's youth on behalf of our Chinese communist adversaries. Some Silicon Valley executives saw a foreign rival encroaching uncomfortably on their social-media turf and decided that joining the hawkish consensus against TikTok could be a prudent decision for their business and their politics. Later, Senator Mitt Romney and Senator Mark Warner would separately say that the surge of pro-Palestinian activism on TikTok—including gruesome videos of Israeli atrocities in Gaza—helped galvanize establishment opposition to the platform.[1]

In August 2020, President Trump had issued an executive order targeting TikTok and WeChat, the latter a popular Chinese messaging app with an estimated 3.3 million users in the United States.[2] The order addressed TikTok as a national-security threat in the ongoing cold war with China: "[TikTok's] data collection threatens to allow the Chinese Communist Party access to Americans' personal and proprietary information—potentially allowing China to track the locations of Federal employees and contractors, build dossiers of personal information for blackmail, and conduct corporate espionage."[3]

The executive order threatened TikTok with a ban if they didn't divest themselves from their Chinese ownership. TikTok's leadership and the Trump administration discussed a plan to sell the app to Walmart and billionaire Oracle founder Larry Ellison, one of Trump's political benefactors. That effort ultimately ran aground in court. Meanwhile, TikTok sought to fend off future Trump attacks and takeover bids by beefing up its US operations and promising that it would take measures to ensure that the vast troves of American consumer data the site harvests would remain stateside, in Texas.

The movement against TikTok exemplified the shifting political winds in Silicon Valley. As we have seen, during the Obama administration, the tech industry developed a profitable revolving-door relationship with the security state. In 2013, Edward Snowden's revelations of mass domestic surveillance—often with the assistance of big tech companies—disrupted that relationship. End-to-end encryption—making data in transit unreadable by snooping parties—became table stakes for many tech companies. Some talked a big game on privacy. Others actually challenged secret surveillance orders in court.[4]

But most tech companies made their peace with the US surveillance state and still did business with foreign dictatorships, as did the VCs funding the new wave of startups. Some bid for contracts that would make them paid-up partners in the kind of mass surveillance they publicly claimed to abhor. Customer surveillance remained the preferred business model. Without curbing mass data collection, Silicon Valley could never challenge the national-security edicts of presidents and intelligence agencies. It would only grow closer to them.

Perhaps that's what the tech industry wanted. Following Trump's 2016 election, leading executives expressed their desire to partner with a new administration whose chaotic authoritarian designs were clear from day zero. Some, like Oracle CEO Safra Catz and IBM CEO Ginni Rometty, offered the president their open support. Others, like Mark Zuckerberg, enjoyed private meetings with Trump. Most tech chiefs went along quietly or offered bursts of disagreement that quietly faded. On January 28, 2017, Google co-founder Sergey Brin attended a protest against Trump's Muslim ban at SFO airport. "I'm here because I'm a refugee," said Brin, who was born in the Soviet Union.[5] By the end of the Trump administration, as Covid-19 raged in the US, Brin had resigned his position at Google and moved to a private island, reportedly one of several he owned near Fiji.

If there were to be any politics of dissent in the tech industry, it would have to come from people below the executive class. As discussed in the "Thiel and the New Alignment" chapter, a nascent political awakening seemed to be happening around this time in tech—interest in unionization, a refusal to contribute to the military-industrial complex, a general discomfort with the social, political, and mental health effects of social-media platforms, particularly on young people. But it was a scattered sense of political consciousness, tamped down by company leaders who maintained intelligence-agency-style "insider threat" programs that vigorously surveilled employees for potential whistleblower activity or communications with journalists. The big tech companies became so comfortable with working for intelligence agencies because they had become intelligence agencies themselves. Mass surveillance, institutional secrecy, the employment of former intelligence officials and operatives, a constant vigilance against threats internal and external, fleets of lawyers—these became core characteristics of companies like Facebook, Amazon, and Google. Perhaps they were simply following the authoritarian trail blazed by other large multinationals, but they set a new standard in what they could provide the national-security state: a virtually complete record of human communications and activity. Collecting that information was core to their business. And in return, the tech companies would develop the kind of relationships and lucrative government contracts that would make them paid-up members of the new, digitally enabled defense-industrial base.

It was in this context that a faction of tech leaders decided to go to war against TikTok. Perhaps the most visible—certainly the most militant—was Jacob Helberg, the Palantir advisor who interviewed his boss Alex Karp in that Capitol Hill defense forum discussed earlier. Helberg was another prominent Silicon Valley player who had undergone his own public political transformation. In 2020, Helberg raised money for Pete Buttigieg's run in the Democratic presidential primary. Four years later, he donated $1 million to Trump campaign PACs and committees, telling the *Washington Post*, "Trump was right on a lot of make-or-break issues for America."[6] Helberg and Trump disagreed on TikTok, but they were both China hawks, and Helberg hailed from the same tech industry clique as future Republican vice president JD Vance.

In the run-up to the TikTok ban, Helberg and billionaire venture capitalist—and Democratic donor—Vinod Khosla published an open letter to US senators calling TikTok a Chinese "weapon of war" and "programmable fentanyl whose effects are under the control of the Chinese authorities." This wasn't about free speech or data privacy, the letter stated. According to Helberg and Khosla, "cognitive warfare is a new theater of war in the 21st century." Using the wonkish language of the tech defense hawk, they warned, "The CCP is deploying technologies that spread narratives and ideas with viral coefficients and enable panoptic state surveillance powered by advanced models. This is a theater of war pervasive in today's world."[7]

The language seemed overheated. As with the disastrous, decades-long global war on terror, Helberg, Khosla, and their many like-minded confreres seemed to be looking to concoct a borderless, unending conflict that affected everyone. Whether we acknowledged it or not, China was attacking us, not just collecting consumer data or conducting mass surveillance but prosecuting a whole new theater of war. We had no choice but to respond.

The same logic, more politely expressed, undergirded the chip war with China, in which the US sought to limit China's access to advanced semiconductors. It's an expensive, dangerous, and potentially endless conflict. How does one "win" a race over semiconductor production or AI development? The economic war being fought with China—via sanctions, government pressure on tech firms, and covert means—seems foolish, unsustainable, and economically disruptive. It makes genuine "kinetic" conflict between the two sides more likely, not less. It also inspires some pretty unhinged suggestions, like the notion we should draw up plans to bomb the world's most important chip manufacturer in the event of a Chinese invasion of Taiwan.

In this heady atmosphere, US tech executives styled themselves as hardened national-security experts. Helberg was one of them. So were Elon Musk and David Sacks, especially with their interest in Ukraine. In Musk's case, it was at least partly a financial interest, with his Starlink satellite internet terminals being used by frontline Ukrainian soldiers (and, via the magic of the black market, by Russian forces as well). Sequoia Capital partner Shaun Maguire, who denounced Trump after January 6 before becoming a passionate supporter two years later, liked to cite his time working as a civilian contractor for DARPA in Afghanistan. There were many others—the Palantir alumni and a16z American dynamism boosters and defense tech profiteers and the Anduril skunk works planners cooking up lethal AI-powered drones. Together they formed a new cadre of militant, nationalistic engineers, executives, and investors who were ready to devote themselves to the growing cold war with China.

Looming in this constellation was Eric Schmidt, the former Google CEO and chairman who, more than any other tech executive, embodied this union between Silicon Valley and the national-security state. Schmidt might have been a Democrat, but his role was more supranational, another oligarch on an authoritarian tilt, profiting from war, dispensing his bleak panoptic vision of the future to policymakers.[8] His general secrecy and his role in bridging industry with the military hardly seemed like democracy-fortifying efforts.

Schmidt might have had more experience and a bigger portfolio than Helberg, but he spoke at times with the same bravado that inspired concern about who might be driving high-level US national-security and industrial policy. In 2024, at an appearance in a class at Stanford, Schmidt bragged that he was a "licensed arms dealer,"[9] referring to his drone company, White Stork, whose existence he refused to publicly confirm.[10] He talked about going to the White House to discuss artificial-intelligence policy. He talked about using AI for war-fighting. Schmidt seemed to have found a way to deal with the moral and legal complexities. "Because of the way the laws work, we're doing this privately and then this is all legal with the support of the governments," said Schmidt. "It goes straight into the Ukraine and then they fight the war."[11]

This was how a popular video-sharing app could be drafted into a global contest of superpowers. And it's how both Democratic and Republican presidents could come to see TikTok as a pressing national-security issue requiring drastic intervention.

But all that was before Trump met billionaire Philadelphia financier Jeffrey Yass.

A top Republican donor, Yass publicly discouraged Trump from running in the 2024 election. Yass initially supported Florida governor Ron DeSantis before spreading his bets between Vivek Ramaswamy, Chris Christie, and Tim Scott. But as Trump once again steamrolled his primary competitors, Yass reached out and asked him to speak at a retreat for a powerful right-wing business PAC, the Club for Growth, which had pulled in $61 million in donations from Yass since 2010. The Club for Growth also happened to be employing former Trump advisor Kellyanne Conway to lobby on behalf of TikTok on Capitol Hill.

The retreat seemed to go exactly as planned. Praising Yass as "fantastic," Trump emerged as a critic of a TikTok ban. "If you get rid of TikTok, Facebook and Zuckerschmuck will double their business," Trump posted in March 2024 on Truth Social. "I don't want Facebook, who cheated in the last Election, doing better. They are a true Enemy of the People!"[12]

If wars are how Americans learn geography, then elections are how they learn about plutocracy. Within the country's donor-driven political system, each election brings different billionaires into the public eye—chemical magnates, software executives, hedge fund tycoons, reclusive scions to old banking fortunes.

For the 2024 election, whatever hesitation some of the country's elites might have felt about supporting Trump, soon on his way to being a multiply convicted felon, quickly proved to be kayfabe—a pose easily dispensed with, once the conditions were right. By June 2024, after Trump had dispatched his rivals, assumed control of the RNC, and survived a criminal conviction without a dip in his base's support, it was clear that the party of business, more than ever, belonged to Trump. Democrats' frenzied rhetoric about Trump as a threat to democracy seemed to matter less to the nation's tycoons than the prospect of low taxes and a more business-friendly administration. (Not that any of them were doing poorly under Biden.)

It didn't take long for it to become clear that many of the country's ultra-rich would sidle up to the bar again for another round of Trump. "Never mind: Wall Street titans shake off qualms and embrace Trump," went a June 10 headline in *Politico*.[13]

For a crucial period in 2024, Jeffrey Yass was the moneyman of the moment—the Koch or Gates or Walton who, by sheer fact of his billions, felt able to lean on the levers of democracy. His vast wealth, geopolitically sensitive business interests, and right-wing institutional connections placed him squarely in the middle of Republican fundraising efforts and policy debates. It allowed him to gain the ear of Donald Trump.

Born in 1956, by 2024 Yass was the richest man in Pennsylvania, with an estimated fortune of about $28 billion derived from options trading and venture capital investments—including a sizable interest in TikTok. Local politicos and activist groups had long faced off against him and his bottomless war chest in fights over education, social welfare, and unions. Arielle Klagsbrun, deputy campaign director at the Action Center on Race & the Economy (ACRE), described Yass as a "next generation Koch brother … someone who is rigging the rules to privatize our schools while also not paying his fair share of taxes."[14]

"His disdain for teachers' unions, in particular, is profound," said Klagsbrun, characterizing Yass's influence as "corporate authoritarianism in our democracy."[15] ACRE pushed Pennsylvania elected officials to refuse to take money from Yass in the 2024 cycle. That was a tough ask.

Yass didn't openly support Trump in 2020, instead giving tens of millions of dollars to the Club for Growth and conservative PACs, but it didn't take long in the next presidential cycle to realize that Trump was still the only game in town for Republican voters. That presented an opportunity.

By March 2024, Yass had become the leading Republican donor of the campaign cycle. His poll position would be challenged by other right-wing billionaires, like Timothy Mellon, an heir to a Gilded Age banking fortune, who donated at least $197 million, mostly to PACs supporting Donald Trump (he also tossed $25 million to Robert F. Kennedy Jr.'s campaign).[16] But Mellon was famously "reclusive," and Yass was the sort to meet with politicians directly, recommending specific policies, while funding influential think tanks and lobbying groups. He was in the mix. In the first few months of 2024, Yass and his wife, Janine, had given more than $46 million to conservative groups and candidates, according to Open Secrets. They had a history of big giving: the couple doled out $56 million in 2022 and $30 million in 2020. Their 2024 bill would top out at about $101 million.[17]

In 2012, Susquehanna International Group, the trading and investment giant co-founded by Yass, made an early investment in ByteDance, TikTok's Chinese parent company. By 2024, as the TikTok debate flared up again, this time under the Biden administration, that stake amounted to about 15 percent of the company and was worth an estimated $40 billion—possibly much more. A bit under half of that holding—somewhere in the neighborhood of $18 billion—belonged to Yass personally.

Yass had an enormous financial interest in ensuring that TikTok could continue to operate legally in the United States. Both the Trump and Biden administrations had made moves to ban the platform. If ByteDance were forced to sell TikTok, then Yass could be well-positioned to assume a larger ownership share. In the meantime, Yass was showering Republicans, right-wing PACs, and big-business groups with millions of dollars in donations, and he was educating them, just as he had done with Trump, on the value of TikTok.

Yass checked many of the boxes expected of the post-Citizens United billionaire class. He was passionate about "school choice" and less passionate about paying taxes.[18,19] He was financially and ideologically invested in the charter school movement, saying that many Philadelphia teachers at "government schools" were "horrible" and overpaid.[20] He called the Democratic Party an "evil political actor."[21] He was on the board of the libertarian Cato Institute and idolized Milton Friedman, whose 1962 laissez-faire tract *Capitalism and Freedom* was a core text in Yass's conversion to conservative economics.

The son of two accountants, Yass grew up in the Bronx. He was a math major at SUNY Binghamton and a gambler. After college, he tried to make it as a professional poker player in Las Vegas. He and some friends made hundreds of thousands of dollars implementing a sophisticated betting scheme at racetracks across the country. After one track kicked them out, Yass sued the track owner in federal court. He lost.

Yass eventually landed on Wall Street, where he was mentored by Izzy Englander, a highly regarded hedge fund trader. Yass started trading options on the Philadelphia Stock Exchange and soon invited some of his college poker buddies to join him. They founded Susquehanna, which grew into a dominant player in options trading. It also had some lucrative interests in finance and tech. Poker remained a huge part of Susquehanna's game-theory-driven culture. The company hosted a series of games for employees, and several Susquehanna quants won bracelets at the World Series of Poker.

Like many fintech moguls, Yass nursed a fierce hostility toward public education, which he attributed to his libertarian mentor Friedman. "He was the guy I respected most," Yass said at a December 2023 gala for the Yass Prize, which awarded millions of dollars to charter schools. "As a gambler, I go with the smartest guy. And he was the smartest guy, I thought."

Yass believed that students in publicly funded schools were "slaves," rather than the "customers" they should be. At the 2023 gala, he said that he hoped that, decades from now, people would look back in astonishment at the fact that some parents didn't have access to charter school vouchers. "That's like looking back and thinking, in 1850 how did you allow slavery? How did something so disgusting exist?" (Timothy Mellon, the banking heir, has compared welfare to slavery.[22] Likening things to slavery that are very much not like slavery seems to be a right-wing mega-donor trope.)

Trump was the most prominent Republican to come around to Yass's view on TikTok, but he was far from the first. Vivek Ramaswamy used to call TikTok "digital fentanyl."[23] But he eventually had the same epiphany that Trump later experienced. During the summer of 2023, Ramaswamy received millions of dollars in donations from Yass—and sure enough, come September, he launched his own TikTok account, saying he wanted to reach young people. Ramaswamy said that he was against banning the app, as were Kentucky senator Rand Paul and other nominally libertarian recipients of Yass campaign donations.

Less fortunate fundraiser-lawmakers in the GOP and the Democratic Party continued to demonize the social-media app as a first-order threat to national security. It was a bipartisan effort, supported by political factions on both sides of the proverbial aisle and by Silicon Valley elements, like Palantir advisor Jacob Helberg, who met with lawmakers and stoked hawkish concern about the CCP spy app living in American teenagers' phones.

Amidst America's crude sound-bite-driven politics, the battle around TikTok was reduced to a Sinophobic moral panic, rather than a complex debate about data sovereignty, free speech, the contested definition of "disinformation," and big tech's pioneering use of surveillance as a business model. Banning TikTok seemed like a crude policy response when America's tech giants—and its intelligence community—collected vast amounts of consumer data, and when numerous other Chinese apps remained on

American consumers' phones. But with a majority in the Senate and Republican allies in the House—Yass's money had traveled far but not far enough—the Biden administration had the votes to pass a ban and chalk it up as a win. And so it did. On April 24, 2024, President Biden signed the Protecting Americans from Foreign Adversary Controlled Applications Act, which granted the president broad latitude to ban and force the sale of social-media companies deemed "to present a significant threat to national security."[24] It's a law that could be used for much more than just prying TikTok away from its Chinese ownership, potentially allowing the president to shut down access to any app with minimal pretext.

As the Biden administration was making progress on antitrust matters, particularly through Lina Khan's Federal Trade Commission, it seemed incongruous to engineer the forced sale of a major social-media company to the same tech moguls and financiers whose acquisitive appetites the FTC was attempting to keep in check. A TikTok ban/forced sale was politically unpopular, censorious, a distraction from more pressing political crises, and certain to be challenged in court. But that's the policy that President Biden chose to embrace. Assuming the law survived legal challenges and the presidential transition, the TikTok ban would be a victory for the national-security directorate, cementing American corporations' tech sovereignty at a cost to American consumers.

Whatever the outcome, Jeffrey Yass could claim a major financial conquest. Given the platform's popularity, there was too much money at stake not to make a deal. That meant that Yass could eventually emerge from this imbroglio with either a greater stake in TikTok or billions of dollars in profit on what was reportedly a low seven-figure investment. The price was going to be high. Former Trump Treasury secretary Steven Mnuchin was one of several politically connected financiers who said that he wanted to form a group to buy TikTok. Parking lot mogul Frank McCourt, who bankrupted the Dodgers baseball team and walked away richer than ever, announced his interest in acquiring the platform.

Yass also made another deal with Trump that provided an essential financial lifeline when it seemed like the presidential candidate might be running out of cash. In March 2024, after extensive delays, SEC investigations, an outside accountant busted for fraud, and at least two guilty pleas for insider trading, Trump Media & Technology Group finally consummated its SPAC merger with the blank shell company Digital World Acquisition Corp (DWAC). As it turned out, Susquehanna Group was "the biggest institutional shareholder" of DWAC, owning about 2 percent.[25] When the merged companies went public under the ticker symbol DJT, Yass's stake was worth tens of millions (not to mention the several billion of paper wealth Trump could now claim). A few months later, Susquehanna sold its stake, though it later bought back in.[26]

The former president had a paper-thin ego, but he was easily persuaded—particularly with a dizzying array of legal fees and court fines before him. His reconciliation with Elon Musk—with whom Trump had traded public insults—was proof of that. A similar parley happened between Yass and Trump over the things that mattered: money and the policies needed to make even more of it. Yass's largesse was no doubt why Trump was reportedly considering Yass as a potential Treasury secretary. Having made peace with Trump, Yass got his turn with the tiller of Republican policy.

With one foot in finance and another in tech, Yass reflected the shifting character of the Republican Party's big-business wing. Trump was about to select JD Vance, a former venture capitalist and Yale Law School graduate, as his vice presidential running mate. Vance wouldn't have gotten there without a big assist from Elon Musk, Peter Thiel, and the venture capitalists who were beginning to influence the course of Trump's campaign.

17

The Road to Vance

On July 13, at an outdoor rally in Butler, Pennsylvania, a gunman named Thomas Matthew Crooks was able to get a clear line of sight on Donald Trump from 443 feet away.[1] Crooks fired eight shots, clipping Trump's ear and killing one rally attendee, before a law enforcement sniper took him out. Captured live in full high-definition video, the sight of a bloodied Trump raising his fist and shouting "Fight!" proved as galvanizing an image for perpetually online VCs as it did for the MAGA faithful. Elon Musk, who had promised as recently as March that he would not directly support a candidate, announced after the shooting that he "fully endorse[d]" Trump.

The attack became subject to the usual cycles of accusatory spin and roving speculation that attended any major media event. Prominent Trump supporters blamed the assassination attempt on Democratic rhetoric about Trump being a danger to democracy. The Secret Service was headed by a woman, which in MAGA minds could only mean a DEI hire. The attempted murder became proof of Trump's disruptive power against the deep state. "They" were out to get him at any cost.

"Tucker was right," wrote David Sacks, referring to Tucker Carlson's prediction that someone would try to assassinate Trump.[2]

"100%," responded Shaun Maguire, a partner at Sequoia Capital.[3]

Blaming President Joe Biden for inflaming the political climate, Vivek Ramaswamy wrote, "The only thing more tragic than what just happened is that, if we're being honest, it wasn't totally a shock."[4]

"You very much predicted this," replied Musk.[5]

"I badly hoped I would be wrong," wrote Ramaswamy.[6]

For Maguire, a former liberal who had become radicalized by what he described as a dishonest media and elite establishment that lied about Trump, July 13, 2024 was a momentous occasion. He posted on X at least 51 times that day about the assassination attempt, continuing late into the night. Like some of his peers, he speculated that there was a deep-state plot afoot and that "this shooter will almost certainly be discovered to be a member" of Antifa, the leaderless leftist protest movement. "The world still doesn't appreciate how coordinated and motivated Antifa is," wrote Maguire. "It should have been designated a terror organization long ago."[7]

"100," wrote Musk, using the emoji indicating full agreement.[8]

The most troubling thing that Maguire posted in connection with the assassination attempt concerned an "election prediction" he had posted about five weeks earlier. The original prediction post was a jumble of letters, numbers, and symbols—an encrypted message. "Too spicy for plain text," Maguire wrote at the time.[9]

A few hours after the July 13 assassination attempt, Maguire posted the decrypted version of his message. It read:

> Optimal strategy is for Biden to be assassinated by a "MAGA supporter"
> Breeds maximum sympathy
> Michelle and Gavin each have huge baggage, no time for it to come out

Maguire then offered a retrospective gloss on his "prediction":

> 6 weeks ago I posted this
> I got the target wrong, but the means correct
> The stakes of this election have always been assassination
> Wake up [American flag emoji][10]

As a prediction, it was a bizarre and macabre piece of conspiracism. It sounded more like a hypothetical recommendation—a plan—for a ruthlessly corrupt Democratic Party to beat Trump by assassinating its own candidate. With the "optimal strategy" suggestion, Maguire perhaps understood how his "spicy" post could be interpreted, so he posted an encrypted version of his thought experiment that he could later unveil to validate himself. As for what he meant by "the stakes of this election have always been assassination," I had no idea. Clearly he thought the situation was trending toward violence. He seemed ready for it.

"The media has lied to you about everything," wrote Maguire, whose employer Sequoia Capital put $800 million into Musk's purchase of Twitter.[11] "Trump has been [fighting] for America. While the media and deep state machine has been spinning it the other way—you have been manipulated on every single topic."[12]

Peter Thiel might have claimed that he was sitting out the 2024 election, but his baton had been passed to a band of venture capitalists and tech CEOs best known by the general public for these kinds of X posts: Elon Musk, Joe Lonsdale, David Sacks, Marc Andreessen, Shaun Maguire—i.e. the men who appear in this book. They were all very rich and controlled a lot of capital beyond their own.

By August 2024, they were wielding increasing influence over the Trump campaign: Sacks spoke at the Republican National Convention in Milwaukee. Jacob Helberg advised Trump on TikTok and AI policy. Chamath Palihapitiya was one of a number of tech notables who attended a Trump dinner at Sacks' San Francisco mansion, where the group pushed Trump to choose Vance as his running mate.

Musk's endorsement would prove crucial to Trump's campaign, but his backing was a fait accompli. The two men had been speaking frequently in the previous months, and their bitterly reactionary politics aligned. Musk had been quietly supporting right-wing political organizations run by Trump advisor Stephen Miller, such as Citizens for Sanity, which, during the 2022 midterm elections, aired ads that "accused Democrats of promoting sex-reassignment surgeries for children and portrayed illegal immigrants as causing crime waves and draining economic resources."[13] Within days of Musk's endorsement, the *Wall Street Journal* reported that Musk was committing a remarkable $45 million per month to America PAC, a new pro-Trump super PAC that would also be supported by Palantir co-founder Joe Lonsdale, Mark Zuckerberg castoffs Tyler and Cameron Winklevoss, and several members of the PayPal Mafia.[14] Donning their "Dark MAGA" hats, the tech authoritarians were all in, and they were bringing their money with them.

Two days later, sporting a white bandage covering the wound where a bullet had grazed his ear, Trump stood triumphantly onstage at the Republican National Convention. There he unveiled as his vice presidential nominee Ohio senator JD Vance, a former venture capitalist and the *Hillbilly Elegy* author who owed his 2022 Senate victory to a $15 million campaign-cash infusion from Peter Thiel, his longtime employer and mentor. For the tech industry, the Vance selection was sensational. "WE HAVE A FORMER TECH VC IN THE WHITE HOUSE," crowed Delian Asparouhov, a partner at Thiel's Founders Fund who once drew notice for sharing a comic by the neo-Nazi cartoonist known as StoneToss.[15] (Asparouhov later said that he did not know of StoneToss' other work.)[16] "GREATEST COUNTRY ON EARTH BABY."[17]

Musk, who had been agitating privately for Trump to choose Vance, celebrated the pick on X. "Resounds with victory," he wrote.[18] Vivek Ramaswamy posted wistful, supportive remarks about being drinking buddies with Vance at Yale Law School.[19] Using the term of endearment favored by his fellow mega-rich *All-In* podcast hosts, Chamath Palihapitiya celebrated the news: "A Bestie adjacent as the VP?!?!?!"[20]

Overnight, Vance's appointment as the VP candidate became a seminal moment for the Silicon Valley elites. Many Americans knew Vance as a "hillbilly" made good, but for America's right-wing tech class, he was also one of them.

If Silicon Valley conservatives had already turned on the money spigot for Trump, the Trump assassination attempt and Vance's ascension prompted them to fully open the tap. Marc Andreessen and Ben Horowitz, who headed the highly influential VC firm bearing their names, announced on their podcast that they would be donating to pro-Trump PACs. Following the long tradition of rich guys who value tax cuts above all else, the billionaire VCs cited a Biden administration proposal to tax unrealized capital gains as their personal breaking point.

They also described what they saw as a breakdown in the implicit bargain between big tech and the political overclass. The deal used to go something like this: Tech guys would innovate, build cool stuff, and get rich. They'd pay some of it back via foundations and philanthropic work and, sure, the minimum legally required tax payment. The government and regulatory state would cheer from the sidelines and clear the runway for takeoff. In the minds of Andreessen and Horowitz, that bargain had broken down. Additional capital gains taxes, Lina Khan's activist FTC, and the SEC's crackdown on crypto fraud and securities law violations were unacceptable breaches of norms.

It wasn't just venture capitalists, tech executives, and Elon Musk who were putting their wealth behind Trump. The libertarian-minded cryptocurrency industry was dominating that cycle's political giving. The industry's super PACs were swimming in cash. Salivating at the chance to overthrow an adversarial regulatory regime, crypto leaders called for their customers to make their voices heard as single-issue voters. By August, when Trump was laying on the flattery as the keynote speaker of the largest annual Bitcoin conference, the influence of crypto donors became impossible to ignore.

Despite being relatively small in terms of revenue—and having experienced the disastrous 2022 collapse precipitated by multibillion-dollar frauds like FTX, Celsius, and Terra— the crypto industry had a lot of money to deploy to shove their regulatory priorities across the finish line. They had been lobbying Congress and state houses for months, showing as much zeal for influence-peddling as Sam Bankman-Fried ever did. Fairshake, the PAC funded by Coinbase, Ripple Labs, Jump, and other top players—including Andreessen Horowitz and Winklevoss Capital Management—raised more than $204 million.[21]

Fairshake spent millions to advance its political agenda. As the tech critic Molly White wrote on her site *Follow the Crypto*, which tracked crypto political spending, Fairshake was focused on a single issue: "installing crypto-friendly politicians and ousting those the industry views as a threat."[22] Vance happened to be a crypto devotee who had been circulating a draft bill that one lobbyist told *Politico* was almost too friendly to the crypto industry and would come across as excessively "partisan."[23] The crypto industry got their man on the ticket, and Vance and other Republicans were lined up to be beneficiaries of Fairshake's massive war chest.

These were the powerful political and monetary currents now being tapped by the Trump campaign. It was not much different from the plutocracy practiced by the Koch brothers, the Mellons, Miriam Adelson, and numerous other members of the donor-class, but now it came with a shiny Silicon Valley wrapper. For old money and new, their interests aligned, as Donald Trump became the standard bearer for the venture capitalists' techno-fascist political project described throughout this book.

The linchpin of this relationship, the one whose years of political work made this new alignment not only possible but somehow logical, was Peter Thiel, the venture capitalist. After spending decades accruing wealth and power and influence as Silicon Valley's proudest contrarian, Thiel provided essential financial support to the 2016 Trump campaign, becoming its conduit to Silicon Valley. He chose who sat at the table for the Trump Tower meeting with tech CEOs in December 2016. He proposed candidates for administration appointments, though some of his choices, like Network State-propagandist Balaji Srinivasan as head of the FDA, didn't pan out. While Thiel was supposedly out of politics—at least as a donor—by the 2024 cycle, he was still interviewed frequently on TV, criticizing the efficacy of the Trump administration but never quite denouncing its policies or its figurehead. Thiel's ideas and disciples were seeded throughout Team Trump and the larger Republican Party. Thiel didn't speak at the 2024 Republican

National Convention, but his friend David Sacks did, along with Hulk Hogan, the retired wrestler whose lawsuit in response to the publication of a video of him having sex with a friend's wife—a suit secretly funded and directed by Thiel—bankrupted Gawker Media, a Thiel nemesis. Silicon Valley's most ideologically influential venture capitalist may not have been an official supporter of the 2024 Trump campaign, but his influence was pervasive. And when his mentee was selected as the vice presidential nominee, Thiel had one of his own poised to enter the Oval Office. It was an effort that, in one way or another, Thiel had been working toward for decades.

TECH'S MOST INFLUENTIAL AUTHORITARIAN

In a 2009 essay, Thiel outlined his political vision, reflecting a worldview that seems to have persisted to this day. It started with fundamental issues of who is allowed to govern and to what end. This was the essay where, as we heard earlier, Thiel presented his blunt conclusion that "freedom and democracy" were not "compatible." Thiel preferred the open freedom of the unfettered market, perhaps under the dictatorship of a benevolent sovereign. Thiel complained that "the vast increase in welfare beneficiaries and the extension of the franchise to women" had been difficult for the libertarian cause. He was frustrated that an "unthinking demos"—that is, ordinary voters—guided electoral politics. When he was later accused of opposing women's suffrage, *Cato* published a comment from Thiel in which he didn't apologize so much as reiterate his desire to escape the heavy shackles of democracy: "While I don't think any class of people should be disenfranchised, I have little hope that voting will make things better."[24]

Thiel had long been disappointed that humanity hadn't achieved a *Jetsons*-like future of infinite abundance. One of his popular mantras went: "We wanted flying cars, we got 140 characters." (Thiel's friend and PayPal colleague Elon Musk fixed that issue by doubling X's character limit.) The *éminence grise* of the powerful network of investors and executives known informally as the PayPal Mafia, many of whom supported Donald Trump, Thiel spoke of politics—and death, for that matter—as something that could be "escaped," leading to a utopian place of true freedom. His investments and political donations flowed accordingly, making him one of Silicon Valley's most influential investors and conservative political operators while blazing a trail for a new crop of reactionary venture capitalists and tech executives who embraced the MAGA movement. Thiel was there first, investing in explicitly right-wing companies like Palantir, Rumble, and Anduril, dining with white nationalists such as Kevin DeAnna, sponsoring far-right writers like Curtis Yarvin, and founding startups dedicated to supporting the surveillance state.[25] Although he claimed to be a committed libertarian, after 9/11, Thiel spoke frequently of the need for the tech industry to partner with the national-security state in order to fight the global war on terror. With Palantir, his data analytics startup, Thiel did just that, becoming an intelligence contractor whose software was used from Kandahar to Kyiv.

Among his peers, Thiel was early to support Trump. In 2016, he spoke at the Republican National Convention, announcing himself as a proud gay Republican. After the release of the *Access Hollywood* tape in which Trump bragged about sexually assaulting women, Thiel offered a public show of support with a $1.25 million donation.

By the time of the 2024 presidential cycle, as a liberal activist group began investigating Thiel's activities, the billionaire decided he wanted out.[26] He expressed disappointment less in Trump's policies than in the chaos of his shambolic administration. When Trump asked for a multimillion-dollar campaign donation, Thiel said no, reportedly leading to a rift between the two.[27]

But in pay-to-play politics, disputes are easily papered over. In June 2024, Thiel said he would vote for Trump if someone put a gun to his head.[28] After that, he said that he couldn't make a case for Trump, but he could make one against Biden.[29]

That was before Trump chose Ohio senator JD Vance as his running mate. In *The Contrarian*, his biography of Peter Thiel, the journalist Max Chafkin described Vance and Blake Masters as "extensions" of Thiel, men who owed their careers and much of their political thinking to Thiel's influence. (Masters lost his 2022 Senate election before losing a congressional primary in 2024.) Some politicians were friendly to right-wing Silicon Valley oligarchs like Thiel, but Vance had fashioned himself directly in Thiel's image. They were friends and colleagues. Thiel became Vance's patron when the younger man was feeling professionally adrift. Suddenly, the billionaire hard-liner seemed on the verge of getting the sort of power he had long sought.

Although he made his bones as a tech executive and financier, Thiel had been writing and speaking publicly about his bugaboos—identity politics, women, democracy, higher education—since he was an undergraduate at Stanford University in the late 1980s, when he founded the *Stanford Review*. Despite denouncing American campus culture and funding a fellowship to pay entrepreneurs to skip college, Thiel remained involved with Stanford as a guest lecturer and as one of its most famous alumni/critics. Over the years, Thiel hired many former staff members of the *Stanford Review*. And he was still, in the year 2024, giving talks at elite colleges about "the diversity myth"—the title of a book he published in 1995 with David Sacks, Thiel's putative replacement as Trump's top Silicon Valley supporter. "We're still in this Groundhog Day," Thiel said in February 2024 to a conservative student group at Harvard. His book felt "incredibly prophetic," he said. "We were basically right. Very little I would change on the particulars."[30]

If we were in a Groundhog Day situation, it might have been in part because powerful people like Thiel couldn't let go of certain political obsessions. Thiel had been lamenting the influence of leftist identity politics for more than 30 years. He was still complaining about being forced to read—in college, 35 years earlier—certain academically *en vogue* books, like Aimé Césaire's postcolonial retelling of *The Tempest*, and the autobiography of Rigoberta Menchú, a Guatemalan indigenous rights activist who won the Nobel Peace Prize. But Thiel liked to play his hits, and over time, he found a receptive audience for his repetitively aired grievances.

Thiel had described his "utopian" yearning to transcend politics and create a place of true freedom. In practice, that had meant pursuing highly ideological efforts to provide alternatives to existing institutions, and the cumbersome regulations and systems of law enforcement and criminal justice overseeing them. Where the state lacked capacity, that's where Peter Thiel thrived, as shown by the intelligence-contracting success of Palantir. In one of Thiel's offices, the journalist Barton Gellman observed, there sat a sculpture in which a figure resembling the billionaire was trying to kill a lion labeled "fair elections" and a dragon labeled "democracy."[31]

There had never been much subtlety in Thiel's approach. He wrote what he believed. He gave interviews to everyone from CNBC to college Republican clubs. He funded right-wing, anti-regulation candidates who aspired to pass policies that would help his business interests. At times, those candidates were people Thiel had previously employed. Thiel invested in an anti-woke bank and an anti-woke dating app, the latter helmed by John McEntee, a first-term Trump appointee who was booted from his White House job for his gambling problem. Both quickly failed. (McEntee was a prominent player in Project 2025, the policy playbook devised by dozens of conservative organizations in preparation for a second Trump administration.[32])

Thiel allocated his growing capital to create the sort of world he wanted to live in. He invested in seasteading and charter cities initiatives that aimed to overcome the legal strictures of the nation-state by creating autonomous corporatist nations, either on the open sea or on land carved off from countries with weak governments. He put millions into life extension research and said that he wanted to overcome death itself. Since his PayPal days, Thiel had talked about his belief that companies and individuals could issue their own currencies, free of government control. In the years that followed, he invested heavily in cryptocurrencies and in crypto exchanges around the world.

Some of Thiel's bets worked out. He was Facebook's first outside investor and after the company's 2012 IPO, he sold most of his Facebook holdings, netting him hundreds of millions of dollars.

But he would have made far more if he had held onto his stake for even a year or two. One of his hedge funds folded during the 2008 financial crisis, but Founders Fund, his VC firm, became a Valley powerhouse. And Thiel's mode of thinking—his ruthless imperiousness, his congenital contrarianism—became a model for a generation of tech authoritarians.

In Thiel's venture approach to politics, he managed to hedge his bets by spreading his money widely. Masters didn't hit, but Vance did—unbelievably so. Having never fully broken with Trump, Thiel was handed a way back in—a more direct line to power than he'd ever had before. Most importantly, key parts of his political project, like smashing the administrative state, had been taken up by his allies in Trump's inner circle. No one had embraced Thiel's ideas with more commitment than JD Vance.

BECOMING JD VANCE

In 2011, JD Vance, then known as James David Hamel, was attending Yale Law School when Thiel came to give a talk. At the time, Vance was a Marine veteran and Ohio State graduate who had emerged from meager economic and social circumstances in southern Ohio to attend a top law program that served as a finishing school for future members of the power elite. Vance had grown up steeped in evangelical Christianity but in college he drifted into Sam Harris-style atheism—a common enough path for a young man in the place and time. His colleagues saw him as politically conservative but not radically so. That would change.

Thiel's subject matter was his typical fare. He spoke about the illusory satisfactions of chasing prestige and competing with one's peers over a limited pot of rewards while the larger society faced technological stagnation and decay. For Vance, whose beliefs were proving to be malleable, it became a formative experience. In attempting to escape his traumatic upbringing, Vance had allowed himself to be driven by the mindless pursuit of academic achievements and professional credentials. Rather than aspiring for a career as a federal judge or a partner at a white-shoe law firm, as so many of his classmates did, he realized that he dreaded his future as a lawyer. Despite being a product of the same milieu that Vance now inhabited, Thiel offered another way. "Peter's talk remains the most significant moment of my time at Yale Law School," Vance wrote in a widely cited essay in a Catholic magazine.[33]

There was another aspect of Thiel that Vance liked. "He was possibly the smartest person I'd ever met, but he was also a Christian," Vance wrote. "He defied the social template I had constructed—that dumb people were Christians and smart ones atheists."[34] Vance later converted to Catholicism. And he reached out to Thiel, who would transform his life.

Since receiving this insight about how the ruthless pursuit of meritocratic striving might corrode one's soul, Vance's course hadn't wavered. If anything, he climbed the meritocratic ladder with more vigor. Blessed by one of the country's most powerful venture capitalists, Vance ascended through prestigious jobs in law and tech. He published *Hillbilly Elegy*, a bestselling memoir that made emotional appeals to the same liberal elites he would later claim to despise. It was turned into a successful Hollywood film. After working for Thiel's Mithril Capital, Vance opened his own venture capital firm, Narya (with backing from Thiel, it too took its name from JRR Tolkien's *The Lord of the Rings*) and became very wealthy. He helped Thiel start a right-wing Republican tech donor network called Rockbridge.[35] In 2022, he was elected to the US Senate and, two years later, he was anointed as Donald Trump's running mate. At age 40, he was the first millennial on a presidential ticket and was duly elevated to the position of heir apparent to the MAGA movement.

Vance owed it all to Thiel, who became "a good friend." Thiel helped a young Vance parachute into a Silicon Valley executive job—"it was a favor for Peter," one insider told the *New York Times*—and has charted a golden path for him ever since.[36] When Vance was not working directly for Thiel, his ventures were bankrolled by him. And he benefited from Thiel's connections, becoming close with venture capitalist David Sacks ("one of my closest friends in the tech world") and Donald Trump Jr., among other MAGA notables.[37]

Thiel was an intellectual guide for a generation of tech industry conservatives. He was a dutiful reader and popularizer of his intellectual heroes, including the philosopher René Girard, whom Thiel studied under at Stanford. (Because of Thiel's name hovering near him, Girard had come to be seen as a right-wing thinker—to the dismay of his many liberal and leftist devotees.)

Vance wrote that his eyes were opened by Girard's theory of mimetic rivalry, which held that people mimicked the desires of others, lusting after things that they were told were desirable. A person couldn't avoid being influenced by mimetic desire, according to Girard, and in this Hobbesian vision, the frenzy of competition could spill over into violence. The solution was what Girard called the scapegoat mechanism: finding an outside force against which rivals could unite and enact violence.

Vance had his own history of mimesis, as demonstrated by his writings and public life. As an Ohio working-class kid learning at the knee of his grandmother, whom he calls Mawmaw in his book, a Marine public affairs officer selling the Iraq War, a callow college student indulging in the new atheism's debate-me-bro narcissism, and as a burgeoning member of the coastal elite at Yale Law School, Vance exhibited a tendency to take on different personas. He changed his name several times. (He became JD Vance shortly before graduating law school.) With Thiel, who blended authoritarian futurism with Christian devotion, Vance found something close to a final form. It's no wonder, then, that Vance supported Trump's plan to present an "alternate slate" of 2020 electors and that, after an unconvincing spin as a never-Trumper, he was willing to play caddy to the aspiring dictator. Democracy was not on the list of Thiel-ian values.

As a leading representative of the so-called New Right, Vance incorporated other ideological influences into his political program. He cited Curtis Yarvin, the reactionary, monarchist writer whom Thiel had sponsored for years and who argued for an American dictator or "CEO." Vance aligned himself with right-wing, "anti-regime" Catholics like Patrick Deneen and Rod Dreher, who questioned neoliberal economic orthodoxies because they impeded the formation of religious, conservative communities. The New Right preached limited economic populism—for example, that a family should be able to survive on one parent's income—but in the service of regressive goals like limiting reproductive rights and pushing women to stay at home. Vance, who said that he thought there should be a nationwide ban on abortion, showed himself comfortable with this mix of retrograde religious social conservatism tethered to modest economic reform.[38]

Speaking at a high school in 2017, Vance suggested that women had been empowered at the expense of children and families. "This is one of the great tricks that I think the sexual revolution pulled on the American populace, which is the idea that like, 'well, OK, these marriages were fundamentally, you know, they were maybe even violent, but certainly they were unhappy,'" said Vance. "'And so getting rid of them and making it easier for people to shift spouses like they change their underwear, that's going to make people happier in the long term.'"[39] Vance's relationship with Trump, like Thiel's, had been characterized by a sense of opportunism. In a 2016 Facebook exchange with a former roommate, Vance wrote of Trump, "I go back and forth between thinking Trump is a cynical asshole like Nixon who wouldn't be that bad (and might even prove useful) or that he's America's Hitler."[40] In public, Vance called Trump "cultural heroin" and presented himself as a never-Trumper.

That changed when Vance decided to run for the Senate and needed Trump's support. In a 2021 meeting at Mar-a-Lago, Thiel brokered a truce between Vance and Trump, in which Vance admitted he had been wrong about the former president, who then publicly endorsed Vance. In November 2022, Vance won his Senate race and from there was off, on the fast-track toward the heights of political authority. "JD, you're going to be doing this for a long time," said Trump at the 2024 Republican National Convention. "Enjoy the ride."

It's patently disturbing that Vance would compare Trump to Hitler and then be willing to dispense with whatever concerns he might have once had. Vance claimed publicly that he'd changed his mind about Trump, that—in the classic MAGA tradition—he realized that he had been bamboozled by a dishonest media. Though he'd once called Trump a bad person, Vance discovered that he was wrong and that his disagreements with Trump were more about aesthetics than policy. It was a form of rationalization that would be deployed by other never-Trumpers, who realized that they had no future in the Republican Party unless they embraced its leader, who was wildly popular with voters and the base of party activists.

Vance's conversation with his former roommate also revealed his apparent regard for President Richard Nixon, an insecure, canny "cynical asshole" who deeply resented the Eastern Establishment that, as an outsider from humble beginnings, he had to flatter and fight in his ascent to power. Vance, a smart, cynical guy from working-class Ohio who quickly mastered the folkways of East and West Coast elites while simultaneously holding them in contempt, might have been able to identify.

In November 2021, at a speech at the National Conservatism Conference, Vance lambasted the American university system that had been essential to his rise to prominence. Flashing a big grin, he quoted what he called the "wisdom" of Nixon: "The professors are the enemy."[41]

The quote came from a secretly recorded conversation between President Richard Nixon and national security advisor Henry Kissinger in late 1972, when they plotted a massive bombing campaign to force North Vietnam into a more favorable negotiating position. Operation Linebacker II unleashed a horrific amount of firepower on the north, killing thousands of civilians. Swedish prime minister Olof Palme called it a crime on par with some of World War II's most awful massacres. As for pushing North Vietnam toward better terms, most scholars agreed that the bombing campaign did no such thing.

It wasn't the outcome of Nixon's policy that appealed to Vance. It was the disregard for elite opinion with which the 37th president prosecuted his plan. Like Nixon before him, Vance knew who his enemies were: the very members of the liberal establishment whom he'd wheedled into giving him a seat at the table. And like Thiel, Vance had joined a governing order—a "regime"—that he claimed to want to overthrow. As a product of the tech industry, Vance would find full-throated support from the cryptocurrency moguls who were flooding the Trump campaign with hundreds of millions of dollars of backing. Crypto companies were running one of the most expensive political-influence operations the country had ever experienced. Ironically, their actions most resembled the failed political-lobbying campaign of FTX founder Sam Bankman-Fried, who would watch the 2024 election campaign cycle play out from a prison cell. Only two years earlier, Bankman-Fried had been on top of the world, donating fantastic amounts of money to politicians of both parties while leading a charm offensive on Capitol Hill. It all fell apart for Bankman-Fried, but his former crypto colleagues seemed to think they could essentially run his program over again, this time with the goal of electing Donald Trump.

18

Didn't the Last Guy Go to Prison?

The first time I met Sam Bankman-Fried, or SBF, the founder of the FTX cryptocurrency exchange, was during a conversation over Limoncello-flavored seltzers in a conference room of a luxury Manhattan hotel. It was July 2022, and crypto's chief man-child, who was allegedly worth 32 billion real dollars built on an empire of celebrity-endorsed fake money, was posing for a magazine cover shoot and taking interviews with journalists, part of the duties bestowed upon a mogul who seemingly had the world in his hands.

The second time I met Sam Bankman-Fried was almost exactly a year later, alone in a long hallway in the Daniel Patrick Moynihan Courthouse in Lower Manhattan. He was a criminal defendant in one of the largest fraud cases in US history, and I was wandering the cavernous 27-story building, trying to find the courtroom for one of his pre-trial hearings. I wasn't planning on just stumbling into him there, with no one else around, not even a lawyer or a court security officer or his devoted parents. I wasn't sure if he recognized me, but he had bigger concerns. (As part of SBF's playing of the media, he maintained a list of favorite journalists and I wasn't on it.) Embarrassingly unprepared—here was my chance with the moment's protagonist—I asked him if he knew where the courtroom was for the day's proceedings. He responded with an indifferent shrug and bent down to tie his shoes. I found my own way.

A few weeks later, back at the courthouse, I sat in the gallery as a judge accepted the prosecutor's argument that Bankman-Fried had tried to intimidate two witnesses, including by leaking to the *New York Times* the personal writings of his ex-girlfriend Caroline Ellison, who was the CEO of Alameda Research, his crypto hedge fund that also served as a vehicle for embezzling stolen FTX customer funds. It wasn't his first offense: the prosecution also contended that Bankman-Fried had tried to convince a former FTX executive to talk so they could coordinate their stories.

I have spoken of the collapse of FTX before in this book, and Bankman-Fried's name has appeared more than once. It is worth looking more closely at what actually happened—because it demonstrates how the corruption wrought by the convergence of tech money and crypto politics has been bipartisan.

Bankman-Fried grew up in Palo Alto, the son of laureled, well-connected Stanford legal scholars. His whole life had been gilded by privilege and the cosseted imperviousness to consequence that comes with it. At Jane Street, the prestigious financial firm where Bankman-Fried worked after graduating from MIT, he lost $300 million in a poorly conceived bet pegged to the 2016 presidential election. Still, it wasn't his money, and he retained his job—and his halo of genius. Major institutional investors would later trust him with billions more.

After his December 2022 arrest in a fraud that centered around the theft of more than $8 billion in FTX customer funds, Bankman-Fried agreed to be extradited to the United States from the Bahamas, where his business was based. Upon arriving stateside, he was again granted the fruits of privilege, avoiding pre-trial detention in favor of somewhere more comfortable: his parents' home in Palo Alto. Bankman-Fried was able to receive friends and to strategize over his defense. His childhood bedroom became a site of regular pilgrimage for some of the country's top tech journalists. Periodically the routine would be broken up by required court dates, and America's newly notorious grifter would fly with Mom and Dad to New York City for hearings like this one.

But this hearing turned out to be different. Bankman-Fried had committed acts of witness intimidation and tampering, according to Judge Lewis Kaplan, a stentorian 78-year-old who had handled major terrorism and securities fraud cases. Undeterred by previous judicial warnings, Bankman-Fried seemed inclined to do it again. Bankman-Fried had "shown a willingness and desire to risk crossing the line … wherever the line is," said Kaplan.

Judge Kaplan remanded Bankman-Fried into custody. The fallen wunderkind wouldn't be going back to his cozy Palo Alto warren. A pair of muscled security officers approached Bankman-Fried and told him to empty his pockets and take off his belt. When they told him to take off his shoelaces, the enormity of the moment seemed to hit him. His face pale, he slowly bent down to remove his laces. I thought of watching him tying his shoes in the hallway a few weeks earlier. His mother, Barbara Fried, hurried to the low barrier that separated the defendant and his lawyers from the gallery. The marshals warned her to stay back. She sobbed as her son was led away.

The judge's order wasn't unexpected, but it pierced the veil of impunity that had surrounded Bankman-Fried with a shock that could be felt among the assembled observers. In the YOLO-minded, trollish world of crypto, where nothing was serious except the ruthless pursuit of money, Bankman-Fried operated with a particular blithe arrogance, buying interests in expensive startups the way most people splurge on a sushi dinner. If you were his friend—or perhaps a lover—he might have invested half a billion dollars in your crypto hedge fund. He might have created a new token and let you in on it before it debuted on public markets. SBF did what he wanted, operating according to a sociopathic code that was marketed as rigorously quantitative and ethical. There was supposedly no situation where he wasn't calculating odds and assessing the expected value of his decisions. Yet he often acted like a spoiled child, not a hyper-rationalist fintech visionary. On Twitter, he told an annoying gadfly to sell him their crypto tokens and fuck off.[1] He famously played video games during VC pitch meetings—and the investors, to their everlasting discredit, ate it up. He even treated his arrest like a joke, as he initially continued tweeting, gossiping with journalists, and publishing rambling, supposedly exculpatory essays on Substack. Pre-trial detention helped put an end to that.

Corporate and political impunity are among the defining features of our age. In what has become a notorious emblem of our national decline, no bank CEOs were prosecuted following the 2008 financial crisis. Through 9/11, the Iraq War, Hurricane Katrina, mass surveillance, torture, Covid-19, climate change and environmental despoliation—in response to major crimes and crises, the US produces no shortage of blue-ribbon commissions of silver-haired notables promising to get to the bottom of things. But there is practically no accountability, much less arrests of high-level government officials or corporate officers, a small irony given our outrageously carceral society. The US criminal justice system is designed to imprison poor people—not billionaire financiers or presidents. For that reason, every stage of Sam Bankman-Fried's prosecution—from the raid on his Bahamas penthouse to his extradition to the revocation of his bond to his eventual prosecution and conviction—took on a growing air of unreality. You wouldn't have been cynical for thinking he would walk away, right up until the jury convicted him on all charges.

Elon Musk, David Sacks, and other members of their clique said so publicly, though their comments were generally slathered in partisan disgust. "SBF was a major Dem donor, so no investigation," Musk wrote on Twitter a few days after FTX collapsed.[2] "Who's more protected, SBF or Hunter Biden?" asked Sacks in July 2023, around the time that I ran into Bankman-Fried in that courtroom hallway.[3]

Fortunately, these men were wrong. Bankman-Fried was convicted (and so was Hunter Biden, for that matter). The system, in its current mangled formulation, worked, putting away a major fraudster while forcing guilty pleas from several of his co-conspirators. The Southern District of New York's District Attorney's Office, which handles some of the most significant federal criminal cases in the country, gave Bankman-Fried the treatment meted out to other defendants who were indicted around the same time: ex-Honduran president Juan Orlando Hernández (drug trafficking), hedge fund titan Bill Hwang (fraud, market manipulation), and the mercurial Chinese businessman and intelligence asset Miles Guo (fraud). Contrary to how he had been treated his entire life, Bankman-Fried was not special in the eyes of the court. His high-profile prosecution was a refreshing corrective to the belief that rich political donors could get away with almost anything.

But it was far from a complete accounting of the corruption wrought by the FTX fraud. I worry that that complete accounting will never be performed. The powerful prefer it that way.

The crime wave is white collar. Violent crime has been overall declining for decades. Billions more are lost each year to wage theft—bosses depriving their workers of overtime pay, for instance—than to shoplifting rings, which were hyped in the Covid years as a menace devastating cities' shopping districts. Tax evasion is a greater threat to American democracy than any foreign meddling. The rule of law may be at its ragged end, but mostly as it applies to those in the upper income brackets. Prosecuting elites has become almost unthinkable. As a result, for the political right, the criminal prosecution of Donald Trump for his array of crimes seemed like a politically motivated farce. Only banana republics put former presidents in jail! But so do democracies—South Korea, France, South Africa, Brazil—when their leaders commit crimes. Prosecuting a president or a CEO can be a suspicious anomaly compared to business as usual; it might also be a form of equality under the law.

The ethical genius character played by Sam Bankman-Fried was a fabrication, abetted by a credulous media and paid-for celebrity supporters. He did do some things well, like taking advantage of the corruption that had cracked America's political institutions. Bankman-Fried was a prolific political donor—both overtly and, it later emerged, through dark money and other subterranean methods. He gave tens of millions to Democratic politicians and organizations. He became buddies with Representative Maxine Waters and met privately with regulators and then-Senate majority leader Mitch McConnell. In an interview, he bragged that he might give up to $1 billion in the 2024 election cycle. After his arrest, *CoinDesk* reported that Bankman-Fried had given money to at least a third of Congress. According to Signal screenshots used as evidence in his criminal trial, it appeared that Bankman-Fried had also exchanged private messages with US senators.

Judging by all available evidence, Bankman-Fried had supervised a political-influence operation that included major violations of campaign-finance law. It was an important part of the government's first indictment against him, which counted eight charges, including "conspiracy to defraud the Federal Election Commission and commit campaign finance violations."[4] Allegedly, Bankman-Fried used stolen FTX customer funds to covertly funnel money—including through straw donations—to state and national politicians on a massive scale. And he had help: some of his top executives would later plead guilty to campaign-finance charges.

The original indictment against Bankman-Fried was replaced a couple of times by superseding indictments. At one point he faced 13 charges. This is common in big criminal trials, where the state may acquire more evidence to add charges to an indictment between the initial arrest and the beginning of the trial. Sometimes it goes the other way and charges might be removed in a superseding indictment. By the time Bankman-Fried went to trial in October 2023, the campaign-finance and bribery charges were gone, supposedly to be brought back for a second trial, in March 2024, focusing on corruption. Bankman-Fried had allegedly paid a $150 million bribe to Chinese law enforcement officials to unfreeze more than a billion dollars' worth of seized crypto—a clear violation of the Foreign Corrupt Practices Act. Caroline Ellison testified to this fact in court. And Bankman-Fried had overseen a political-influence operation that implicated his colleagues, professional political operatives, an unnamed New York politician, and, according to a civil suit, even his mother. It needed to be accounted for.

It never happened. On November 2, 2023, after less than five hours of deliberation, Bankman-Fried was convicted on seven counts of conspiracy and fraud. By the new year, prosecutors announced that they would not be pursuing a second trial for bribery and campaign-finance violations. The public might never know the full scope of his political operation or where all the money went. And there was little to discourage bad actors in crypto—or any other industry—from similarly leveraging a corrupt system.

When Bankman-Fried was at the height of his power, his public dealings were potentially just as disturbing as whatever backroom illegalities he was indulging in that day. In 2022, Bankman-Fried made numerous publicized trips to Washington, DC, testifying in front of Congress and meeting with senators, congressional representatives, and regulators from key agencies like the Commodity Futures Trading Commission (CFTC) and Securities and Exchange Commission (SEC). Much of this wheeling and dealing happened in the open—chronicled in news articles, tweets, and Instagram posts, sometimes by the government officials themselves, who seemed oblivious to the potential optics of a crypto billionaire having chummy meetings with the people who were supposed to regulate his industry.

But embarrassment and self-awareness have never been part of America's political culture. The guiding mantra is more like "never apologize, never explain." Billionaires pose arm in arm with politicians from both major parties because that's simply the default. Their money funds the elections and determines party agendas, and to even question this fact signals a naivete that many decided to dispense with after the Supreme Court's 2010 decision in *Citizens United v. FEC* ruled that corporations could spend unlimited amounts of money in support of political candidates (provided that they didn't coordinate with or donate directly to a politician's campaign). That resulted in an explosion of super PACs, as big businesses were granted "corporate personhood" and First Amendment rights that made them even more influential political actors.[5] It has become impossible to imagine an American electoral system that isn't defined by billionaire bankrolls and corporate giving.

On Capitol Hill, Bankman-Fried found an open door. He wasn't just another powerful billionaire—if a newly crowned one—but one who could provide guidance for policymakers about a novel industry many of them didn't understand. It might have once seemed like an obvious scandal for elected representatives to invite a CEO to tell them how to best regulate his industry, but that ethical framework had been rendered quaint. Bankman-Fried was such a familiar and influential presence on the Hill that one circulating draft piece of legislation acquired the nickname "Sam's bill."

Some crypto leaders chose a different tack. They didn't want to cooperate with lawmakers at all. They had no interest in playing donor games with PACs or glad-handing with politicians they didn't respect. They were steeped in libertarian ideology that made that kind of negotiation anathema. The whole point of crypto was to separate money from the state. As Peter Thiel wrote of the early days of PayPal, "we were all obsessed with creating a digital currency that would be controlled by individuals instead of governments."[6] Crypto true believers had the same dream: money that wouldn't be under the dominion of geriatric senators who had no idea what they were voting on. Crypto was about freedom, not compromise.

Some in the industry supported Bankman-Fried's greasy-palmed charm offensive. Some simply disliked him personally or found him to be a manipulative business partner and would openly celebrate his fall. Bankman-Fried's lobbying push could have been very lucrative for him and his companies, but in its broader goals, it would also have benefited some of his competitors by expanding crypto's access to US banks and US customers. As it was, a number of major crypto exchanges, like FTX, operated offshore in jurisdictions more associated with tax evasion than consumer protection. There they offered a wider range of tokens, leverage (the ability to borrow money from the exchange to make bigger bets), and risky digital financial products. They touted decent trading volume and the ability to win or lose a lot of money.

In comparison, their American counterparts, like FTX.US and Binance.US, were derelict flea markets where no one shopped—distracting American regulators from the fraudulent behavior happening at their overseas equivalents. This was deliberate. Binance adopted something it called, in an internal presentation prepared by a consultant, the "Tai Chi strategy." It was a classic "bait and switch," as *Forbes* described it.[7] The idea was that Binance.US would be served up to regulators as a compliant exchange trying to do the right thing under US law. Binance.US had to be ready "to accept nominal fines in exchange for enforcement forbearance," according to the presentation—redirecting the energies of US law enforcement away from the mothership, Binance.com. Meanwhile, customers would be funneled to the offshore exchange, which, with its distributed global operations, could operate with greater latitude. For a time, the strategy worked quite well.

FTX, which received an early investment from Binance, operated in much the same way. Bankman-Fried controlled dozens of overseas shell companies registered in tax havens around the world. The bulk of FTX's revenue came from its global operations, not FTX.US. But through its partnerships with Tom Brady, Gisele Bündchen, Shaquille O'Neal, and other celebrities, it had conquered the US in terms of brand awareness. Because of regulatory concerns—i.e. that their offshore product offerings were probably illegal in the US—FTX.US offered fewer ways for crypto holders to bet on tokens. If FTX was going to reach its full potential, Bankman-Fried had to find a way to bring the crypto casino onshore. That meant changing the laws regulating cryptocurrency and derivatives markets. And to do that, Bankman-Fried had a universal solvent that he applied to every problem: a ton of money.

By 2022, the cryptocurrency industry was impatiently awaiting what it called "regulatory clarity." There was a regulatory turf war going on between two of the country's financial regulatory agencies, the SEC and CFTC—the kind of bureaucratic battle played out via boring policy memos, years-long civil suits, enforcement decisions, and lobbyist-written legislation. The SEC was trying to assert its regulatory responsibility over crypto by arguing that some tokens qualified as securities. The CFTC, an agency with a fifth of the budget and far fewer staff, had already ruled that Bitcoin qualified as a commodity, like corn or oil. Bankman-Fried and like-minded peers thought that they would get more generous treatment from the smaller regulator, so they pushed for the CFTC to have the crypto regulatory mandate. Bankman-Fried testified before the Senate Agriculture Committee, which oversaw the CFTC, and he hired officials from both the Ag Committee and the CFTC. Over a period of 14 months, Bankman-Fried had 10 meetings with CFTC chair Rostin Behnam.[8] The two also exchanged messages.

Bankman-Fried had everything he needed to push through a regulatory overhaul that would expand crypto's ambit in the US, bring the crypto casino onshore, make it easier for crypto companies to bank and access US dollars, and provide himself with more access to lucrative derivatives markets. By the fall of 2022, Bankman-Fried seemed on the verge of getting what he wanted. Even as several multibillion-dollar crypto companies collapsed amidst accusations of fraud and money laundering, Bankman-Fried was ostensibly thriving, bailing out competitors and reveling in his very public politicking.

But then it all fell apart. On November 2, 2022, *CoinDesk* reported on a leaked balance sheet from Alameda Research, Bankman-Fried's crypto hedge fund that doubled as a venture capital firm, buyer of Bahamian luxury real estate, and a general clearing house for whatever the youthful mogul wanted to spend his stolen billions on—which included buying a Bitcoin mine in Kazakhstan, an AI startup, and the loyalty of a huge swath of Congress.[9] The leaked balance sheet smashed the lie that, while many of its peers were struggling, Alameda was in good shape. In fact, its finances were a mess. Most of its assets were in crypto tokens, and not major ones like Ethereum and Bitcoin. Instead, Alameda was holding billions of dollars' worth of "Sam's coins"—crypto tokens that Bankman-Fried had either created or invested in. Most of the coins were FTT, the house token for Bankman-Fried's FTX exchange. Although Alameda could never find a buyer for all the tokens it held—it would cause their value to plummet—it "marked to market" its FTT tokens, treating them as far more valuable than they were. The company likened owning FTT tokens to holding equity in FTX. Pledging the tokens as collateral, Alameda received multibillion-dollar loans, in cash and crypto, based on the marked-up value of FTT and other lesser tokens, which no one on the open market really wanted to buy. Essentially, Bankman-Fried's $32 billion empire was built on a foundation of illiquid, overvalued fake money—and, it would soon emerge, a massive fraud.

The publication of the balance sheet was a sensation, becoming the talk of the crypto industry and the financial press that had buoyed Bankman-Fried's reputation. Still, no one outside of a few senior FTX executives seemed to know that the company was missing more than $8 billion in customer funds. Bankman-Fried had authorized Alameda to secretly withdraw money from FTX customer accounts, money which Alameda then spent, gambled away on bad crypto bets, and funneled to politicians. That customer money was supposed to be segregated, untouched. Things quickly got out of hand. Few people knew that Alameda was surviving on high-interest loans that it had taken out from lenders who themselves were teetering from the industry-wide instability. These lenders had been calling in their loans for repayment, which spurred Bankman-Fried to dip even further into FTX customer funds. The collapse was already in motion.

Within days of the balance sheet leak, the industry's most powerful player entered the fray: Changpeng Zhao, also known as CZ, the co-founder and CEO of Binance, the world's largest crypto exchange. Zhao and Bankman-Fried had been friends and colleagues. Zhao made an important early investment in FTX, and in many ways Bankman-Fried's corporate fiefdom seemed modeled on Zhao's. But as Bankman-Fried's star rose in the crypto firmament, he began to clash with Zhao. When FTX sought to acquire a crypto company in Gibraltar, local authorities requested information on its investors. Binance, which had no official headquarters and operated through a hazy array of globally distributed shell companies, wasn't inclined to share information about its operations, especially its banking practices. Bankman-Fried decided to buy out Binance's ownership share in FTX. Rather than using real dollars, the deal was conducted mostly in FTT and BUSD, a Binance "stablecoin" whose value was supposed to remain at a constant $1. Bankman-Fried solved his problem of being entangled with a shady overseas operator, but he did it by handing his rival a large amount of FTX's house token. If Binance ever decided to sell the FTT tokens, they might crash its price. In return for a short-term advantage, Bankman-Fried had given Zhao the means to potentially destroy his company's finances.

Bankman-Fried continued to behave recklessly, engaging in wild spending and extreme risk-taking while relying on his arrogance to guide himself through choppy waters. In the months leading up to the balance-sheet leak, Bankman-Fried and his executives had begun publicly criticizing Zhao, joking on Twitter that the Binance chief couldn't match FTX's DC lobbying muscle because Zhao was afraid to step foot in the United States. Bankman-Fried was also rumored to be trying to serve up Binance and Zhao to US authorities—a potential distraction from his own crimes. (Binance would later be fined $4.3 billion for banking and money-laundering violations while Zhao would plead guilty to similar crimes and receive a sentence of four months in federal prison.)

On November 6, 2022, Zhao deployed the weapon that Bankman-Fried had carelessly handed him a year earlier. "Due to recent revelations that have came [sic] to light, we have decided to liquidate any remaining FTT on our books," Zhao wrote on Twitter, adding that the sale would be done over months to minimize impact on the market.[10] "Regarding any speculation as to whether this is a move against a competitor, it is not," Zhao added. "Our industry is in it's [sic] nascency and every time a project publicly fails it hurts every user and every platform."[11]

FTX hadn't yet failed. But with his announcement, Zhao had helped speed up the inevitable collapse. His announcement was another bomb going off in a week of crypto industry pyrotechnics. The price of FTT began to plummet in anticipation of Zhao potentially dumping millions of tokens on the market. Alameda CEO Caroline Ellison cheekily offered on Twitter to buy all of Zhao's FTT tokens for $22 each. FTX customers began withdrawing their funds—dollars and crypto—sparking the crypto exchange equivalent of a bank run. Within two days, FTX was on the verge of running out of money, and the company shut down withdrawals—the surest sign that a crypto company was headed toward the abyss.

That day, Bankman-Fried announced that he had agreed to sell FTX to Binance, to his rival Zhao. The deal was non-binding and dependent on Binance completing its due diligence on the company. It was a remarkable defeat, a complete abdication by someone who only weeks earlier had been publicly insulting the man he was now trusting to pick up the pieces of his shattered empire. One day later, on November 9, Binance announced, "As a result of corporate due diligence, as well as the latest news reports regarding mishandled customer funds and alleged US agency investigations, we have decided that we will not pursue the potential acquisition of FTX.com."[12]

Zhao had humbled Bankman-Fried by forcing him to the edge of bankruptcy, making him surrender his company to him for pennies on the dollar. Then he added the *coup de grâce* by backing out and allowing the crumbling edifice of FTX to collapse under the weight of its own contradictions. With it went the fortune and future of the world's richest 30-year-old.

"In the beginning, our hope was to be able to support FTX's customers to provide liquidity, but the issues are beyond our control or ability to help," said Binance in an announcement.[13] In other words, too much money was missing. There was nothing to be done.

In a long Twitter thread, Bankman-Fried fessed up to making mistakes. "I'm sorry," he wrote. "That's the biggest thing. I fucked up, and should have done better."[14]

It was one of many apologies he would issue and, like all of them, unconvincing. He went on to make excuses for his companies' failure, citing in part overleveraged trades made by poorly supervised subordinates. (He would basically stick to that explanation even after his conviction.) Addressing "a particular sparring partner"—clearly Zhao—Bankman-Fried wrote, "well played; you won."[15]

At about 4 a.m. on November 11, facing pressure from his lieutenants, the company's high-powered lawyers, and millions of jilted customers, Bankman-Fried signed a form that sent FTX and Alameda into bankruptcy. He almost immediately regretted the choice, claiming coercion and that he had a rescue plan that could be deployed. But few believed him. It was too late for regrets.

A month later, Bankman-Fried was arrested and, after a short spell in a grim Bahamian prison, agreed to be extradited to the United States. The subsequent trial ended in his conviction on seven charges related to the $8 billion theft. The trial also exposed massive political corruption—the aforementioned nine-figure bribe paid to Chinese intelligence officials and what both prosecutors and the judge described in court as one of the largest campaign-finance violations in US history.

On December 30, 2023, SDNY prosecutors announced that Sam Bankman-Fried, who had yet to be sentenced for his first trial, would not face a second trial. "Proceeding with sentencing in March 2024 without the delay that would be caused by a second trial would advance the public's interest in a timely and just resolution of the case," prosecutors wrote to Judge Kaplan.[16] They were concerned that a second trial would delay repayment for FTX customers and creditors (lawyers and investigators had been scouring FTX's accounts for assets that could be sold off or returned). The reasoning seemed sound and in line with precedent, but it also meant that perhaps the most significant campaign finance crime in American history would simply be brushed aside. What was there to stop someone from doing it again?

When Sam Bankman-Fried was sentenced on March 28, 2024, I was in the courthouse, this time watching via video from an overflow room. I wouldn't stumble upon him alone in a hallway again. It had been about eight months since Bankman-Fried had experienced even the relative freedom of house arrest, and it would be decades before he was free again.

Judge Kaplan's ruling was sweeping and unrelenting in its criticism of Bankman-Fried, whom he saw as a deceptive, manipulative operator who, in his greed for money and power, hurt a lot of people. He said that Bankman-Fried had committed perjury at least three times.

After his conviction, Bankman-Fried fired his lawyers and hired new ones. One of those new lawyers, Marc Mukasey, who had represented Donald Trump and confessed fraudster (and Bankman-Fried business associate) Alex Mashinsky, got up to give a first and last defense of his client. Mukasey said that Bankman-Fried was a better person than he had been portrayed in court and the media. He was an "awkward math nerd" who "loves video games and veganism, and he's compassionate to animals and children." And now he had "lost everything."[17]

At one point, Mukasey wandered into a seemingly unnecessary and too detailed anecdote about Stefan Irving, a pediatrician who was a serial sexual predator targeting children. "I know it's a different kind of case, and I know Irving was a bit of an older guy, but I respectfully submit that if you're judging by the average person in the street, no reasonable person would say that Sam is even half as dangerous or irredeemable or incorrigible or as bad as Stefan Irving, who got 21 years," said Mukasey. It was a bizarre, creepy example to invoke—another incident in which Bankman-Fried and his lawyers seemed totally out of sync with the arguments made in the court.

Finally it was Bankman-Fried's turn to rise and say something. He said that creditors deserved to be paid back and, speaking in general terms, offered an apology. "I failed everyone that I care about and everything I care about too," said Bankman-Fried. He praised some of his former colleagues, including Gary Wang and Caroline Ellison, who had testified against him, and reminisced about what they had built together. "I threw all of that away," he said. "It haunts me every day."

But then Bankman-Fried said something revealing that, like his lawyer's odd statements, showed that he wasn't up to the gravity of the moment. "I made a series of bad decisions," he told the court. "They weren't selfish decisions. They weren't selfless decisions. They were bad decisions."[18]

He went on to explain that those decisions "culminated with a bunch of other factors"—a liquidity crisis, his own mismanagement—to bring down the whole thing. He still thought "FTX would have survived" if he had made better decisions. Despite having signed forms to place his companies into bankruptcy, he still denied that they were bankrupt. If he had had more wisdom and time, he could have saved everything. There had always been "billions more than is necessary," he claimed, to pay back all creditors in full.

Bankman-Fried ended with what sounded like a hymn to himself, to his own squandered potential: "I guess there is a big opportunity in the world to do what the world thought I would do, what it hoped I would do, at least for a while, what I hoped I would do for the world, not what I ended up doing." The world had big dreams for Sam Bankman-Fried—at least the worlds of fintech and politics in which he proved himself an expert wheeler-dealer and social climber—and he had big dreams for himself.

Dreams tend to collapse when you steal $8 billion in customer funds, said Nicolas Roos, the prosecutor whose statement followed Bankman-Fried's wistful lament. His theft harmed hundreds of thousands of people. "He said trust me," said Roos, describing Bankman-Fried as a fraudster who lied to investors and customers alike. "This was not, as was suggested, a great business that had a problem at the end. This was a business that was pervaded with criminality throughout."[19]

Recalling a comment about Bernie Madoff, Roos said that Bankman-Fried wasn't "inhumanely monstrous. He is monstrously human."[20] He gave every indication that he didn't accept responsibility for his crimes and that he would pursue similar efforts again. Roos asked for a sentence of 40 to 50 years.

Judge Kaplan seemed to agree with Roos's character assessment of Bankman-Fried as a remorseless liar whose "goal was power and influence." Bankman-Fried had also committed "the biggest political financial crime in history," said Kaplan. "He did it because he wanted to be a hugely, hugely politically influential person in this country."[21]

Judge Lewis Kaplan sentenced Bankman-Fried to 25 years in federal prison—less than prosecutors asked for but a definitive penalty.

The public knew by then that there would be no further investigation into the political-influence campaign directed by

Bankman-Fried. Despite the campaign finance crimes, the nine-figure bribe paid to Chinese law enforcement, and prosecutors' suggestions, in some filings, that FTX/Alameda employees engaged in drug trafficking and sex trafficking, this would be Bankman-Fried's only criminal trial.

Some of his colleagues would still go down for the political operation, though its details weren't fully aired in court. Nishad Singh, FTX's director of engineering who testified about the missing $8 billion in Bankman-Fried's trial, pleaded guilty to six charges, including "conspiracy to defraud the United States by violating campaign finance laws."[22]

Ryan Salame, the head of FTX's Digital Markets division who helped direct the conservative side of the company's political giving, pleaded guilty to making illegal political contributions, defrauding the Federal Election Commission, and conspiring "to operate an unlicensed money transmitting business."[23] In his plea, he acknowledged that he had lied to a bank and that no attorney had advised him to do so. He acknowledged that he was familiar with campaign finance law and knew that his straw donations were in violation of the law. Unlike several of his colleagues, he did not cooperate with prosecutors against Bankman-Fried and said that if subpoenaed to testify, he would invoke the Fifth Amendment to avoid self-incrimination.

Salame was sentenced to seven and a half years in federal prison and required to pay more than $11 million in forfeiture and restitution.[24] (While at FTX, Salame bought six restaurants in his hometown in the Berkshires and attempted to withdraw millions of dollars in cryptocurrencies as the company collapsed.)

Once he had already been sentenced and was waiting to report to prison, Salame's official story changed. He claimed on X that the public's understanding of the campaign-finance operation—and the overall FTX fraud—was completely wrong. Yes, Salame had pleaded guilty, as many defendants did when considering the long odds of a trial. And yes, FTX, under the direction of Bankman-Fried, had donated prolifically to politicians of both major parties, sometimes using cutouts and other dubious means. But their activities had been blessed as legal by "internal and external legal teams, political consultants, and accountants."[25]

On X, Salame blamed FTX's lawyers, who came from high-powered firms like Sullivan & Cromwell and Fenwick & West. "The lawyers did tell me to borrow money instead of sell my own crypto to fund my political endeavors (which is what I have said) and the lawyers did review all of the transactions, entity structure, everything I was a part of in 2019 / 2020," wrote Salame.[26] He added that the charges of bank fraud—such as disguising FTX's account at Silvergate Bank as a fake electronics retailer called North Dimension—were spurious: "No one lied to a bank, we just did what the bank told us to do at every turn. and no one lied to lenders, everything was transparent with all our lenders (including the assets and how they were valued)."[27]

I didn't entirely believe Salame's protestations. He was trying to save himself and his partner Michelle Bond, with whom he had a young child. Bond would soon be charged with campaign-finance violations related to her unsuccessful run for Congress—another beneficiary of FTX's illicit largesse.

But somewhere in Salame's deflections, there was a kernel of truth that pointed toward something important. It was less about Salame's individual guilt or innocence than the larger conspiracy of forces that helped drive a fraudulent company toward enormous heights and then, after it crashed, let some of the potential co-conspirators walk away untouched, with the full extent of their crimes uninvestigated. As attested to by the number of civil lawsuits filed against FTX, company insiders, celebrity endorsers, investors, Sam Bankman-Fried's parents, and FTX's lawyers at Sullivan & Cromwell, there was potentially a great deal of illegal behavior that had still gone unexamined, including allegations that Alameda, when based in Hong Kong, had facilitated billions of dollars in Chinese capital flight and money laundering.

As long as that fuller accounting didn't happen, illiberal, authoritarian forces would leverage institutional corruption. So of course Coinbase could run back the SBF playbook two years later with virtually no pushback. Was it all kosher this time?

Few bothered to check. As the tech critic Molly White reported, Coinbase was possibly in violation of campaign-finance laws that prohibited government contractors from making political donations. Coinbase had given $25 million to Fairshake PAC, among other donations, and the company was also a government contractor, paid by the US Marshals Service to hold and sell Bitcoin that it seized from criminals.[28] (This Bitcoin would be incorporated into a future national stockpile under Trump.)

Diving into the minutiae of the relevant law, Coinbase responded that it didn't officially qualify as a government contractor because it was paid from an asset forfeiture fund, not by funds appropriated by Congress. But White and her lawyers at Public Citizen, a progressive, nonprofit consumer rights organization, thought that Coinbase was in fact being paid with funds appropriated by Congress. With their help, White filed a complaint with the Federal Election Commission—knowing that the organization could belabor its decisions and tended not to be a strong enforcer of campaign-finance law.

Would anyone investigate?

TRUMP'S CRYPTO CONVERSION

When Sam Bankman-Fried went down, it seemed that the broader public had been saved from an aggressive, amoral mogul who was just starting to put his political project into motion. Thankfully he hadn't yet consolidated his gains or managed to cause even more damage. The laws and regulatory measures he supported were shelved or lost out to other political priorities. As crypto markets cratered, anything associated with Bankman-Fried's name was verboten.

It couldn't last long. By the spring of 2024, crypto asset prices had miraculously recovered and the industry was on the march again, barnstorming state capitals across the country and holding the same DC power broker meetings presided over two years earlier by the now-imprisoned Bankman-Fried. Coinbase, which had previously tried to rally its customers against crypto-skeptical politicians, led the charge. Its CEO Brian Armstrong posted a photo of himself in the Capitol, declaring: "I met with more than a dozen Dem and GOP Senators in DC over the last 48 hrs to discuss creating clear rules for the crypto industry and consumer protection for crypto users. There's strong bi-partisan momentum to get this done in the Senate now that FIT21 has passed in the House. Glad to see the voice of the crypto voter having an impact."[29]

The voice of the crypto voter, in this case, was that of a billionaire CEO.

Coinbase had bankrolled a lawsuit against the Treasury Department's decision to impose sanctions on Tornado Cash, a cryptocurrency "mixer" that acted as a money-laundering service for North Korean hackers who broke into crypto companies' systems and stole hundreds of millions of dollars' worth of tokens. For the industry, Tornado Cash was important as an expression of financial privacy and financial freedom. It was just open-source code. It didn't matter that its main utility was money laundering and that one of its most prolific users was the North Korean government.[30]

As Coinbase battled the political establishment, the company was dealing with its own internal issues. In 2018 and 2019, an exodus of Black employees led to accusations that Coinbase had created a hostile work environment. After Minneapolis police murdered George Floyd, Armstrong equivocated on how to address dissent within his firm, which was starting to experience employee walkouts. In a Twitter thread, he used the phrase Black Lives Matter, said he was getting "educated" on issues, and offered support for Black employees.

But the company environment soon changed.[31] Armstrong deleted his Twitter thread.[32,33] He announced that Coinbase wouldn't have anything to do with "social activism." A new policy limited political talk in company Slack channels. Coinbase removed "racial intolerance" from the "Prohibited Uses" section of its user agreement.[34] Coinbase was "a mission-focused company," Armstrong declared in a blog post, and it wouldn't be distracted from it.[35] Anyone who wasn't happy could take a severance package and go, he told employees in a company-wide email.[36] About 5 percent of Coinbase's employees accepted his offer.[37]

Armstrong set Coinbase on a path to be an ostensibly apolitical "mission-focused company," but the mission of passing crypto-friendly financial regulations turned out to be pretty political. By 2024, Coinbase was one of the leading donors to Fairshake PAC, which was laser-focused on defeating Democrats opposed to the industry's regulatory agenda. And Armstrong was one of the faces of that effort.

As the CEO-led lobbying offensive proceeded, hundreds of pieces of legislation were submitted for consideration in state legislatures. Industry executives and VC firms gave hundreds of millions of dollars to PACs fighting for crypto's political priorities. By the middle of 2024, crypto had emerged as the biggest political donor among all industries—more than healthcare or defense or pharma—despite its relatively small size and a general lack of legal-use cases for crypto beyond speculating on token prices. Nearly all of the hundreds of millions of dollars raised by crypto PACs would go to support Trump, Republicans, and a handful of pro-crypto Democrats.

Their coffers full of crypto industry donations, members of Congress started talking again about their love of Bitcoin, which on the Republican right had become almost an article of faith, a righteous challenge to the government institutions they wanted to control. Senator Ted Cruz bragged on X about buying a few Bitcoin-mining machines as parts of his sun-scorched state, with its overstretched energy infrastructure, were suffering from periodic blackouts. Senator Cynthia Lummis became a laser-eyed true believer, putting some of her wealth into Bitcoin, speaking at crypto conferences, and urging the US government to buy and hold Bitcoin.

Even Donald Trump found religion in crypto. As president, Trump declared Bitcoin a scam, essentially on economic protectionist grounds. He didn't like that it might compete with the US dollar. But as venture capitalists and top tech executives lined up behind Trump, his opinions shifted. Perhaps one of the Silicon Valley billionaires now bankrolling his campaign had a Jeffrey Yass-style conversation with him, this time about the electoral value of pandering to crypto voters. Trump emerged as a convert. "With your vote, I will keep Elizabeth Warren and her goons away from your Bitcoin, and I will never allow the creation of a central bank digital currency," said Trump at the Libertarian National Convention.[38]

For crypto enthusiasts—a small but voluble contingent—Trump's direct appeals were manna from heaven. Many of them already supported Trump. His embrace of crypto made his victory seem all the more important. He even had talking points down about subsidiary issues like a central bank digital currency—a government-issued digital dollar that right-wing coiners feared would become a tool for a system of Chinese Communist Party-style social control. Clearly someone with fluency in crypto industry concerns was whispering in the former president's ear, offering arguments convincing enough that Trump would end up starting several of his own crypto ventures.

The crypto lobby was doing a lot more than influencing crypto legislation and funneling talking points to Trump. It had a massive, nine-figure war chest, friends in Congress, and a chorus of online supporters. And it had gained some wins: Fairshake had already spent millions to help defeat Democrats Jamaal Bowman and Katie Porter in their primary campaigns.

On social media, committed Bitcoiners became vocal, single-issue voters. For crypto bag holders, the issue was about their wallets, yes, but also their financial freedom. To the general public, crypto could often seem scammy or ridiculous (I co-wrote a book about that). But in the minds of crypto partisans, it was the ultimate vehicle for individual liberty. The freedom to transact was freedom itself, the initial condition from which all other freedoms flowed. And they shared the same kind of anti-government sentiment that animated MAGA reactionaries and anti-tax conservatives like Grover Norquist. With its faux-populist message—throw a brick at Wall Street, sponsored by Silicon Valley and the Saudi sovereign wealth fund!—crypto became a vehicle for expressing political resentment against a rotten status quo.

In late July in Nashville, during the largest annual Bitcoin conference, which had previously played host to major announcements like El Salvador's adoption of Bitcoin as an official currency, the Republican Party and crypto cemented their relationship. Fresh off surviving an assassination attempt and now struggling to figure out how to politically attack Vice President Kamala Harris, who had just taken Biden's place at the top of the Democratic ticket, Trump took the stage to preach to the Bitcoin faithful. He began with friendly callouts to industry notables, including MicroStrategy CEO Michael Saylor, who two months earlier had agreed to a $40 million settlement with the District of Columbia for tax fraud.[39] The overall performance was very Trump, with off-the-cuff quips about how "most people have no idea what the hell it is."[40] But the speech's core message read as if written by a crypto lobbyist, promising Bitcoiners everything on their political wish list: better access to US banks; an end to enforcement actions by the SEC and Department of Justice; establishing a favorable regulatory framework; and generally providing a clear path for the crypto industry to do what it wanted.

"From now on the rules will be written by people who love your industry," said Trump.

Echoing a proposal already aired by Senator Lummis and Robert F. Kennedy Jr., Trump said that if he were elected again as president, he would establish a strategic national Bitcoin stockpile. He would retain the Bitcoin that the government seized in criminal investigations and possibly use government funds—public money—to buy more Bitcoin, which would pump the token's price and benefit the very wealthy tech industry donors who had been pouring money into his campaign.

Todd Phillips, a lawyer and professor at Georgia State's J. Mack Robinson College of Business, described the shoddy economic thinking that would cast Bitcoin as a commodity in need of stockpiling: "Bitcoin is nothing like petroleum. The latter is an input into real-world goods and services. The former is not an input into anything. The purpose of a strategic bitcoin reserve is simply to require the Fed [to] buy bitcoin, sending its price higher for speculators already holding."[41]

A national Bitcoin stockpile was an astonishing suggestion: a direct transfer of public wealth to crypto industry whales, all to inflate the price of a digital token that, even after 15-plus years of searching, had no use case beyond speculation and being the reserve currency for global cybercrime. That the proposal happened to be completely against Bitcoin's libertarian founding purpose, separating money from the state, was no small irony. But few Bitcoiners seemed to care when there was potentially so much money to be made. When Trump repeated his promise to fire SEC chair Gary Gensler, the industry's ultimate villain, the ecstatic crowd chanted the former president's name.

Before leaving the stage, Trump signed off, saying, "Have a good time with your Bitcoin and your crypto and everything else that you're playing with." The transactional nature of his speech couldn't have been more clear: having once dismissed Bitcoin as a scam, he now cared about it because he could campaign on it and accept political donations in it. He might have even held Bitcoiners in contempt ("and everything else that you're playing with"). It didn't matter. For true believers like Nic Carter, a venture capitalist and influential crypto personality, it was "everything we could possibly ask for and more."[42] He called it "probably the most bullish single political event in bitcoin history."[43]

He was right. Trump and the crypto industry were in total political and economic alignment. In the coming months, their fortunes would rise together.

Days after Trump's star turn at the Nashville Bitcoin conference, Kamala Harris's campaign reached out to crypto industry leaders in an attempt to "reset" the relationship—the kind of language that was once used to describe a rapprochement between the United States and Russia under President Obama. Harris was from California and had an amicable history with the tech industry (her brother-in-law and close advisor Tony West was chief legal officer for Uber). The Harris campaign was probably worried about the incredible amounts of money flowing from the crypto industry to Trump-aligned super PACs. Perhaps, her campaign thought, they could redirect some of that flow to themselves. On a call for a group called Crypto for Harris that featured some top Democrats, Senate Majority Leader Chuck Schumer said he wanted to pass a crypto law by the end of the year. "Crypto is here to stay no matter what," said Schumer. "So Congress must get it right."[44]

In the compromised world of political fundraising, it wasn't an unreasonable idea, but was it an effective strategy? Whatever modicum of support the crypto industry might have offered to friendly Democrats, it came at a cost to the party's constituents, who would have to deal with the eventual fallout of the party of consumer protection forsaking its mandate to further legalize an industry that had much more in common with sports gambling or payday loans than finance. When the next bubble popped and voters' digital fortunes evaporated, it would be on Democrats, too.

Most importantly, the crypto industry, angry at what it perceived as persecution from the Biden administration, had little interest in boosting Democratic politicians and absolutely no interest in the Democratic Party's other economic and political priorities. The two sides were political adversaries, probably irreconcilably so. But only one side understood that. When the crowd in Nashville chanted Trump's name, it confirmed what had been clear for months: one of America's shadiest industries, which couldn't survive without bending the law in its favor, was all in for the Republican nominee. With its bankrolls inexplicably flush, it would spend hundreds of millions of dollars to help get Trump elected and to defeat any other politicians who opposed its agenda.

The crypto industry would have an excellent ally in Elon Musk, who, by the time Trump left Nashville, was stumping full-time for the once and future president. Musk was a crypto fan—he had aligned himself with Dogecoin, which he bought and pumped on social media—and he now held the reins of X, the crypto industry's preferred social-media platform. Spending almost half a billion dollars in direct political donations, Musk and the crypto industry had the potential resources to push Trump over the finish line. But even the richest man in the world had financial backers whom he relied on, who propped up his businesses, bought his debts, and traded political favors with him. It was time to find out who some of them were.

19

Best to Be Low-Key

It had cost about $46.5 billion for Elon Musk to acquire Twitter[1]—a transaction that he initiated, then publicly tried to back out of, before acceding under legal pressure. The court-mandated disclosure of some embarrassing, or at least revealing, Musk text messages may have nudged the affair to its conclusion. It was a costly acquisition, highly leveraged. The money was cobbled together from $20 billion in Musk's assets, $13 billion in loans from big banks (which soon found that they couldn't move them off their books), $6 billion in loans to Musk himself, and more than $7 billion in commitments from investors who would be shareholders of the new private enterprise.

In a May 2022 SEC filing, Musk listed a number of his planned Twitter co-investors and their equity stakes, so we had some idea of who was helping him buy the company. Saudi Prince Alwaleed bin Talal, Twitter's largest outside shareholder, had initially been publicly critical of Musk's offer and then, perhaps after a talk with Saudi crown prince Mohammed bin Salman, announced that he supported Musk and would happily roll his shares into the new entity. Other reporting—including those previously mentioned text messages revealing, for instance, a $2 billion commitment from Oracle founder Larry Ellison—helped fill in some of the sources of money.[2] But gaps remained. And once Twitter went private that October and Musk set about slashing and burning the divisions of the company that offended him, there was no official list of its shareholders, or the legal names of the trusts, funds, LLCs, and other corporate entities holding their shares. The shareholder list that X had filed under seal in multiple civil cases contained that crucial information, which was why I had lawyers helping me try to convince a judge to unseal the document.

People had a right to know who owned a company with such a prominent role in shaping public discourse, both in the United States and around the world, especially leading up to a crucial presidential election. A company that had been caught up in censorship disputes around the world; that was penetrated by Saudi agents who channeled sensitive customer information to their Saudi government handlers; that tolerated massive bot farms promoting foreign propaganda; that had been accused of putting Chinese and Indian spies on the payroll; and that eliminated teams responsible for ensuring the site's safety and integrity—such as it was. The newly renovated X's self-proclaimed role as a guarantor of free speech meant that we should know which outside entities—and which foreign governments—might be able to exert influence on the company and its speech policies.

Musk called himself a "free-speech absolutist," but his business dealings tended to be filtered through the usual veil of corporate secrecy, legal threats, nondisclosure agreements, encrypted chats, and fleets of powerful attorneys that protect very powerful people. He denounced "lawfare" while widely practicing it.

With X, he sometimes compromised his free-speech militancy, agreeing to content restrictions in Brazil, Turkey, and other important overseas markets—to say nothing of the deals he made in authoritarian countries for SpaceX and Tesla. Musk banned journalists from X when they displeased him, and he ordered the reinstatement of the accounts of Nazis, white supremacists, grifters, and a QAnon-adjacent influencer named Dom Lucre who'd posted a screenshot from a video of a child being sexually abused.[3] In explaining his intervention, Musk claimed that Lucre tweeted the post out of concern for the victim. In many instances, these far-right accounts were ones he was familiar with or which were suggested to him by the extremists he already followed and conversed with regularly. Together, his interventions for far-right users reflected his shifting politics and his public embrace of bigoted beliefs on race, gender, immigration, crime, and other issues. When Musk told someone who touted the anti-Semitic Great Replacement theory, "You have said the actual truth," it was just one conversation like so many others he had been having publicly on X.[4] For those following his descent, it was another reminder that the list of Musk's similarities with earlier industrialists like Henry Ford and Howard Hughes might also include their pathologies.

Legal proceedings are rarely defined by their brevity. In civil litigation, the party with more money and a bigger cadre of highly paid lawyers has an overwhelming advantage. If they don't win outright, they aim to exhaust their adversary—their nerves, their bankroll, their appetite for conflict. If you're going to sue someone, settle in. It can be a journey through bureaucratic challenges, a flurry of motions, pointless delays, and daunting appeals. It can be emotional and wring you dry of any latent idealism you may have maintained about the legal system's ability to hold malefactors to account. And if you're fortunate enough to win, good luck collecting what your opponent owes you.

The occasional lawsuit threat aside, I've managed to stay out of the defendant's chair in my journalism career. I had filed dozens of Freedom of Information requests and had experienced that initial sense of optimism that a government system may finally be leveraged for public transparency—only to find that, after years of waiting, your request is denied or you're sent a pile of redacted documents. Challenging X in court felt like a similarly quixotic venture.

My legal effort to unmask X's investors was a motion to intervene, not an entire lawsuit, but my adversary had infinitely more resources than I did. When I asked Reporters Committee for Freedom of the Press (RCFP), a small nonprofit legal organization with a distinguished history of supporting First Amendment causes, to help me, I figured that the process could take months or years, perhaps ending in frustration. Selfishly, I hoped the situation would be resolved before this book went to press. I didn't think that it would take less than a month—or that it would work.

On August 20, 2024, Judge Susan Illston of the Northern District of California ruled in favor of a motion to intervene that we filed in a civil case called *Anoke v. Twitter* in order to unseal a list of X's shareholders. *Anoke v. Twitter* was one of the many civil lawsuits resulting from Elon Musk's chaotic takeover of the company and his mass firing of thousands of employees—from the four fired senior executives suing for $128 million to lower-level employees who didn't receive promised severance or claimed that they were forced to break laws to fulfill Musk's mercurial edicts. In *Anoke v. Twitter*, X's lawyers filed the list under seal in 2023.

We got a quick ruling in our favor, but that didn't mean it was over. X could, and probably would, appeal. But hours after Judge Illston's ruling, the filing containing the list appeared on the online court docket, visible to anyone logged into the public court system. I'm still not exactly sure what happened, but apparently it's a matter of a clerk clicking to change permissions on a limited-access filing, so it's possible that someone at the court prematurely made the list available. The error, if it was one, was soon noticed by reporters at the *Washington Post*, who wrote an article about the list's contents.[5] Given that I was still in active legal proceedings involving X, my attorneys recommended that I sit back for a couple days as the situation played out.

Soon, it didn't matter. The list was everywhere, published in hundreds of media outlets, becoming grist for debate, memes, misinformation, and—I hoped—researchers, regulators, and journalists looking into a powerful tech company openly in the tank for the Republican candidate for president.

Transparency, free speech, and challenging power being core tenets of journalism, the potential civic value of the list seemed self-evident. Why did someone want to keep this information secret? And why shouldn't it be public? When I finally obtained the list, which enumerated the legal names of about 95 entities owning a piece of X (but not the size of their holdings), it began to fill in the picture of whom Musk depended on for cash and the networks he moved in. It was a window into a political and economic formation with increasing purchase on our world. And it was laden with clues: the more I looked, the more I learned.

I divided them into categories. It all started, of course, with Elon Musk. He was the majority owner of X through a trust he controlled. He was followed by Jack Dorsey, the former Twitter CEO and major shareholder who helped deliver the company to Musk, and a host of other tech and finance figures.

There was a fleet of venture capitalists, friends of Musk who were consistent investors in his various enterprises. Venture capitalists were winners of the passive-income lottery, making big bets with other people's money and pocketing handsome fees while knowing that most of their investments would fail, but a precious few might hit big. For the VCs considering chipping in for Musk's Twitter deal, it didn't matter terribly if the price was high. They were supporting a friend, colleague, and industry doyen with growing political power, and they wanted in on the next Musk investment opportunity *after* Twitter. Whatever the eventual fate of this particular acquisition, they needed a seat at the table. (Many of them, it should be noted, were frequent posters like Musk, investing in a product they used obsessively.)

Some of these firms had close relationships with authoritarian governments, like Saudi Arabia and Qatar, who were direct investors in X. Andreessen Horowitz received hundreds of millions of dollars from Saudi Arabia to invest on their behalf in US tech startups and was in talks with the kingdom about creating a $40 billion AI investment fund.[6] VCs served as laundromats for a class of kleptocrats, princelings, and other global elites, who could funnel their fortunes into one of America's most celebrated industries. Silicon Valley VCs and their foreign investors often shared a general disregard for democratic governance. In the Saudi crown prince, they saw a counterpart who demonstrated the same benevolent authoritarian style that they enacted in their business lives—but on an even grander scale, with unchallenged power. VCs published chatty manifestos about their technological aspirations;

MBS offered his own consultant-approved economic development plan known as Vision 2030. The two sides had much in common.

"Saudi has a founder," Ben Horowitz said at a 2023 tech conference featuring Saudi government representatives. "You don't call him a founder. You call him his royal highness."[7]

Saudi Arabia's ailing king and ambitious crown prince were hardly "founders" of a state that, in its current form, had been inaugurated in 1932. But the rhetoric was not just flattery. It resonated in tech circles where, inspired by Thiel-sponsored figures like the writer Curtis Yarvin, an increasing number of people believed that the US would be better off under a dictatorial CEO figure, not an elected president. It may have once sounded silly, but dictatorship often does to someone still living in the last throes of democracy. If Trump were elected, Musk had the potential to become that kind of figure.

Gulf dictatorships were good business partners. They had enormous resources and an urgent need to diversify their economies and exercise influence in power centers like Washington, DC and Silicon Valley. Their money washed all over the tech industry, especially in the years after 9/11, and Musk's business empire—from Tesla to SpaceX to X to xAI—got its fill.

One of the shareholders on the list bore the inscrutable name Q Tetris Holding LLC. A quick search revealed its nature. Q Tetris Holding LLC was registered to a high-rise office building in Doha that housed the Qatar Investment Authority, Qatar's sovereign wealth fund. The directors for Q Tetris Holding listed in public filings worked for the QIA. This was the ownership entity for the Qatari government's reported $375 million share of X. You may remember seeing Musk, standing glumly with arms crossed, attending the World Cup in Qatar in December 2022. He was joined at the time by a bunch of Qatari notables and another expert wheedler of Gulf dictator cash: Jared Kushner.

There was one Gulf-linked venture capital firm that fascinated me more than the others. VYC25, as it was called on the shareholder list, was the ownership vehicle of Vy Capital, a UAE-based venture capital firm run by Alexander Tamas, a German entrepreneur who became industry-famous as an aide to Russian tech mogul, Facebook investor, and former Kremlin ally Yuri Milner. Already you can see the various connections and national affiliations piling atop one another, a thicket of potential geopolitical and cross-border financial intrigue.

Vy was the kind of firm that was called "secretive" because journalists didn't know much about it. To be fair, it maintained a small footprint—a discreet office in Dubai and a Los Angeles outpost for entrepreneur John Hering, its US representative, who shared an office with Sequoia, which invested $800 million in Musk's Twitter purchase. According to SEC filings, Vy had more than $6 billion under management, much of it through funds registered in the Cayman Islands. The firm, which reportedly drew some of its backing from Chinese private equity firms, had invested billions of dollars in Musk's companies.

John Hering, who previously founded Lookout, a cybersecurity company backed by Vy, didn't list his affiliation with Vy Capital on his LinkedIn or X pages. Yet he was the one apparently making deals on behalf of Vy in the US, including with Elon Musk, to whom he became close. He regularly posted in praise of Musk's ventures, celebrating a successful SpaceX rocket launch by saying, "We just punched a hole in the matrix."[8] Hering was one of the first donors to Musk's America PAC, indicating that his support for Musk ran beyond business. As if to confirm their tight alignment, three weeks before the 2024 presidential election, Hering posted on X, "All in."[9] To anyone following Musk—who had used the phrase to describe his support for Trump and whose friends and political allies ran a popular podcast with the same name—it was clear what he meant.

Strangely, despite this massive outlay of support, no one from Vy Capital was on the boards of any Musk companies. And Alexander Tamas had talked to associates about winding down his VC investments, which included startups all over the world, along with prominent US brands like Reddit.

There were other peculiar players in the X orbit, especially from the crypto world. Olivier Janssens, a wealthy Bitcoiner, might have been best known for once partnering with Roger Ver, nicknamed Bitcoin Jesus, to "[purchase] sovereignty from a government to create the world's first Free Society."[10] It was exactly the kind of arch-libertarian, profit-chasing polity discussed in the chapters on charter cities and California Forever. Janssens' Free Society never materialized, but he became a pitchman for a private-jet company that took payment in Bitcoin. At the time that Janssens' ownership stake in X was disclosed, his friend Bitcoin Jesus was awaiting possible extradition to the United States on criminal charges for failing to pay $48 million in taxes.

The crypto giant Binance was a singular case, and not just for its role in taking down Sam Bankman-Fried. One of the more laughably corrupt companies around, Binance had been caught trading on its own exchange—a form of potential market manipulation—and funneling billions of dollars in revenues to Swiss and Maltese companies controlled by Changpeng Zhao and a mysterious company executive whose role the company obfuscated. Despite the instability surrounding Binance, the company still managed, somehow, to maintain its pole position as the world's biggest cryptocurrency exchange by volume.

I had reported on Binance for a couple of years and closely followed investigations from colleagues at the *Wall Street Journal*, Reuters, and the crypto press. I had never encountered another company like it. Binance was supposedly worth tens of billions of dollars, but it had no official headquarters and was notorious for dissembling about the nature, and even the location, of its operations. Binance Capital Management Co.—which put $500 million into Musk's Twitter buyout—was registered in the Cayman Islands, with an office address on a residential street in Malta. Binance CEO Changpeng Zhao was known to spend a lot of time in Dubai, where Binance apparently had an office. That is, until Zhao went to prison.

With Binance under investigation in at least a dozen countries, a serious legal confrontation with the US government seemed all but assured. In November 2023, Zhao pleaded guilty to money-laundering violations and Binance agreed to pay the Department of Justice a fine of $4.3 billion for allowing its platform to become a financial clearing house for militias and insurgent groups, money launderers, sanctioned oligarchs, and other "bad guys."[11] It was one of the largest corporate fines in US history. Zhao received a slap-on-the-wrist four-month term in a US federal prison. By the fall of 2024, he was released. Zhao left the country, likely never to return to North America.

Binance was still being sued by the SEC and faced investigations around the world. Zhao had nominally stepped back from operating the company, but he was believed to be its majority owner. In mid-October, he was back in Dubai and posting on X—the platform he partially owned, and which served as a key vector for pumping the value of the meme tokens and digital penny-stock equivalents that traded on Binance. (As an investor in the $250 million-plus category, Binance was reportedly promised access to closely held X user data, which might help the company analyze and shape crypto trends.) In late October, at Binance's annual Blockchain Week conference in Dubai, Zhao received a raucous ovation. He told the crowd that while he was no longer running Binance, his "shareholder rights" were still respected. He was still interested in crypto, he said, but he now wanted to focus his efforts on education and philanthropy.

There were other names on the X shareholder list whose inclusion seemed baffling, whether judging by morality, logic, or business sense. A few of them I branded the Inexplicably Rich. Andrea Stroppa was an Italian cybersecurity researcher who appeared to first grab Musk's attention in May 2022, when he professed to have specialized knowledge about Twitter's bot problem. At the time, Musk was obsessed with the issue of bots, claiming that Twitter was awash with inauthentic activity. To be fair, he was correct, but he seemed to misrepresent the issue in his attempts to drive down the acquisition price or to scotch the deal entirely. After he acquired the company, Musk claimed that the bot problem had been dealt with, but for many users, the problem only got worse.

After that May 2022 exchange, Stroppa and Musk tweeted frequently at each other, with Musk publicly thanking Stroppa for his "important work" on Twitter. Stroppa said that he'd assisted Musk's staff in addressing child sexual exploitation on the platform. (After his takeover, Musk fired 80 percent of the engineers working on trust and safety and dissolved a trust and safety advisory council.)[12]

A 2024 article in *La Repubblica* called Stroppa "Musk's man in Italy" and highlighted his support for right-wing Italian prime minister Georgia Meloni, who met with Musk. It's not clear how Stroppa came about his wealth or his stake in X. He didn't respond to a request for comment.

By Elon Musk's standards, the investment firms Glacier Ventures, Litani, and G64 Ventures should have been small fry. Yet they bought in—that is, they were allowed to buy in on a deal that Musk told his friend Larry Ellison was so "oversubscribed" that he would have to "reduce or kick out some participants." (Musk still asked Ellison to double his initial $1 billion offer, and Ellison quickly agreed.)[13]

Did Musk need their money? Two years after Musk closed his Twitter acquisition, Glacier Ventures' website said that they were still currently raising their first fund. Litani was a small Chicago-based venture capital firm with investments in food and biotech startups (its managing director didn't respond to a request for comment). G64 Ventures was another small firm that typically made investments for less than half a million dollars and didn't list X among its portfolio companies. Perhaps they had more money than they publicly demonstrated. Or maybe Musk, who was not nearly as liquid as his $200 billion-plus estimated fortune would suggest, needed to tap some deep sources for cash.

Less surprisingly, a number of financial firms and professional investors bought in, though some eyes widened on Wall Street when it was revealed that Fidelity had invested in X across at least 25 different funds. Fidelity soon announced that it had written down its investment in X by 79 percent.[14]

A number of money managers and friends of Musk bought not for their investment firms or their clients but for themselves. Bill Ackman, the hedge fund billionaire who developed a sideline as a cranky social-media essayist, owned $10 million worth of X through his nonprofit foundation.

There were some notable names missing. Peter Thiel, Keith Rabois, and other pro-Trump members of the PayPal Mafia didn't chip in, nor did Thiel's Founders Fund—although, typical of the industry's circular networks of cash and influence, Founders Fund was an investor in X investor 8VC. According to some of the court-disclosed texts, former PayPal exec and LinkedIn co-founder Reid Hoffman told Musk that $2 billion was "probably doable." Musk welcomed his contribution but—maintaining the pretense that the deal was oversubscribed—said that he would "just cut back others" to accommodate Hoffman. It appears that Hoffman never invested.

Musk's friends David Sacks, Antonio Gracias, and Jason Calacanis were absent, even though they advised Musk on the acquisition and sat in the Twitter "war room" as he shredded the company roster. In April 2022, Sacks wrote to Musk, "I'm in personally and will raise an SPV [Special Purpose Vehicle]," rather than invest through Craft Ventures, his venture capital firm. Musk later liked a message that Sacks wrote: "Best to be low-key during transaction."[15] Did one of the unidentified shell companies belong to Sacks?

In text messages, several of Sam Bankman-Fried's friends and allies dangled a potential multibillion-dollar investment in front of Musk. Morgan Stanley banker Michael Grimes urged Musk to meet with the crypto mogul. Bankman-Fried was denied entry. "He set off my bs detector," Musk posted on the day FTX filed for bankruptcy.[16]

"It took me a fair bit of time to come to terms with the fact that Elon and I actually aren't all that much alike," Bankman-Fried wrote to me in a September 2022 Twitter direct message. Bankman-Fried claimed that the texts released by the Delaware court weren't the full content of his communications with Musk.

It was probably best for Musk—and everyone—that he never vibed with Bankman-Fried. But he found plenty of other partners: close friends, longtime business consiglieres, C-list internet personalities, Middle Eastern tyrants, and the venture capital firms that washed their bloody billions. It was an eclectic group, and still incomplete until some of the offshore trusts and shell companies could be traced to their ultimate beneficiaries.

My attention kept returning to X's relationship with Saudi Arabia, which started long before Elon Musk acquired the company and persisted under his ownership. It was about more than Prince Alwaleed bin Talal, the major company shareholder and billionaire Saudi industrialist who had bent to Crown Prince Mohammed bin Salman's will during a dark imprisonment at the Ritz-Carlton Hotel in Riyadh. It was about money and influence, a host of unresolved, and maybe unresolvable, legal issues, and the ways that foreign governments exerted influence in Silicon Valley. And because few people wanted to talk critically about it, the saga remained an exemplar of the dark geopolitics underpinning both X and the larger tech industry.

The issue of espionage and foreign influence in Silicon Valley made for exciting investigatory stories, but it was still poorly explored terrain. Seven years after the Twitter spy ring was ostensibly dismantled, the Saudi government was still a major shareholder. The company had experienced its share of embarrassing hacks, including one by a group of teenagers who hijacked prominent accounts, like Jack Dorsey's, to promote a crypto scam. Mudge, the cybersecurity expert who held a senior role at Twitter, appeared before Congress to offer whistleblower testimony about the company's numerous ethical lapses and its poor security architecture. "Twitter's security failures threaten national security, compromise the privacy and security of users, and at times threaten the very continued existence of the Company," Mudge told Congress in September 2022, a month before Musk's acquisition finally closed.[17]

According to the *Washington Post*, anyone who invested more than $250 million in Musk's Twitter acquisition received special access to sensitive data about the company and its users.[18] Six investors were known to qualify: Saudi Prince Alwaleed bin Talal, the Qatari sovereign wealth fund, Binance, UAE-based Vy Capital, Sequoia Capital, and CIA contractor Larry Ellison. What did they get?

There were other connections between X and Middle Eastern autocracies, some of which had gone unnoticed. 8VC, the venture capital fund led by Joe Lonsdale (he of the intergenerational nondisclosure agreements and contempt for the "homeless industrial complex"), had three limited partners. These LPs were the investors who provided the bulk of the firm's investment capital. They included The Daniel B. & Florence E. Green Foundation—a private family foundation—and the University of Michigan endowment. The third was J.A.S. Ventures, a practically unknown investment firm based out of Abu Dhabi. 8VC and J.A.S. appeared to share a lawyer from the Abu Dhabi office of powerhouse firm Baker McKenzie.

There was little public information connecting the two firms. On LinkedIn, an entrepreneur named Sean Nasiri listed himself as co-founder of J.A.S. Ventures, which he described as "the venture practice of a prominent family based in Abu Dhabi."[19] In a LinkedIn post from the summer of 2024, Nasiri remarked that he founded J.A.S. Ventures in 2021 with a man named Ahmed Alsuwaidi.[20] The Alsuwaidi family was indeed very prominent in the UAE—a lineage of businessmen and statesmen who had played major roles in the UAE since the modern state's founding in 1971. Ahmed Alsuwaidi was a big fish: a senior vice president at Mubadala, the UAE sovereign wealth fund that was also a major tech investor. Like many of its peers, then, 8VC was a conduit for money from Gulf states. It's not clear how much J.A.S. Ventures might have put into 8VC. But some portion of 8VC's Opportunities Fund II—which, according to SEC filings, raised about $743 million—went to Musk's acquisition of Twitter.

While I had been focused on Prince Alwaleed bin Talal (and the Saudi crown prince looming over him), there appeared to be another Saudi entity on the X shareholder list: T. One Holdings LLC. In corporate filings with the Delaware Secretary of State, T. One Holdings LLC listed Nassr Haj Ali Bek as its authorized person. His address was in the Al Sulaimaniyah district of Riyadh, Saudi Arabia. It wasn't clear who Bek was. Someone with his name was a director of companies registered in Canada and Malta. A LinkedIn account indicated he had received an MBA in Canada before working for four years in the business division of a Saudi media company. From there, he claimed, he went on to Alawaal Financial Services, a major Saudi bank, where he wore the equally lofty title of Head of Corporate Finance & Investment Services. Bek didn't respond to my messages.

My effort to unseal the X shareholder list was a tiny drop in the ocean of litigation facing Musk and X. US courts were supposed to offer an opportunity for redress for people victimized by large corporations like this one. Some of the former employees whom Musk summarily fired would probably reach decent settlements with the company or eventually receive some compensation under California labor law. But even that was not assured. Musk's aggressive legal campaign included a lawsuit against the National Labor Relations Board that questioned the constitutional authority of the country's top labor regulator. It was war on all fronts, and Musk would continue to fight lawsuits brought against Twitter/X's previous management.

With regard to X's relationships with illiberal governments, the US legal system offered little succor, especially when the offenses occurred at the intersection of corporate power and national-security interests.

Since President Franklin D. Roosevelt formed a compact in 1945 with King Abdul Aziz ibn Saud, the founder of the House of Saud, the US and Saudi Arabia had been close allies. It was a devil's bargain—protection for oil, to put it crudely—a relationship that ever since has been a driving force in US domestic politics and its imperial activities in the Middle East. Over the decades, the US government intervened in official investigations and judicial processes—from the long-redacted 27 pages of the 9/11 Commission Report to a lawsuit by a Saudi ex-intelligence chief against MBS—in order to protect its autocratic ally.[21]

The Saudi government and its billions were welcomed in the US, especially by Silicon Valley venture capitalists and executives. In a photo from June 2016, a grinning Crown Prince Mohammed bin Salman can be seen standing with 14 tech industry luminaries—including Reid Hoffman, Peter Thiel, Marc Andreessen, Sam Altman, and Michael Moritz. The photo—which was taken at a San Francisco dinner where MBS, who had just invested $3.5 billion in Uber, discussed business opportunities with the American financiers—was published in the *Wall Street Journal*. The photo was credited to Bader Al Asaker, the MBS aide who led the Twitter spy ring.

When Musk acquired Twitter, there were rumblings that the Committee on Foreign Investment in the United States (CFIUS) might investigate the deal. "CFIUS has the responsibility to review transactions that could result in an American business being controlled by a foreign person," wrote Senator Chris Murphy in a letter to Treasury secretary Janet Yellen. "I call on CFIUS to immediately conduct a review of the recent changes in Twitter's ownership and governance. It is essential to our national security that public officials and citizens alike can continue to rely on this platform to be a neutral platform, free of foreign influence."[22]

In his letter, Murphy specifically cited concerns about the Saudi government using its investment "to silence government critics and human rights activists, or to further state-sponsored disinformation campaigns." According to the *Washington Post*, the investigation never happened.[23] (CFIUS records are not subject to Freedom of Information requests.)

That investigatory work fell upon activists, journalists, and victims of Saudi transnational oppression. They didn't have much luck. Or more accurately, the system wasn't set up to help them. It existed to stymie them.

The courts seemed to have no remedy for transnational repression conducted by an autocratic government that was accused of having bought, infiltrated, spied, and exploited its way into the heart of a prized Silicon Valley company, one whose animating purpose was supposed to be synonymous with personal freedom. Twitter, in the interest of self-preservation and avoiding expensive legal settlements, would never acknowledge its own negligence or potential liability. Twitter might have become X, buttressed by Elon Musk's militant devotion to free speech, but the Saudi government ownership and influence remained—indeed, appeared more prominent than ever. The new company's army of lawyers would continue to fend off Saudi dissidents' attempts to hold it accountable, with several lawsuits dismissed outright by judges.

With all its baggage and biases, this was the X that Musk would deploy in 2024 in service of electing Donald Trump. Trailed by lawsuits and a miserable reputation; overrun by ads for scam dropshipped products and assorted bots (crypto, porn, inscrutable AI conversationalists); amplifying the posts of its angry right-wing owner and his dues-paying users; salting the discourse with bad information, AI-generated fakes, and bad-faith hysteria about crime and migrants; infiltrated by authoritarian foreign governments; presided over practically 24/7 by Elon Musk—this ridiculous, debauched platform was one of the most powerful media tools that a power-hungry mogul could ever have in his political arsenal. And he was quite clear about what he wanted to do with it.

20

Someone Has to Win

It made sense that Donald Trump would find common cause with the men in this book. Their concerns didn't always match, but their worldviews and attitudes did. Trump shared with Thiel, Musk, Sacks, Lonsdale, and other tech oligarchs the frisson of cultural resentment, the constant desire to troll his enemies as he wore his bigotries on his sleeve, ever the insult comic. He was a macabre cynic, describing a fictional America overrun with crime, drugs, disorder, and violent migrants. In Trump's imagined universe, Hannibal Lecter, the serial killer from *The Silence of the Lambs*, was as real as whatever distorted migrant crime story he was regurgitating that day. The question of truth was superfluous, especially since in Republicans' view Democrats had already polluted the epistemological landscape with arguments over "disinformation"—a category most Republicans refused to acknowledge as real. No, what mattered was that everything had gone to seed and that Trump, in his meandering stage performances, could reliably tick off the enemies of the people that had brought America to its current fallen state: Democrats, communists, the Democrats who were actually communists, transgender people, migrants, the deep state.

Trump's allies in tech didn't play the character nearly as well—many of them were insufferable whiners on X—but they had enough money to keep the performance going. Still, they revealed the essential poverty of the MAGA vision. It was one thing when

Trump demagogued about America's ruined cities from a hastily constructed stage next to a Midwestern airstrip (he never wanted to be among the hoi polloi for long), or when he ranted on Truth Social about the very unfair terms of a debate. Trump's fans were familiar with his belligerent prima donna persona. They looked to him for bleak doomerism and rants about migrant invasions. He was their voice, as he had told his followers.

Somehow, the ability of Silicon Valley elites to raise massive amounts of cash or found successful social-media companies had created a sense that any industry was ripe for their mastery. They had the skills and knowledge to remake whatever they put their attention to—taxis, healthcare, hotels, defense contracting. Now it was the government's turn. For those not directly attracted to Musk's bigoted X rants, this was his appeal as a Trump ally. By sheer dint of his genius, he would make things better—cut government waste, fire inefficient bureaucrats, sprinkle whatever fairy dust magic he had. Trump promised the public that he would "fix everything."[1] Musk could actually do it.

There wasn't much proof that venture capitalists and tech moguls possessed this kind of infinitely applicable meta-skill. It seemed hypocritical for a group that claimed to value meritocracy. But hypocrisy, a lesser cousin of lying, was no longer a social crime. No one cared. Musk didn't know much about government, except as a contractor who benefited from more than "$38 billion in government contracts, loans, subsidies and tax credits."[2] His skills as a businessman—even if sometimes in dispute—did not automatically translate to reforming federal agencies or serving a public that wasn't lining his pockets. Nor should they. But as I wrote in the New Alignment chapter, this was a group that disclaimed experts except when it suited them.

When David Sacks published long, angrily discursive posts on X about the supposed failures of President Joe Biden's Ukraine policy, one might have thought that his and the public's time would be better served if he applied to the foreign service. Instead, he posted policy briefs as if he were auditioning to be Trump's next national-security advisor. Perhaps he was.

If we were going to democratize knowledge and the public sphere, we should have been welcoming outsiders and autodidacts offering their voices. But some voices were far louder than others, and not every opinion was offered in good faith. Power is self-certifying: it legitimizes its wielder. And with Trump potentially returning to power, tech's leading lights were ready to rule.

"Our high skilled immigration system is frozen in time and not responsive to the market," wrote Aaron Levie, the CEO of cloud storage company Box, in an X post. "We have far more demand for the top talent to work for and start companies here than we let in. It's a bipartisan issue that politicians don't touch. Someone like Elon finally could do it."[3]

There was no reason to think that Musk was especially suited to this task, except that he was an authoritarian outsider on the cusp of acquiring tremendous power.

Musk himself was an immigrant, but the man who demanded draconian crackdowns on migrants had not always followed immigration law in his own life. In 1995, Musk, a Canadian citizen, arrived in the US to attend a PhD program at Stanford. His visa status didn't allow him to work. Musk decided not to enroll in the PhD program after all, and went to work for Zip2, a startup which created guides for cities and later was acquired for $300 million. He recruited his brother Kimbal to join him there, without valid work authorization—a potential crime. In 1996, employees and investors at Zip2 implored Musk to sort out his immigration situation, worrying that it could be a threat to the company and its ability to go public. The following year, the Musk brothers worked with an immigration lawyer to receive work visas allotted to Canadians under a provision of the North American Free Trade Agreement.[4]

In a 2013 conference appearance, Kimbal Musk said that he and his brother illegally resided in the US when they were working at Zip2. Elon tried to brush off his brother's comment. "I'd say it was a gray area," replied Elon. "We were illegal immigrants," said Kimbal, sounding more insistent.[5] In a podcast interview, Kimbal once said that they had been in the US illegally. Elon acknowledged Kimbal's comment and said that he was supposed to only be doing "student work."[6] In yet another podcast interview, Kimbal said that he once lied to US border officers about why he was entering the country (to see a David Letterman taping, rather than his intended business meeting). One expert told the *Washington Post* that Kimbal's actions could be considered "fraud on entry," earning him a permanent ban from entering the United States.[7] These immigration violations could also be used as a pretext for revoking Elon Musk's citizenship.[8]

Despite what Aaron Levie suggested, immigration was an animating issue for Musk not because he thought he could streamline the process but because he had strongly felt views about who deserved to be in the country. Believing that the United States was under siege by hordes of migrants from the Global South whom Democrats ushered across the border as part of a larger conspiracy to create a one-party state, Musk promoted the most odious lies and unfounded claims about migrants, doing so in lockstep with Trump, Vance, leading Republican officials, and right-wing media figures.[9] Musk wasn't a technocrat; he was an ideologue.

Raised in apartheid-era South Africa, Musk's feelings on race and the politics of privilege might be summed up by a meme he shared. The picture showed a white man on horseback returning home, with a doll in his hand, to his excited daughter. Next to him were the words: "Your ancestors weren't villains. Don't apologize for them to people who hate you." The Rabbit Hole, the account that posted the meme and which was a Musk favorite, added "Historical guilt is dumb." Musk re-shared the post with his audience, adding a simple "Yes."[10]

Musk had been accused of being racist in his business dealings. Black former Tesla employees claimed that they were kept in their own segregated area and blocked from receiving promotions.[11] In a major lawsuit filed by 5,977 Black workers at Tesla's Fremont factory, the plaintiffs claimed that they faced a hostile work environment riven by discrimination, racist taunts, and harassment.[12] Several other lawsuits, including one filed by the Equal Employment Opportunities Commission, have accused Tesla of maintaining a racist work environment where Black employees face retaliation for reporting racist abuse, while the n-word could be seen scrawled in spots around the Fremont Tesla factory. In 2023, a jury awarded Owen Diaz, a Black man who used to work for Tesla, $3.2 million for the mistreatment he faced.[13]

The executive overseeing this troubled work environment was the person who Levie thought would be particularly suited to overhauling the "high skilled immigration system." Notably, Levie was not talking about immigration generally but about the well-trained engineers from India, China, South Korea, and other countries whom the tech industry relied upon. Under Trump's potential mass deportation regime, this special class of immigrants might be protected, at least by their big tech patrons. Others wouldn't be so fortunate.

As for Musk, who was surely Levie's intended audience, he liked the idea.

"I agree," he replied in a post published at 2:42 a.m.[14]

As F. Scott Fitzgerald remarked, the rich aren't like you and me, and their social-media fear-mongering rang hollow for some. The country had serious problems, but Trump and right-wing tech donors described a Democrat-wrought Sodom and Gomorrah that did not match what a lot of people saw in their daily lives. In this country of immigrants and their descendants, many people either didn't know any undocumented migrants or interacted with them daily—at grocery stores, farms, warehouses, restaurants, and throughout the so-called service economy—without noticing, much less being physically threatened with violence. If anything, migrants were vulnerable people who had often experienced terrible abuse and trauma on their perilous journey to the United States, where they struggled to make a living in the shadows of an economy that needed their labor but could have them deported at any moment. (As it happened, more people were deported under President Joe Biden than in President Trump's first term.) Some of them also paid taxes.

But the appeals of Trumpism were built on libidinal emotions and alternative facts, and they were powerful enough to propel him to the highest office—twice, it would turn out. In the eyes of too many voters (and non-voters), Democrats focused on identity politics or social issues or Trump as an existential threat to the democratic order—without realizing that, just maybe, some people weren't very happy with the current order of things. They were broke, exhausted, hollowed out by the relentless petty demands of the post-industrial economy. They saw Democratic politicians who spent their time in office getting rich on legalized insider trading, rather than walking in picket lines. Instead of finding class consciousness or the bonds of solidarity, some found the prickly comforts of a reactionary cynicism bordering on nihilism. And some were consumed by hatred, radicalized by a rotten political culture and a tech media machine that kept them algorithmically hooked on more and more extreme and sensationalist media. Neither party had an answer for this predicament, but one was able to leverage it.

The Democrats built their appeal on an assumption that they deserved their authority, that their righteousness was self-evident, that progress could be incremental and boring, and that most material issues were downstream concerns. The endorsement of a celebrity or a mid-tier Republican official meant more than that of a union leader.

Democratic politicians didn't take positions so much as they gently circled them. What did Kamala Harris stand for, besides opposing Trump? When asked on *The View* whether she would do anything differently from President Joe Biden, the unpopular incumbent she replaced as nominee, Harris said no. She then modified her answer: actually, she would have a Republican in her cabinet.

That refusal to distinguish oneself traveled poorly on social media, failed to activate the politically indifferent people that Democrats needed to bring to the polls, and didn't offer a tangible, positive vision of material progress. The Harris campaign promised, basically, more of the same, which didn't appeal to the millions of working-class people who were still struggling in what they were constantly told was a good economy for which they should be grateful. They would eventually vote for Trump in greater numbers than they did in 2020. Nor did it appeal to Muslim Americans in Michigan or an increasing number of Latino men. Their identities did not make them automatic Democrats. Americans of varying backgrounds and ideological stripes didn't want a new, younger Biden, with slight policy variations. They wanted radical change—a break from the calcified order—which only one candidate would claim to offer.

In the face of a say-anything candidate whose followers existed in a mostly separate epistemological reality, Democrats wielded consultant-approved talking points that managed to say nothing at all. Whenever a national Democratic politician did seem to stumble on a genuinely original way to communicate with the public, a gut-level remark that cast into relief the absurdity of our political predicament, they didn't seem to last. The talk of Republicans as "weird"—as creepy and invasive in their perverse desire for control over women's bodies, for example—ended with the kind of suddenness that indicates a memo was circulated from on high. Attempting to rally voters to fight off an incipient authoritarianism, Kamala Harris's campaign began with cries of "We won't go back" and ended with a promise to put a Republican in her cabinet. Rather than campaigning heavily with popular labor leaders like Shawn Fain and Sara Nelson, Harris's most frequently used surrogates in the last days before the election were billionaire Mark Cuban and neoconservative Liz Cheney. Harris would go on to win a smaller percentage of Republican voters than Joe Biden did.

"The Democratic Party has become a metropolitan, college-educated party," longtime Democratic consultant David Axelrod told the *Washington Post*. "And even though it retains its commitment to working people, it approaches them sometimes in a spirit of a missionary—that we're here to help you become more like us. Implied in that is disdain. I don't think it's intended, but it's felt. And I think Trump has exploited that."[15]

With a feckless opponent, a demagogue can have an easy time, especially when he lies relentlessly and is backed up by powerful allies in tech and media. A billionaire like Trump can present himself as a populist savior for a benighted working class abandoned by Democratic elites. These were the kinds of fictions that powered Trump's MAGA movement.

The supposed migrant invasion was one of several deceptive inventions by Trump, the conservative press, and social-media influencers, who, adopting an age-old tactic, thrived by scaring their audience. If the country was overrun by dangerous migrants, as the conservative political establishment and media-sphere claimed, then only Trump, who promised the harshest of crackdowns, could cleanse the country of the problem.

To some it might have seemed strange or disturbing. Where was this invasion? Wasn't it clear that every viral video panicking about migrant crime had all the authority of a chain letter? But there were plenty of people who did believe it, because they existed in a mostly siloed-off informational and political environment. Racist wish-casting also played a role—there's a certain drama in thinking you're under attack, that you're engaged in a potentially heroic struggle against an obvious enemy.

Against this depressing political horizon, it seemed to voters like me that the stakes were fascism—underwritten by the tech billionaires—or another exhausting round of electoral politicking that might delay the country's backslide into authoritarian rule. Even as the swapping out of Joe Biden for Kamala Harris injected a new dynamism into the race, it was hard to have faith in a Democratic Party that often governed like George W. Bush-era Republicans. If democracy was indeed on the ballot, as President Biden liked to claim it was, then it was a battered democracy, broken by corruption, inequality, elite impunity, unlimited corporate money, endless war, an out-of-touch ruling class, and the repressive policies of people like Donald Trump. Thankfully, we had been spared the worst of Trumpism the first time round by the incompetence of its namesake and his rogues' gallery of advisors. The next Trump administration would be worse.

Trump had repeatedly expressed his wish to be a dictator and to do away with elections. He talked about using the military to dispose of his enemies. He was surrounded by a who's who of constitutional subversives and right-wing radicals, the intellectual and bureaucratic foot soldiers of a political project that would attempt to consolidate power in a president immune from legal judgment, purge the government of millions of disloyal workers, use the military to deport 20 million individuals, and create a database of pregnant people to track violators of a national abortion ban. Among various other potential crimes and civic outrages, they also wanted to invade Mexico to fight drug cartels.

Some of tech's richest leaders decided they were onboard with this political program. They would devote their fortunes, their corporate networks, and their formidable influence to making it happen. They believed in it, or they denied it would be as bad as those hysterical liberals claimed. Their critics all had Trump Derangement Syndrome. Then they acquired a bad case of Musk Derangement Syndrome. The Democrats, backed by their own cadre of self-interested billionaires, were no better, they said.

Maybe it was worth it to chisel away at the corporate tax rate and land a blow against the administrative state and the woke mind virus. Elon Musk seemed to think so. The man who, in 2017, stepped down from two Trump advisory councils to protest the president withdrawing from the Paris Climate Accords had changed.[16] Seven years later, he would tell the venture capitalist Vinod Khosla, who was worried about Trump's refusal to take climate change seriously, "As you know, sustainable energy production and consumption is growing very rapidly and is tracking to exceed use of hydrocarbon fuels. That will happen no matter what Trump does."[17]

Musk's answer was ignorant or deliberately obtuse, refusing to consider Trump's wholesale climate denialism—the same denialism that Musk once publicly opposed.

By October 6, when Musk jumped and yelped onstage during Trump's return rally at the site of his attempted assassination in Butler, PA, it was obvious that the mogul was all in, as he described it to Tucker Carlson. If Trump didn't win, Musk said, "I'm fucked." He wondered how long his prison sentence might be and if he'd be allowed to see his kids. Even if they were unmoored from reality, Musk's dark jokes reflected the truth: he saw the stakes as incredibly high. He was right.

Who knows if these two arch-authoritarian personalities truly liked each other, but it was clearly to their benefit to act like it (Less than six months into the second Trump administration, we saw how tenuous their bond was when their relationship collapsed). Calling him a "super genius," Trump embraced Musk's cultish image as a technical visionary with ambitions reaching beyond the stars. The flattery became mutual: Musk, who spoke in the scaremongering register favored by reactionary venture capitalists and Trump himself, routinely described the Republican nominee as the only person who could save America from civilizational collapse. Either Trump would win, or this would be the last election, as Democrats illegally funneled migrants into the country with a plan to give them citizenship and institute a permanent Democratic Party majority.

True to his word, Musk did all he could to promote Trump's candidacy.

Animated by political rage, Musk posted day and night about Trump and the apocalyptic condition of the nation. Displaying all of the media literacy of a man twice his age, he amplified every fact-free conspiracy, every outrageous attempt to demonize trans people or migrants or a minority community. "Wow," went a typical Musk repost, appending his stamp of approval for his hundreds of millions of followers—a good chunk of them bots—and the news organizations, influencers, YouTubers, and Tesla devotees who generated content based off them. It was an ongoing performance: the richest man in the world freaking out about the decline of man and society, and doing everything he could to scare you—*you*—into believing that he knew the way through.

Some saw this version of Musk as a self-evident farce, but Musk had spent years building up a cult of personality that projected an image of himself as a swaggering entrepreneur. He had an audience who would follow him anywhere, and as he fell into radical right-wing circles on social media, millions of regular people were happy to make the journey, too. In his role as chief curator of this reactionary space, he connected his followers to a larger network of right-wing techies and anonymous anime fascists. Often responding to posts from sycophantic strangers, Musk reflected right back at them their panicked anger, their misogynistic outrage and racist memes, their angry impatience for a technologically advanced, *cooler* future—a future that they believed had been denied to them by Democrats, woke activists, and other cultural enemies.

For Musk, Trump meant access to the highest levels of power. He also offered protection: a way to preserve Musk's lucrative government contracts as officials began publicly worrying about his influence, and numerous regulatory agencies investigated his operations. If Trump won with Musk's help, then Musk's legal concerns—a lengthy list to which Musk seemed to be adding potential violations of campaign finance and lottery laws—would mostly go away.

Trump promised Musk a form of authority unlike any previous big donor. Trump touted Musk as a future "secretary of cost cutting" running a Department of Government Efficiency—or DOGE, according to the eye-rolling acronym they created in reference to the dog-themed crypto token. This unprecedented role would give him carte blanche to remake the administrative state, to tackle the apocalyptic threat of "the woke mind virus." The post would grant Musk total authority to dismantle agencies he didn't like—which, in practice, meant booting masses of middle-class government workers out of their jobs and slashing regulations that attempt to check corporate power. Maybe Trump would give Musk—who already had more than $11 billion in rocket launch contracts with NASA—full control over the US space program or the Space Force. Musk, Trump, and Republicans might find common cause in ending protections for trans youth and the healthcare programs that served them.[18] Musk's ability to disrupt Americans' lives would be vast.

It sounded like Shadow President Elon Musk.

We had never seen the American plutocracy operate quite like this. The richest person in the world spent the homestretch of the 2024 presidential campaign providing a degree of public and financial support for a candidate unprecedented in the annals of pay-to-play American electioneering. Not since Howard Hughes secretly funneled cash to Hubert Humphrey, Robert F. Kennedy, and Richard Nixon during the 1968 presidential election had an unstable, flamboyant billionaire industrialist exerted such an influence on a presidential race.[19]

While the media sometimes portrayed Musk as a political newcomer, he had been sharpening his grievances for years and donating money quietly to right-wing political organizations. In 2022, he gave $25 million to Citizens for Sanity, a group connected to Stephen Miller, the Trump advisor who longed for an era of mass deportations and stripping immigrants of their US citizenship. Citizens for Sanity used the money to pay for political ads denouncing trans healthcare policies and hyping migrant crime. The following year, David Sacks brokered a meeting between Musk and DeSantis. "Musk and DeSantis found common ground on their stances against diversity, equity and inclusion initiatives," reported the *Wall Street Journal*.[20] Anti-wokeness had become core to their politics. Musk later gave $10 million to a pro-DeSantis group.

By late summer 2024, Musk had adopted an all-hands approach to the election. He shifted his base of operations to Pennsylvania, where he assembled a war room of advisors and political consultants to strategize how to win the crucial swing state. His America PAC emphasized collecting voter data in such states, and employed dissembling tactics that quickly drew investigations from state authorities. Musk joked about traveling around Pennsylvania and personally canvassing neighborhoods. Instead, he did the rich man's version of door knocking, unleashing his PACs to hire canvassers on the ground.

In the frenetic few months in which Musk became the closest thing to a second Republican presidential candidate, it was hard to tell at times which of his initiatives was working, which merely attracted media coverage, and which might one day land him in a deposition chair. He began giving away $47 to each registered swing state voter who signed a petition supporting the First and Second Amendments—which may have violated election law because it was contingent on recipients being registered voters. Then Musk moved the dial to 11, announcing a $1 million giveaway each day for a different registered swing state voter. Progressive Philadelphia district attorney Larry Krasner tried to stop it, arguing that Musk was running an illegal lottery, but a judge disagreed. The show continued, with Musk presenting giant novelty checks at live-streamed town halls to winners who were randomly selected. As legal scrutiny increased, America PAC changed its policy again, claiming that the million-dollar winners were paid spokespeople, not random lottery winners. That might also be illegal, Krasner and his allies suggested, but it didn't matter. The giveaway ran through election day.

As Musk stumped for votes, rambling through his vision for transforming society, the performance seemed desperate. Maybe Musk really was "fucked" if Trump didn't win, as he told Tucker Carlson. There was so much on the line—self-interest above all else—which was reflected in the neediness of his public appeals, a pleading desire for us to feel, as he did, that Trump's election was crucial for the survival of Western civilization. As a political operator, Musk deployed the tech modus operandi of move-fast-and-break-things—including, perhaps, campaign finance law—a growth-hacking mentality in which cutting corners was fine as long as it quickly scaled the product.

For a time, it sounded like Musk's shambolic but well-funded political operation was stumbling. Besides the controversial data collection practices and the cash giveaways, it turned out that one of America PAC's subcontractors was abusing the temp workers hired to be canvassers. The workers, many of them Black, were hired through ads that led them to believe they would be doing some kind of nonpartisan political polling. Instead, after they signed NDAs, they learned that they would be working for the Trump campaign. They were flown to swing states and driven around in moving vans that didn't have seats. They had nigh-impossible door-knocking quotas that would determine if they got paid (another America PAC subcontractor had already been caught lying about their canvassing numbers). When some canvassers complained to a *Wired* reporter about their working conditions, they were allegedly fired and left in Michigan, unpaid, with no flight home.[21]

Like numerous other labor scandals connected to Musk, the story was outrageous but didn't stick. Nor did it seem to matter when Musk repeatedly posted false information about Harris, whom he called a communist responsible for flying in millions of illegal migrants to vote.[22] It did not matter when Musk's money was discovered to be propping up an astroturf website called Progress 2028, which presented a fictional Kamala Harris-authorized political document designed to distract from concerns over Republicans' draconian Project 2025 governance plan.[23] There was little sustained backlash when 404 Media discovered that another Musk-funded PAC was microtargeting Jewish and Muslim neighborhoods—sometimes within miles of one another—and showing them different ads designed to turn them against the Democratic Party.[24] The ads misrepresented Harris's policy positions, and the organization sent out text messages to potential voters in which they falsely claimed to be affiliated with the Democratic campaign.[25] These tactics had become almost expected in dark-money electioneering, on both sides.

At every level, Musk was flooding the zone with money, misinformation, and deceptive tactics. He was acting upon what had become a social-media truism: lies travel more quickly and more widely than the truth. You can spread bullshit faster than the other side can debunk it. And when caught, just ignore the issue and move on to a new lie.

As with Trump, Musk's fans seemed to enjoy his impudence—the idea that he could be a juvenile provocateur, upsetting the apple cart of polite expectations, and that he could get away with it. Trump's supporters liked that he was a felon, because they didn't respect the system that had branded him an outlaw. In Trump and Musk, they didn't see oligarchy or elite impunity or corruption. Embodying the false consciousness that makes billionaire populism such an effective political strategy, MAGA voters saw Musk and Trump as working toward liberating people from the shackles of the same establishment that the two men had mastered. They had been in the room with the bad guys—the Clintons, Bidens, Soros, Hollywood. They heard how they talked and schemed. But they weren't them.

As Musk dumped money into Trump politicking, making himself the center of the campaign, the actual candidate became even more bizarre and unhinged. He was stumbling toward a possible loss and prison time. He needed cash for his legal bills. He promised energy CEOs whatever they wanted for $1 billion. He pleaded with evangelical voters to support him this time, assuring them they would never have to vote again. He started selling $399 golden Trump sneakers and watches, and launched another line of Trump-themed NFTs. And now he was about to go all in on crypto, not just rolling out the carpet for the industry but establishing multiple crypto ventures of his own.

DONALD TRUMP GETS ORANGE-PILLED

After his triumphant Nashville speech, Trump's about-face on crypto reached a new level of commitment with the launch of something called World Liberty Financial. It was just three weeks before election day, and rather than talking about social security or foreign policy, Trump was touting another new business. World Liberty Financial was Trump's new crypto venture, an offshore crypto platform peddling the usual promises of financial freedom and easy profit, this time bearing the approving thumbs-up of the most transactional man in politics. That a presidential candidate was talking about usurping the US dollar with cryptocurrencies, including one of his own, almost went unmentioned. It wasn't as if Trump, who had the title of Chief Crypto Advocate at World Liberty Financial, knew what he was talking about when it came to digital currencies. This was another branding opportunity.

World Liberty Financial was a rogues' gallery of hilariously inept hustlers—which is to say, it was like a lot of crypto companies. The last crypto project run by WLF's 39-year-old leader, Chase Herro, had "attracted only a few million dollars and then suffered a devastating hack," according to a Bloomberg article summarizing his exploits. The relatively unknown crypto entrepreneur called himself a "dirtbag of the internet" and seemed to have limitless confidence.[26]

"You can literally sell shit in a can, wrapped in piss, covered in human skin, for a billion dollars if the story's right, because people will buy it," Herro said in a 2018 video. "I'm not going to question the right and wrong of all that."[27]

That seemed to be what Herro and the Trump family were offering. Like all cryptocurrencies, the WLFI tokens had no inherent value, though they were priced at 5 cents each. You couldn't use WLFI tokens for anything or spend them as currency. They were supposed to be "governance tokens," empowering owners to vote on decisions affecting the World Liberty Financial platform, which as of yet, didn't do much at all. And as numerous examples from crypto's short history have shown, "governance tokens" could be a fig leaf for user control, masking who actually controls a crypto project.

In what should have been an affront to all red-blooded Bitcoiners, World Liberty Financial token owners couldn't move their digital assets off the platform or sell them to others—pretty much defeating the point of crypto. "All $WLFI will be non-transferable and locked indefinitely in a wallet or smart contract," read the site's terms of service, which noted that the company would block attempted transfers. "You should assume that the Tokens are non-transferable indefinitely. As the Tokens are non-transferable, the Company has not taken any action to, and has no plans to, create a secondary market for the Tokens."[28]

Some 22.5 billion tokens were set aside for Donald Trump. At the time of the ICO (initial coin offering), they would be worth $337.5 million, at least in theory.[29] With crypto's illiquid markets, it would be hard to sell many of the tokens without crashing the price. Not that he could sell them—unless the company's rules didn't apply to Trump. But free money is free money, and that's basically what World Liberty Financial was to Donald Trump. It would also become the receptacle for foreign crypto entrepreneurs—some with potential legal issues in the US—to put money in the president's pocket.

The terms of the deal between the Trump family and WLF immunized the former president and his kids from liability toward the company. It also set aside 75 percent of revenue for them.[30]

No matter how goofy or ridiculous the team behind WLF, that didn't mean they couldn't make some money. That was one of the animating principles of crypto: keep risking it all until some outside force stops you. And an already overscheduled SEC didn't seem keen on taking on Trump's token sale in the tense days before an election, one whose outcome would determine whether SEC chair Gary Gensler could keep his job. It was an easy play, requiring little of the Trump family.

In the weeks leading up to the election, token sales were tepid, so the company cut its sales goal from $300 million to $30 million.[31] Billions of tokens went unsold.

World Liberty Financial announced its intention to create a stablecoin—a token with a near-constant value, pegged to the dollar. Ostensibly, people would pay WLF $1 per stablecoin, and then those people could take those tokens and trade them for Bitcoin and other crypto. But if you have a digital-money printer, why wait for someone to pay you $1?

Stablecoins had become the profit center of crypto. In the eyes of some, they were counterfeit digital dollars, minted, sometimes without any real dollar backing, by sketchy overseas companies like Tether, which had more than $123 billion worth of coins in circulation. Tether was crypto's most traded token—the $1 chips used at all the crypto casinos—and its most controversial. It had become one of the reserve currencies of global cybercrime, providing a new payment rail that empowered ransomware hackers and text scammers who coerced Americans to send billions of dollars' worth of crypto to criminals overseas. Tether had paid eight-figure fines to US regulators and was banned from doing business in the state of New York. It had long been under Department of Justice investigation, with nothing to show for it by the end of Biden's term. Its executives lived overseas—its two principals were rarely seen in public—and the company had never been audited, despite promising to do so for years.

Tether may have been banned from doing business in New York, but it had a powerful ally there: Howard Lutnick, the billionaire CEO of the financial services firm Cantor Fitzgerald. Lutnick's company managed billions of dollars in Treasury bills that Tether claimed it had bought. Lutnick was also chairman of Donald Trump's 2024 transition team and was floated as a potential Treasury secretary. With Tether under DoJ investigation, it was a potent conflict of interest that had already attracted criticism, even among the ethically loose MAGA right. Two weeks before the election, *Politico* reported, Lutnick had taken meetings on Capitol Hill about a potential Trump administration only to turn around and start talking about Cantor Fitzgerald and his crypto-related business. The brazen break with protocol earned some grousing from anonymous Trump cronies, who were in a power struggle with Lutnick over who would fill presidentially appointed positions related to finance and crypto. "You cannot do that on behalf of President Trump," one "senior Trump ally" told *Politico*.[32]

Lutnick's growing influence with Trump was one of many 2024 campaign season victories for the crypto industry. It meant that the DoJ investigation into Tether would probably go away. And it meant a potential boom for a crypto industry that needed friendly regulations and access to US banks and Wall Street cash to push Bitcoin's value ever higher.

Crypto money—and the corporate power it represented—had become one of the defining forces in the 2024 campaign. Crypto industry PACs and political organizations raised more than $245 million—far more than any other industry during the campaign cycle.[33] It seemed like someone had reactivated Sam Bankman-Fried's 2022 influence campaign, but at a bigger scale. Crypto PACs started splashing money around everywhere, including political ads that made no mention of crypto. The candidates, however, like used-car salesman Bernie Moreno, who was challenging progressive stalwart Sherrod Brown for his Ohio Senate seat, were in the tank for the industry.

Along with blanketing the country with ads, the crypto industry put together events like the "America Loves Crypto Tour," a series of free live music shows in swing states. The shows were sponsored by the Stand with Crypto Alliance PAC, which was launched by Coinbase, the publicly traded crypto exchange whose CEO Brian Armstrong had become a Capitol Hill regular. Stand with Crypto graded politicians according to their crypto friendliness and directed donations accordingly. Bernie Moreno received about $40 million in crypto industry support.[34] Recipients of industry largesse included Democrats who supported the industry's legislative and regulatory agenda. The crypto industry and its PACs were broadly pro-Trump and pro-Republican, in temperament and because the Republican Party, unlike Democrats, didn't need convincing. Republican officials were almost uniformly pro-crypto—a position that had been somehow branded as anti-state and against the polite status quo, even when the rhetoric was coming from billionaires and senators.

It was an astonishing amount of money and influence from an industry that produced very little meaningful economic activity. Crypto hadn't really caught on in the US, but the big companies and their investors seemed to have endless amounts of cash to plough into political campaigns. Portraying themselves as advocates for the millions of Americans who supposedly used crypto regularly but were oppressed by President Biden's SEC, crypto PACs ended up being responsible for almost half of all corporate donations.

The crypto industry struck me as nihilistic in pursuit of its financial interests. They didn't seem to *care* about anything beyond electing Trump and other paid-for politicians, most of them Republican, who would finally free them from the burdens imposed by the SEC, CFTC, and DoJ. The industry was peppered with sovereign citizens, anti-state libertarians, and corporatist financiers dumping worthless tokens on novice investors. Its culture tended to be misogynistic and trollish. Its product's principal use case was crime. Despite the wreckage of the 2022 crypto collapse and a downturn in retail interest, they managed to reinflate the bubble and thought that their unpopular financial program was the one we all needed to get behind.

Crypto diehards claimed to be part of a revolutionary vanguard. Their pursuit of unfettered financial freedom was in the public interest—the freedom that guaranteed all others. "Fix the money, fix the world," went one Bitcoiner mantra. The results of 15-plus years of cryptocurrencies said otherwise. So did Trump's own forays into crypto. In this election, every policy proposal seemed to come garnished with a heaping of self-interest.

21

Election Day

By November 2024, the polling between Harris and Trump was nail-bitingly close. The wish of many people to move on from the garish embarrassment of Donald Trump was powerful, and it might have contributed to Democratic complacency, a feeling that Harris's coronation was all but assured. As one MSNBC host later remarked, unintentionally reflecting the myopia of the Democratic consultant class: "It was a flawlessly run campaign. Queen Latifah never endorses anyone."[1]

Musk had poured in more than $288 million to his own PAC and other pro-Trump organizations.[2] But his overall contribution—with X, his media profile, his massive devoted following, his powerful network—was measureless. On the campaign trail, Musk merged the roles of mega-donor, surrogate, campaign strategist, celebrity endorser, and right-wing social-media influencer to a degree that made the Republican ticket as much about him and his reactionary, tech-futurist ambitions as it was about Trump.

Besides Musk, the Republican ticket attracted the usual big-money right-wing donors. While Democrats would vastly outspend Republicans—leading to questions about where exactly all that money went—the financial support from Musk, Timothy Mellon, Miriam Adelson, and others kept afloat a campaign that was also fighting numerous court battles.

Some argued that part of Musk's value was that he gave permission to other tech leaders to come out as MAGA. It's a tenuous claim—what millionaire or billionaire requires permission for anything?—but there was indeed a social shift happening, especially among the demographics of Trump supporters. Electing Trump once might be dismissed as an aberration, but a second victory, after everything that had happened, would signal that something fundamental had changed in the political firmament.

Elon Musk, David Sacks, and Marc Andreessen watched the election returns come in alongside Trump at Mar-a-Lago.[3] Musk left early, already certain that Trump would win, according to the popular podcaster Joe Rogan.

I don't need to tell you what happened next: they won. Pretty handily, actually. And this time, Trump won the popular vote. MAGA was no longer a political minority imposing itself on the rest of us, an insurgent fascistic movement attacking an ossified establishment. It was the political majority. The Republicans would hold all three branches of government, and they would have the power to remake the country's courts for a generation.

Crypto won big, too. The only industry-sponsored candidate who lost their contest was crypto attorney John Deaton, who was defeated in the Massachusetts Senate race by Elizabeth Warren, crypto's bête noire. (Dan Helmer, a Virginia Democrat running for a House seat who received almost $4 million in crypto industry support, lost his primary.[4]) Forty-eight other crypto-approved candidates won their races—a record that industry leaders wasted no time in bragging about on social media. SEC chair Gary Gensler was probably already looking for a new job. The same went for Lina Khan, the sensationally productive FTC chair who'd reinvigorated her agency's antitrust and consumer protection practices. The vice president-elect was a former venture capitalist who, as a senator only months earlier, had circulated a draft of an industry-friendly crypto regulatory bill among his Senate colleagues. Crypto CEOs could write their own ticket. Sam Bankman-Fried would have to watch his former colleagues complete his political project while serving a 25-year sentence in federal prison.

Donald Trump would get immunity, official or otherwise, for every crime he might have committed. And so would everyone around him, including his new political allies in tech and finance. The dozens of regulatory and legal investigations into Musk's empire would gently dissolve. Every criminal investigation into securities fraud by crypto companies and venture capitalists was in jeopardy. The Consumer Financial Protection Bureau's death watch had already begun.

Whatever its eventual fate as an industry, crypto did something historic: instrumentalizing our political system to get what they wanted while establishing new standards in legalized political corruption. And they did it with a brazenness that would make a Tammany Hall politician blush.

The celebration would be felt in the corridors of power in Saudi Arabia, Qatar, and the UAE. Their Musk investments were secure. They would have a friend in Trump, who was deeply beholden to the Sunni–Israeli axis that opposed Iran. In 2022, Trump's son-in-law, Jared Kushner, received $2 billion in investment capital for his private equity firm from Saudi Arabia.[5] Emirati and Qatari sovereign wealth funds also invested hundreds of millions in Kushner's firm. Qatar bailed out Kushner on a deeply indebted Manhattan office building he owned.[6] Trump was investigated for approving a potentially illegal venture to transfer nuclear technology to Saudi Arabia. The special counsel's investigation into Trump's hoarding of classified documents included subpoenas for documents concerning his business relationships with Saudi Arabia and the UAE, among other countries.[7]

For Musk and his phalanx of reactionary millionaires and billionaires, it was an unmitigated triumph. "Trump will fill his top ranks with billionaires, former CEOs, tech leaders and loyalists," *Axios* reported two days after the election. "Elon Musk, Marc Andreessen, David Sacks, Joe Lonsdale and other tech leaders are helping pick staff and drive policies to quickly expand AI, crypto and other business frontiers."[8]

They had unfettered power and influence. They were going to make so much money.

The stock market and cryptocurrencies surged. Elon Musk's estimated worth passed the $300 billion mark.[9] According to one calculation, the world's ten richest people added $64 billion to their fortunes in one day.[10]

They were proud of their accomplishments. Of course, Project 2025 was the agenda all along, crowed some conservative operators, surprising practically no one.[11] Crypto industry executives and lobbyists bragged that their influence program worked. Their money had won. They had won.

"We're just getting started," wrote Emilie Choi, the president and COO of Coinbase, over a screenshot of a *New York Times* headline about the industry's successful $135 million spending campaign.[12]

The story was the same across much of the country. The forces of techno-capital and right-wing nativism were ascendant.

In San Francisco, incumbent mayor London Breed lost to Daniel Lurie, the Levi Strauss heir whose campaign was funded by $8 million of his own money and a $1 million gift from his mother. Lurie announced that OpenAI CEO Sam Altman would help lead his transition team.[13]

Michael Moritz, the billionaire venture capitalist, had tried for years "to push a more centralized and business-friendly vision of San Francisco," as *Mission Local* described it.[14] Instead he saw a few million dollars go down the drain as Mark Farrell, who was fined $108,000 by the city's Ethics Commission for campaign finance violations one day before the election, finished fourth in the mayoral race. Proposition D, the ballot measure that would halve the number of commissions running San Francisco, became the most expensive ballot measure in city history, receiving $9.4 million in contributions, but it failed to pass.[15]

"Billionaires like Michael Moritz and Bill Obe[r]ndorf and their agenda have been completely rejected by the people of San Francisco," said Aaron Peskin, the leftist supervisor turned third-place mayoral candidate, who had become a villain in the eyes of some tech leaders.[16] Peskin announced that he planned to form a coalition of liberal and leftist organizations to fight the growing power of billionaires in San Francisco politics.[17] That included a few out-of-towners like former New York City mayor Mike Bloomberg, who donated more than $1 million in support of London Breed.[18]

For the District 5 supervisor race, Bilal Mahmood unseated Dean Preston, another leftist bogeyman despised by swaths of the tech elite. Mahmood had tech industry backing, though he diverged from them on some issues, such as his opposition to clearing homeless encampments.[19] (Mayor-elect Lurie did support that policy.)[20] In the other supervisor races, some progressives retained their seats. Several ballot measures supported by progressives, including one pushed by Aaron Sorkin to establish an inspector general for the city, were approved by voters.

The promised centrist Democratic takeover had only partially materialized. "In San Francisco, it was a mixed bag for the local tech takeover," said the journalist Gil Duran. "They didn't get everything they wanted. There are still progressives on the Board of Supervisors."[21]

For San Francisco's ultra-wealthy, it could still be deemed a victory. "It's a great outcome for San Francisco," wrote Garry Tan, saying that his side had "retaken" the Board of Supervisors. "A near clean sweep of moderate Dems."[22]

Tan celebrated the contributions of a clutch of tech-backed nonprofits like GrowSF, friendly journalists like Susan Dyer Reynolds, "and so many more allies." They had pushed the ball forward—or, more accurately, toward Tan's supposedly moderate vision. "It will still take many years," wrote Tan. "This is only the beginning."[23]

Across the Bay, California Forever may have pulled its Solano County ballot measure, but CEO Jan Sramek promised that was a mere bump in the road, a strategic decision in fact. There was little reason to doubt him. Given the billion-plus dollars invested in his project and its generational timeline, retrenchment made sense. California Forever had the land it needed and was settling with the last few holdouts whom the company had sued for price-fixing. As in San Francisco, bending local politics to their will would take more than one election cycle. A few days after the election, California Forever announced the hiring of retired Air Force general Mike

Minihan, who had been a commander at nearby Travis Air Force Base. Sramek was continuing to build out his company network, turning the initial concerns about his venture's proximity to an important Air Force base into an asset.

"Welcoming Gen. Minihan to the team will help us ensure that Travis Air Force Base and the broader community are well served by the project," Sramek said in a statement. "We're also excited to be working with him on rebuilding our defense industrial base right here in Solano County."[24]

With his law school buddy having just been elected vice president, Vivek Ramaswamy seemed on the glide path to joining Trump's inner circle. Two months before the election, he had published another book, *Truths: The Future of America First*, and announced a deal to front a show on Fox News. Like Elon Musk, Ramaswamy had moved the headquarters of his business to Texas, that tax-free bastion of American corporate freedom.

Within a week of his election victory, Trump announced that Ramaswamy and the richest man in the world would be heading something called the Department of Government Efficiency, or DOGE. It was not a real cabinet-level agency—that would take an act of Congress, and this was not so democratic an effort. Essentially, Musk and Ramaswamy's job would be to work with the Office of Management and Budget in order to recommend major cuts to government agencies, services, and personnel. They would have abundant opportunities to privatize government programs and line up their friends' companies (and their own) for lucrative government contracts.

Musk said that he could cut $2 trillion from the government's $6.75 trillion budget—an amount that would exceed all discretionary spending in any given year.[25] Ramaswamy suggested firing any non-elected government employee whose social security number ended in an odd number. That way the cuts would be so broad—and not exactly targeted—that it would avoid issues of gender or racial discrimination, he noted.[26] Eventually, he said, they could slash 75 percent of the federal workforce—an extraordinary number of people that would cripple essential services.[27] (It wasn't lost on me that the CEO who had once fired me from his company was now preparing to execute the largest mass layoff in US history.)

It seemed like a recipe for putting millions of middle-class people out of work and wrecking the economy. That, in fact, was part of the promise—to punish MAGA's enemies, who weren't billionaire robber barons or the boss with his boot on their neck. No, the people's enemies were faceless bureaucrats gumming up the works of the beautiful American capitalist machine, people who worked for departments and programs that the average American could never name. These layabouts had to be made to suffer. And they would.

It was unusual for a politician to promise to make people's lives worse and for voters to thrill to the possibility. Trump described the planned cuts as a necessary shock to the system of government.[28] Musk said that his moves would produce "temporary hardship."[29] They spoke of getting rid of waste and inefficiencies, but Musk, Ramaswamy, and their allies suggested gutting regulatory agencies like the SEC and FDA, cutting healthcare benefits for veterans, and eliminating the Department of Education. Musk was already drafting some of the same friends and advisors—Steve Davis, Antonio Gracias—who had helped him during his Twitter takeover. Now they were part of the shadow president's transition team.

A skeptic might have called their plan what the author Naomi Klein termed "disaster capitalism"—using political crises to overhaul a nation's political economy to benefit elites, exert authoritarian control over the populace, and further the neoliberal project. The oligarchy was presenting itself in the open, but for MAGA voters, who thought that these men were on their side, the possibilities were exciting. The positive vision that Peter Thiel said his allies lacked still hadn't appeared. But a better, more prosperous future was supposed to emerge from the wreckage of the administrative state.

It was hard to see the optimism in their approach. Musk and Ramaswamy would institute "drastic changes," said Trump. "Everyone's taking a haircut here," said Musk, saying the country had to "live within our means." It was clear that that "haircut" wouldn't touch Musk or his incredible wealth.[30]

What would they do with their power, these unelected change agents? They wanted low taxes, no regulation, enormous investments in AI and defense tech to "deter" China. They wanted to banish wokeness in all its forms. They wanted free-speech absolutism and an end to censorious liberalism, but they also wanted to imprison leakers and take away licenses from media organizations they resented. They wanted to prosecute advertisers for engaging in a supposed criminal conspiracy by choosing not to advertise on Elon Musk's X. They wanted an end to all regulatory and legal investigations that might harm their interests. They wanted personal liberty, so they elected a party that regulated women's bodies and was a slave to corporate power. They wanted free markets and government bailouts and perhaps a charter city in Greenland. They wanted it all—on their terms.

Thiel, who held a pro-Trump election night party at his Los Angeles mansion, seemed fully back in the Republican fold, if not elevated in his influence. After promising to sit out the 2024 election, he had reportedly made a multimillion-dollar donation to a Republican organization and he made sure Trump knew it. Now, Thiel could have a second hack at undermining the state that he continued to profit from as a security contractor. One of his mentees, JD Vance, was a heartbeat away from the presidency. Other members of Thiel's network would find jobs throughout the administration and the military and intelligence apparatus. His companies would surely prosper.

Elon Musk, Thiel's friend and former PayPal colleague, was acting as the potential dictatorial CEO figure that Curtis Yarvin had forecast as an American savior who would put an end to the failed democratic experiment. The day after the election, Musk joined Trump on a call with embattled Ukrainian president Volodymyr Zelensky. (Russian president Vladimir Putin, who according to the *Wall Street Journal* and political scientist Ian Bremmer talked regularly with Musk, might have been interested in what they discussed. Musk denied Bremmer's report that he and

Putin spoke regularly.)[31,32] He spent most days by Trump's side at Mar-a-Lago, receiving high-level briefings, advising on presidential appointments, and sitting in on calls with world leaders. Trump's family took to calling him Uncle Elon.

Musk vowed that his America PAC would stay in business, spending big in the midterm elections and supporting challengers to Republican politicians who were not sufficiently supportive of Trump's agenda. America PAC may have caught flak for its subcontractors mistreating canvassers, its ads targeting certain ethnic and religious groups with opposing messages, and running what the Philadelphia district attorney alleged was an illegal lottery, but there were no real consequences for these actions. Except victory.

Musk's underwater X investment now seemed like an invaluable political tool. Many X users had noted the platform's increasing rightward tilt, encouraged by various feature changes and by Musk himself in his ability to generate trending topics and shape discourse. The "For You" tab on X had become filled with Musk's own posts and those of his ideological allies. A post-election computational analysis by two scholars found that Musk's tweets showed a "significant increase" in views and engagement beginning around July 13, 2024—the day that Musk formally endorsed Trump. Similarly, a group of prominent Republican-aligned accounts showed a boost in views, leading the study's authors to believe that X instituted "platform-level changes that influenced engagement metrics" for the accounts they studied.[33]

Across corporate America, CEOs quickly fell in line. Those who weren't outright Trumpists might have felt that they were being released from the Democratic Party's social expectations. Having already tamped down on employees' political protests, they would no longer donate to Black Lives Matter organizations or demonstrate patience when faced with labor unrest. They could be shameless again.

"Big congratulations to our 45th and now 47th President on an extraordinary political comeback and decisive victory," wrote Jeff Bezos,[34] whose companies competed for rocket, cloud computing, and tech services contracts. Bezos had already telegraphed his acquiescence by canning the *Washington Post*'s planned endorsement of Kamala Harris. (A few months later, Bezos neutered the paper's op-ed department, limiting the range of acceptable publishable opinions.)

The endorsement was not of great importance; Bezos's intervention was. It precipitated hundreds of thousands of subscription cancellations and undermined the newspaper's editorial independence. But it sent the intended message to Trump. Now that Trump had won, Bezos could find some relief in the fact that he hadn't chipped away at his prized newspaper's authority for nothing. There were contracts to be won.

"No nation has bigger opportunities," wrote Bezos. "Wishing @realDonaldTrump all success in leading and uniting the America we all love."[35]

The terrain had been ceded. Now wasn't the time for counter-revolution. "Big Tech's Hotbeds of Employee Activism Quiet After Trump's Victory," read a headline from the *New York Times*.[36]

In what seemed like a powerful exemplar of the political realignment taking place, Donald Trump Jr. announced that he was going to work for 1789 Capital, an "anti-woke" venture capital firm founded by longtime Republican donor Rebekah Mercer, conservative investor Omeed Malik, and Chris Buskirk, who co-founded the Rockbridge Network—the right-wing tech donor organization—with JD Vance.[37] 1789 Capital had already invested in Tucker Carlson's post-Fox News venture, and the firm planned to help build out the "parallel economy" of conservative companies and institutions that were becoming popular on the right.

In the course of my years of reporting I had come to believe that the tech industry's social liberalism had always been a thin veneer, worn away over time by sexism, an authoritarian culture that revered male founders and CEOs, the desire for power, and the ruthless pursuit of profit. By acquiescing to Trump, a corporatist demagogue who would lower their taxes, hand them contracts, and axe pesky regulations, tech could be immune to the imposition of politics, just like Thiel had always wanted. Or that was the hope.

They could pour hundreds of billions of dollars into AI and crypto and autonomous weapons systems, with only the hallowed free market to guide them.

The hosannas poured out from across the tech industry.

"Congratulations to President @realDonaldTrump on his decisive victory," wrote Alphabet CEO Sundar Pichai on November 6. "We are in a golden age of American innovation and are committed to working with his administration to help bring the benefits to everyone."[38]

It's hard to know what Pichai, an Indian immigrant who had ascended to the top of corporate America to lead a company that employed more than 182,000 people and had once been famous for its "don't be evil" motto, was thinking as he published that post to his 5.4 million followers. Donald Trump was promising mass deportations beginning on day one, a policy that could materially affect the tech industry, if not prick its conscience. Sergey Brin, the Google co-founder, protested Trump's original Muslim ban—in person, at San Francisco airport—but had since mostly retreated from view, returning to Google headquarters to work quietly on AI projects. Pichai was the face of Google now, and he was fabulously wealthy and widely respected. He could have said anything he wanted.

But Google had changed. The company had cracked down on internal dissent, firing dozens of employees for silent protests against Google's contracts with the Israeli government. The conglomerate now known as Alphabet was in the middle of a grueling antitrust case that could lead to the partial breakup of the company, and Pichai couldn't be sure that the new Trump administration would be any friendlier than Biden had been. Two months earlier, Trump had said that Google should be prosecuted for "illegally" showing critical stories about him in search results. Soon after that, Trump said that he was worried that a breakup would "destroy" Google and give a leg up to China.[39] There was no telling what a volatile, inattentive president might do.

It was just an X post, but it reflected Pichai's sensitive political position going forward. The old Google was gone. The old Silicon

Valley was gone. Many of Pichai's peers had already congratulated Trump on his reelection, if not actively supported it. And he undoubtedly knew that one person was watching—maybe the only person to whom the esteemed Google chief would ever have to answer besides the president himself.

The response came less than an hour later. "Cool," wrote Elon Musk.[40]

The next month, Pichai would make the pilgrimage to Mar-a-Lago bearing a $1 million corporate gift for Trump's inauguration. Many tech companies and CEOs also made financial contributions. Jeff Bezos gave Melania Trump a $40 million Amazon documentary deal. That agreement was part of an unprecedented post-election flood of cash moving from private industry directly to the president and his family—some $80 million, according to the *Wall Street Journal*, "as defendants settle lawsuits the president previously filed against them and corporations enter into new business ventures."[41]

Pichai was far from the only CEO to hash out business with the new president at his Florida compound—with the now politically ubiquitous Elon Musk sitting across the table. But Pichai's visit was notable for who came with him: Google co-founder Sergey Brin.[42] The former refugee and idealistic startup founder who had protested Trump's Muslim ban had come full circle. It was time to do business again.

Epilogue

When President Joe Biden left office in January 2025, he devoted his farewell address to the problem of American oligarchy:

> Today, an oligarchy is taking shape in America of extreme wealth, power and influence that literally threatens our entire democracy. Our basic rights and freedoms. And a fair shot for everyone to get ahead.[1]

Like President Dwight D. Eisenhower warning the public about "the acquisition of unwarranted influence, whether sought or unsought, by the military-industrial complex," Biden was alerting the people to a political concern that had become a crisis under his watch. The parallels were explicit: invoking Eisenhower's example, Biden said that he was "equally concerned about the potential rise of a tech-industrial complex that could pose real dangers for our country as well."[2]

Now, Biden was handing off the presidency to the very oligarch he had called a threat to democracy. And he would do it with a smile on his face, telling Trump in a White House visit, "Welcome home." Biden's solicitousness toward Trump went beyond politesse, and it revealed his own complicity in the problem he was warning about. Oligarchy had become bipartisan. This was just another wing of the ruling elite taking back the keys.

The oligarchs received their due rewards. Many of the men listed in this book took up positions in the US government or advised Trump on presidential appointments. Playing the role of Goldman Sachs in the Obama days, Andreessen Horowitz began supplying staffers who would be appointed throughout Trump's new administration. Managing partner Scott Kupor was appointed director of the Office of Personnel Management. General partner Sriram Krishnan was named a senior policy advisor for AI.

Jacob Helberg, the China hawk and Palantir advisor, was named the State Department's Under Secretary of State for Economic Growth, Energy, and the Environment. Michael Kratsios, who had worked for various Peter Thiel ventures, became director of the White House Office of Science and Technology Policy. The new SEC chair would be Paul Atkins, a crypto industry consultant.

David Sacks, now a top Trump advisor, was appointed as AI and crypto czar, a position from which he would push Trump to sign an executive order establishing a strategic cryptocurrency reserve that would boost the value of crypto investments made by Sacks and his friends.

Vivek Ramaswamy was treated as the co-head of DOGE, but he seemed to wear out his welcome with Trump and Musk. Offering them his polite support, Ramaswamy officially bowed out of the administration to run for governor in his home state of Ohio.

Elon Musk was the shadow president—or perhaps simply the president, at least until his 130-day term as a "special government employee" was up. Perhaps unsurprisingly, Musk and Trump's relationship fell apart around this time, as the two began criticizing and threatening each one another on social media. But immeasurable damage had been done. And there was more to come. As Joe Lonsdale said on CNBC in June 2020, "we still have a lot of our smartest friends working at DOGE."

Musk had worked to make sure that his influence would last beyond his time in government, particularly regarding the adoption of AI systems from xAI, Palantir, and other favored government contractors. Musk was now widely referred to as the most powerful private citizen in the world. Featuring a cadre of aggressive young coders, lawyers, and tech executives, DOGE immediately began gutting government departments, conducting mass firings, cutting off congressionally appropriated payments, and working its way into core federal logistical, financial, and human resources systems. Panic spread throughout the federal workforce as anything resembling "wokeness" or identity politics was deleted from government websites. The axe came for everything from cancer research to park rangers to weather stations. Federal employees were asked to submit lists of their weekly accomplishments, which would be fed into AI to judge whether they needed to stay in their jobs. In an effort to bypass labor and civil service protections, probationary employees—people who had just been hired or promoted or moved from another agency—were fired en masse. Some were hastily brought back after core government functions began to degrade.

Constitutional scholars accused Musk of launching an administrative coup against the state. It was hard to fault their analysis.

Musk was doing to the federal government almost note-for-note what he had done to Twitter. His slapdash program to purge the federal bureaucracy of the woke mind virus was even led by some of the same people, like Boring Company executive Steve Davis, who had slept at Twitter HQ during Musk's takeover. The ideologically driven austerity program—anti-woke, pro-privatization, faux populist in presenting the world's richest man as the only person who could properly root out waste and corruption—was pretty much the same.

Twitter/X survived Musk's authoritarian revolution—if at a great cost to the site's stability, culture, and usability, and with an assist from Musk's financial backers. After Trump's inauguration, Musk engineered the sale of X to his other company xAI. The deal was an all-stock deal, meaning no money changed hands. The list of X owners I had worked to unseal were now shareholders in xAI, and the social network's finances would be further obscured. X might have been a money-loser, but now it had been rolled into another one of Musk's bets. It didn't matter that X was in a sorry state, or that it lost money, as long as it could now feed data into xAI's artificial intelligence models. And when Musk did need money, he found it from the same reliable group of investors, with xAI raising billions of dollars in fresh capital in 2025.[3]

The federal government was a far more complicated and important interlocking set of institutions. The financial jiujitsu around X wasn't much of an issue for the public. X going down for an hour would be no big deal. If a round of Social Security checks failed to go out, people would die.

We had been so conditioned to expect the worst of government—and so repeatedly failed by our elected officials—that many accepted Musk's reckoning with resignation, if not enthusiasm. In six months as the unofficial head of DOGE, he took a wrecking ball to America's governing institutions, leaving behind incalculable and probably irreparable damage. And he did it without provoking much meaningful opposition, much less the kind of civic uprising the moment called for. One tragedy of Musk's victory was that it seemed to come so easily to him.

Certainly we could do better than this whirligig of a man to dig us out of the rut of societal stagnation, decline, corruption, and mistrust. But we would have to find a way to build that world. For now, we live in Elon Musk's.

Acknowledgements

Thank you to Liz and the kids, Harry, Scott, Loretta, Gary, Rachel, the ghosts of my grandparents, Adam Chandler, Tomasz Hoskins and everyone at Bloomsbury, Eric Lupfer, Reporters Committee for Freedom of the Press, Grayson Clary, Katie Townsend, Ben Wizner, Paris Marx, Edward Ongweso Jr., Ethan Brown, Molly White, Brendan Byrne, Chris Lehmann, Robin Kaiser Schatzlein, Alex Shephard, Ryu Spaeth, Mehdi Hasan, Ash Carter, Spike Carter, Sam Seder, Emma Vigeland, Taylor Lorenz, Imogen Birchard, Christian Lorentzen, Becca Schuh, Dan, Brace Belden, Liz Franczak, Yung Chomsky, Eli Valley, Tony Tulathimutte, Matt Farwell, Evan Hughes, Mike Schapira, Matt Levitt, David Kasirer, Jonathan Kichaven, Adam Boorstin, Ajay Sharma, Michael Libby, Jon Rubenstein, Amrit Dhir, Kyle Berkman, Phil Merkow, David Greenwald, James Block, Zeke Faux, Gabriel Levin, Elizabeth King, Brian Merchant, Arman Safa, Max Chafkin, Justin, Amy Castor, David Gerard, Alex Yablon, Nelson Rauda Zablah, Gil Duran, Ryu Spaeth, Barrett Brown, Jathan Sadowski, Tim Barker, Zach Webb, Chris Shinn, Lips Café, and Jason Greenberg. Thank you (and I'm sorry) to anyone I forgot. Finally, with special gratitude, thank you to those who cannot be named.

Notes

INTRODUCTION

1. https://www.nytimes.com/2025/01/24/world/europe/elon-musk-roman-salute-nazi.html
2. https://www.nytimes.com/2023/06/27/us/politics/vivek-ramaswamy-wealth.html
3. https://www.oilandgas360.com/edenver22-strive-asset-management/
4. https://www.newyorker.com/magazine/2022/12/19/vivek-ramaswamy-the-ceo-of-anti-woke-inc
5. https://www.nbcnews.com/politics/2024-election/vivek-ramaswamy-dropping-2024-presidential-race-rcna133875
6. https://www.instagram.com/reel/CwT8plzItSA/
7. https://prospect.org/blogs-and-newsletters/tap/2023-10-05-invading-mexico-destroy-drug-cartels-heres-how/
8. https://x.com/elonmusk/status/1011666426715766784
9. https://www.yahoo.com/entertainment/ron-160337517.html
10. https://x.com/elonmusk/status/1762567210172911863?lang=en
11. https://x.com/elonmusk/status/1760677431961407672

CHAPTER 1: DECEMBER 14, 2016

1. https://www.washingtonpost.com/politics/trump-recorded-having-extremely-lewd-conversation-about-women-in-2005/2016/10/07/3b9ce776-8cb4-11e6-bf8a-3d26847eeed4_story.html
2. https://www.nytimes.com/2016/10/16/technology/peter-thiel-donald-j-trump.html
3. https://www.vox.com/recode/2021/1/13/22228203/doug-leone-donald-trump-sequoia-capital-capitol-riot
4. https://www.nytimes.com/2016/10/16/technology/peter-thiel-donald-j-trump.html
5. https://www.washingtonpost.com/politics/2022/05/20/larry-ellison-oracle-trump-election-challenges/

CHAPTER 2: THIEL AND THE NEW ALIGNMENT

1. https://www.theatlantic.com/politics/archive/2023/11/peter-thiel-2024-election-politics-investing-life-views/675946/
2. https://www.theatlantic.com/politics/archive/2023/11/peter-thiel-2024-election-politics-investing-life-views/675946/
3. https://www.theverge.com/2023/11/29/23981928/elon-musk-ad-boycott-go-fuck-yourself-destroy-x
4. https://x.com/elonmusk/status/1240754657263144960?lang=en
5. https://www.cnn.com/2020/04/17/tech/elon-musk-ventilators-california/index.html
6. https://x.com/elonmusk/status/1255386895145672705
7. https://www.nytimes.com/2020/05/09/business/coronavirus-elon-musk-tesla-california.html
8. https://x.com/elonmusk/status/1259945593805221891
9. https://www.washingtonpost.com/technology/2020/05/13/tesla-alameda-reopen-plant/
10. https://x.com/DavidSacks/status/1720886430858465560

CHAPTER 3: TECH LIBERTARIANS EMBRACE THE SECURITY STATE

1. https://www.techtransparencyproject.org/articles/eric-schmidt-obamas-chief-corporate-ally
2. https://www.wired.com/story/eric-schmidt-is-building-the-perfect-ai-war-fighting-machine/
3. https://defensescoop.com/2023/09/08/eric-schmidt-led-panel-pushing-for-new-defense-experimentation-unit-to-drive-military-adoption-of-generative-ai/
4. https://www.techtransparencyproject.org/articles/eric-schmidt-cozies-up-to-chinas-ai-industry-while
5. https://www.politico.com/newsletters/digital-future-daily/2024/05/09/dcs-new-ai-matchmaker-eric-schmidt-00157117
6. https://www.politico.com/news/2024/05/01/alex-karp-hill-summit-trump-00155571
7. https://www.cnbc.com/2024/03/13/palantir-ceo-short-sellers-pull-down-us-companies-to-pay-for-coke.html
8. https://www.youtube.com/watch?v=umANP9Ev2B4
9. https://www.politico.com/news/2024/05/01/alex-karp-hill-summit-trump-00155571
10. https://www.businessinsider.com/palantir-ceo-alex-karp-columbia-anti-protests-pagan-north-korea-2024-5
11. https://www.washingtonpost.com/politics/2024/05/14/trump-donors-tech-jacob-helberg/
12. https://www.politico.com/news/2024/05/01/alex-karp-hill-summit-trump-00155571
13. https://cloud.google.com/gov/federal-defense-and-intel
14. https://time.com/6966102/google-contract-israel-defense-ministry-gaza-war/

15 https://theintercept.com/2024/05/01/google-amazon-nimbus-israel-weapons-arms-gaza/
16 https://www.cnn.com/2024/04/23/tech/google-fires-employees-protest-israel/index.html
17 https://www.washingtonpost.com/opinions/2023/05/12/microchips-us-taiwan-strategy/
18 https://x.com/ElbridgeColby/status/1761514916224139737
19 https://x.com/ElbridgeColby/status/1654868358012051459
20 https://techcrunch.com/2024/10/01/palmer-luckey-every-country-needs-a-warrior-class-excited-to-enact-violence-on-others-in-pursuit-of-good-aims/?guccounter=1
21 https://theluddite.org/post/mark-rober.html
22 https://www.wired.com/story/big-interview-trae-stephens-has-built-ai-weapons-and-worked-for-donald-trump-as-he-sees-it-jesus-would-approve/
23 https://www.newcomer.co/p/the-investor-who-called-defense-techs
24 https://www.nbcnews.com/tech/tech-news/thousands-contracts-highlight-quiet-ties-between-big-tech-u-s-n1233171
25 https://x.com/wolfejosh/status/1775729869986373651; https://x.com/wolfejosh/status/1786040878886248819
26 https://x.com/wolfejosh/status/1788977268418900237

CHAPTER 4: THE DIGITAL AUTHORITARIAN STYLE

1 https://www.ft.com/content/cfbfa1e8-d8f8-42b9-b74c-dae6cc6185a0
2 https://www.jpost.com/american-politics/article-783552
3 https://x.com/elonmusk/status/1618744590311501825?lang=en
4 https://www.theguardian.com/technology/2023/dec/01/tesla-swedish-unions-elon-musk
5 https://freespeechproject.georgetown.edu/tracker-entries/elon-musk-fires-twitter-employees-for-criticizing-him/
6 https://fortune.com/2022/11/16/elon-musk-email-twitter-extremely-hardcore-long-hours-high-intensity/
7 https://www.bbc.com/news/technology-64871183
8 https://www.eeoc.gov/newsroom/eeoc-sues-tesla-racial-harassment-and-retaliation
9 http://nytimes.com/2022/08/12/technology/nimby-housing-silicon-valley-atherton.html
10 https://x.com/pmarca/status/1520598108299612166
11 https://x.com/pmarca/status/1520617540052938752
12 https://www.wsj.com/articles/SB10001424052702304549504579316913982034286
13 https://www.newyorker.com/business/currency/tom-perkins-and-schadenfreude-in-silicon-valley
14 https://www.foxnews.com/politics/ramaswamy-pence-clash-after-former-vp-calls-gop-newcomer-rookie-this-isnt-complicated
15 https://x.com/VivekGRamaswamy/status/1749149017122934787

16 https://x.com/jack/status/1518772756069773313
17 https://x.com/pmarca/status/1520214716144316416
18 https://x.com/pmarca/status/1520214716144316416
19 https://x.com/DavidSacks/status/1798883245670707465

CHAPTER 5: KILLING TWITTER, BUILDING X

1 https://arstechnica.com/tech-policy/2023/09/musks-unpaid-bills-dozens-of-lawsuits-try-to-force-twitter-aka-x-to-pay-up/
2 https://www.reuters.com/technology/space/musks-spacex-is-quick-build-texas-slow-pay-its-bills-2024-05-13/
3 https://x.com/pmarca/status/1774547701516152889?lang=en
4 https://www.nytimes.com/2022/11/18/opinion/twitter-yoel-roth-elon-musk.html
5 https://archive.md/SowZ9#selection-1429.0-1429.110
6 https://www.nytimes.com/2023/09/18/opinion/trump-elon-musk-twitter.html
7 https://www.nytimes.com/2023/09/18/opinion/trump-elon-musk-twitter.html
8 https://www.nytimes.com/2023/09/18/opinion/trump-elon-musk-twitter.html
9 https://www.bbc.com/news/world-us-canada-50695593
10 https://techcrunch.com/2022/12/14/elon-jet-the-twitter-account-tracking-elon-musks-flights-was-permanently-suspended/?guccounter=1&guce_referrer=aHR0cHM6Ly93d3cuZ29vZ2xlLmNvbS8&guce_referrer_sig=AQAAADZxhzMMV9hR668I3GKqRRFyou62CSjAo2EoOEu8Q7cPUmfhF_7z1FJ7DFGIGhgxZ-IoING_A2ZXlJNy1UESNZXOoHpeDHtkhdOqwQRZ-CzXhOtLoXQeLlHv94StjXvLGAn2U-Is2MyuUfz9h-KyqnILRrcCL9A7N-RMoVFyG7Bp
11 https://www.washingtonpost.com/media/2022/12/15/twitter-journalists-suspended-musk/
12 https://www.cnn.com/2024/10/23/business/elon-musk-nazi-jokes/index.html
13 https://www.rollingstone.com/culture/culture-news/musk-holocaust-public-workers-union-1235296401/
14 https://www.france24.com/en/live-news/20230419-stamp-of-approval-twitter-s-musk-amplifies-misinformation
15 https://www.reuters.com/world/white-house-condemns-musk-spreading-hideous-antisemitic-lies-2023-11-17/
16 https://www.nytimes.com/2022/10/30/business/musk-tweets-hillary-clinton-pelosi-husband.html
17 https://www.cnn.com/2023/11/20/tech/elon-musk-boosting-pizzagate-conspiracy-theory
18 https://www.cnn.com/2024/09/03/media/elon-musk-x-kamala-harris-trump-misinformation/index.html
19 https://www.theverge.com/2023/2/14/23600358/elon-musk-tweets-algorithm-changes-twitter
20 https://www.theverge.com/2023/2/14/23600358/elon-musk-tweets-algorithm-changes-twitter

21 https://www.theverge.com/2023/2/14/23600358/elon-musk-tweets-algorithm-changes-twitter
22 https://www.theverge.com/2023/2/14/23600358/elon-musk-tweets-algorithm-changes-twitter
23 https://x.com/elonmusk/status/1683656350046232578
24 https://x.com/elonmusk/status/1849718117297246377
25 https://apnews.com/article/twitter-musk-texas-mall-shooting-misleading-claims-c297797d1ebof708cc84d05e0735d8cc
26 https://www.washingtonpost.com/arts-entertainment/2023/05/16/george-soros-elon-musk-adl/
27 https://x.com/elonmusk/status/1724908287471272299?s=20
28 https://x.com/elonmusk/status/1527748229470646272
29 https://x.com/elonmusk/status/1527747040181280448
30 https://www.nbcnews.com/nbc-out/out-news/libs-tik-tok-bomb-threats-oklahoma-library-committee-rcna135369
31 https://www.nytimes.com/2025/02/26/us/politics/elon-musk-doge-x-accounts-activists.html
32 https://x.com/eddie1perez/status/1783457163777646919
33 https://www.theverge.com/2023/11/29/23981928/elon-musk-ad-boycott-go-fuck-yourself-destroy-x
34 https://www.bbc.com/news/world-us-canada-64790657

CHAPTER 6: THE SAUDI INFLUENCE BEHIND TWITTER AND X

1 Author interview with Ali Al Ahmed.
2 Author interview with Areej Al Sadhan.
3 https://www.bbc.com/news/world-middle-east-53677869
4 https://www.vox.com/technology/2023/5/1/23702451/silicon-valley-saudi-money-khashoggi
5 https://www.nytimes.com/2016/06/02/technology/uber-investment-saudi-arabia.html
6 https://edition.cnn.com/2018/10/15/investing/saudi-arabia-global-investments/index.html
7 https://www.wsj.com/articles/saudi-backlash-threatens-u-s-startups-1539707574
8 Author interview with Nader Hashemi.
9 https://www.thedailybeast.com/trumps-publisher-pal-puts-saudi-propaganda-magazine-in-us-supermarkets
10 Author interview with Nader Hashemi.
11 Author interview with Areej Al Sadhan.
12 https://www.cnn.com/2024/05/03/americas/canada-sikh-nijjar-assassination-suspects-intl-latam/index.html
13 https://www.newarab.com/analysis/meet-saudi-mastermind-behind-twitter-spy-scandal
14 https://techcrunch.com/2022/09/13/twitter-whistleblower-mudge-congress/

NOTES

15 https://www.npr.org/2024/10/16/g-s1-28620/texas-judge-elon-musk-x-case-tesla-shares

CHAPTER 7: LEARNING TO HATE THE PLACE YOU LOVE

1 https://www.theinformation.com/articles/in-keith-rabois-silicon-valley-nice-guys-finish-last
2 https://www.theatlantic.com/technology/archive/2013/01/square-keith-rabois-sexual-harrassment/319003/
3 https://www.bizjournals.com/sanfrancisco/blog/2013/01/rabois-odd-anti-gay-slurs-at-stanford.html
4 https://enewspaper.latimes.com/infinity/article_share.aspx?guid=7d571eb8-2efa-4ebd-ae9b-ee59f68191a2
5 https://x.com/elonmusk/status/1658334514462982144
6 https://x.com/elonmusk/status/1642269842555142150
7 https://www.cnbc.com/2021/02/03/chamath-palihapitiya-says-hes-not-running-for-california-governor.html
8 https://davidsacks.medium.com/the-killer-d-a-54d4c4a5135f
9 https://www.youtube.com/watch?v=jaz4RShoqPw
10 https://www.businessinsider.com/silicon-valley-venture-capitalists-at-front-lines-california-recall-2021-5
11 https://www.youtube.com/watch?v=JCJ8EwNPmEI
12 https://x.com/ianbremmer/status/1579941475613229056?lang=en
13 https://www.cnn.com/2022/10/11/business/elon-musk-ian-bremmer-putin-ukraine-intl-hnk/index.html
14 https://podcasts.apple.com/us/podcast/crime-and-chesa-boudins-recall-and-elon-musks/id1532976305?i=1000565554174
15 https://www.rollingstone.com/culture/culture-news/meth-dog-poop-san-francisco-twitter-1234578291/
16 https://www.gofundme.com/f/report-on-chesa-boudin-san-francisco-crime
17 https://x.com/Jason/status/1367933210156404736
18 https://x.com/Jason/status/1673102313945440256
19 https://x.com/davidsacks/status/1455700342981545986?lang=en
20 https://x.com/elonmusk/status/1754999578619707658
21 https://x.com/elonmusk/status/1754978858204385764
22 https://x.com/CNBC/status/1732430744016810431
23 https://www.nationalreview.com/news/peter-thiel-urges-gop-to-move-beyond-nihilist-negation-adopt-positive-agenda-for-america/
24 https://www.nbcnews.com/politics/politics-news/tulsi-gabbard-announces-leaving-democratic-party-rcna51659
25 https://www.sfchronicle.com/bayarea/article/S-F-Mayor-Breed-apologizes-for-comments-about-17523048.php

CHAPTER 8: BILLIONAIRES V. THE PEOPLE OF SAN FRANCISCO

1. https://x.com/elonmusk/status/1794034057824846126
2. https://www.nytimes.com/2024/03/29/business/garry-tan-san-francisco-politics.html
3. https://missionlocal.org/2024/01/garry-tan-death-wish-sf-supervisors/
4. https://img.sfist.com/2024/01/tan-apology.jpg
5. https://www.sfchronicle.com/sf/article/sf-garry-tan-x-threatening-peskin-police-report-18637813.php
6. https://sfist.com/2024/01/31/three-sf-supervisors-say-theyve-received-death-threat-mailers-after-garry-tans-die-slow-tweet/
7. https://www.nytimes.com/2024/03/29/business/garry-tan-san-francisco-politics.html
8. https://missionlocal.org/2024/08/susan-dyer-reynolds-former-marina-times-editor-subject-of-ethics-complaint/
9. https://x.com/garrytan/status/1797420809017041321
10. https://x.com/SusanDReynolds/status/1797410462142976439
11. https://x.com/garrytan/status/1796554990812868637
12. https://x.com/garrytan/status/1799062865351188870
13. Author interview with Gil Duran.
14. Author interview with Gil Duran.
15. https://www.nytimes.com/2024/03/29/business/garry-tan-san-francisco-politics.html
16. Author interview with Gil Duran.
17. https://www.nytimes.com/2024/03/29/business/garry-tan-san-francisco-politics.html
18. Author interview with Gil Duran.
19. https://x.com/elonmusk/status/1770806158497906916
20. https://x.com/elonmusk/status/1799869666946437156
21. https://www.washingtonpost.com/climate-environment/2020/02/23/meet-anti-greta-young-youtuber-campaigning-against-climate-alarmism/
22. https://www.npr.org/2025/01/27/nx-s1-5276084/elon-musk-german-far-right-afd-holocaust
23. https://www.npr.org/2025/01/27/nx-s1-5276084/elon-musk-german-far-right-afd-holocaust
24. https://www.nbcnews.com/id/wbna29881495
25. https://www.politico.eu/article/fascist-visionary-jean-marie-le-pen-france-national-rally-left-wing/
26. https://x.com/jacobhelberg/status/1799914285721596313
27. https://www.cambridge.org/core/journals/perspectives-on-politics/article/testing-theories-of-american-politics-elites-interest-groups-and-average-citizens/62327F513959D0A304D4893B382B992B
28. https://www.phoenixprojectnow.com/thephoenixpapers
29. https://www.theguardian.com/us-news/2024/feb/12/san-francisco-tech-billionaires-political-influence
30. https://www.phoenixprojectnow.com/thephoenixpapers

NOTES

31 https://www.theguardian.com/us-news/2024/feb/12/san-francisco-tech-billionaires-political-influence
32 https://www.eff.org/deeplinks/2020/07/san-francisco-police-accessed-business-district-camera-network-spy-protestors
33 https://www.nytimes.com/2020/07/10/business/camera-surveillance-san-francisco.html
34 https://www.eff.org/deeplinks/2020/07/san-francisco-police-accessed-business-district-camera-network-spy-protestors
35 https://sfstandard.com/2024/03/24/chris-larsen-ripple-crypto-san-francisco-mayor-breed/
36 https://missionlocal.org/2024/02/prop-e-police-surveillance-sf/
37 https://www.sfgate.com/politics/article/billionaire-mom-gives-1m-to-son-s-sf-mayoral-race-18638051.php
38 https://x.com/garrytan/status/1849473492691149058
39 https://www.kqed.org/news/12010904/whos-pouring-millions-into-san-franciscos-expensive-mayors-race
40 https://missionlocal.org/2024/11/michael-moritz-togethersf-sf-elections-november-2024/
41 https://sfstandard.com/2024/03/24/chris-larsen-ripple-crypto-san-francisco-mayor-breed/
42 https://sfstandard.com/2024/03/24/chris-larsen-ripple-crypto-san-francisco-mayor-breed/
43 Author interview with Gil Duran.

CHAPTER 9: A WORKING MODEL

1 https://www.youtube.com/watch?v=yUh9oUEJKwo
2 http://newyorker.com/magazine/2023/02/13/the-astonishing-transformation-of-austin
3 https://reason.com/podcast/2024/04/03/why-palantir-cofounder-joe-lonsdale-left-california-for-texas/
4 https://www.nytimes.com/2015/02/15/magazine/the-stanford-undergraduate-and-the-mentor.html
5 https://www.wsj.com/business/elon-musk-illegal-drugs-e826a9e1
6 https://ciceroinstitute.org/issues/homelessness/
7 https://blog.joelonsdale.com/p/banning-street-camping-gets-people
8 https://nypost.com/2023/12/02/opinion/this-is-how-to-make-homelessness-policy-work/
9 https://www.usatoday.com/story/news/investigations/2019/04/03/alec-american-legislative-exchange-council-model-bills-republican-conservative-devos-gingrich/3162357002/
10 https://www.yahoo.com/news/texas-based-think-tank-upended-110000565.html
11 https://x.com/JTLonsdale/status/1770588244238876858
12 https://blog.joelonsdale.com/p/floridas-homelessness-revolution
13 https://ciceroinstitute.org/confronting-homelessness/

14 https://www.scotusblog.com/2024/06/justices-uphold-laws-targeting-homelessness-with-criminal-penalties/
15 https://therevolvingdoorproject.org/amicus-spotlight-city-of-grants-pass-oregon-v-johnson/
16 https://blog.joelonsdale.com/p/victory-at-the-supreme-court
17 https://apnews.com/article/homelessness-lawsuit-grants-pass-oregon-6aad769dafb15acd52175f2c2a206c29
18 https://www.bloomberg.com/news/articles/2024-06-28/what-the-supreme-court-encampments-decision-means-for-homeless-people
19 https://sfstandard.com/2024/07/15/sideshow-crash-market-street-bike-shop-closing/
20 https://x.com/JTLonsdale/status/1813000586041958440
21 https://x.com/JTLonsdale/status/1813057507754983820
22 https://apnews.com/article/california-newsom-homeless-los-angeles-san-francisco-5b2b3aca9ca56efb444a717d278c1fd9
23 https://www.foxla.com/news/newsom-puts-gloves-personally-help-clean-up-la-county-homeless-camp

CHAPTER 10: FINDING THE EXIT

1 https://twitter.com/elonmusk/status/1840635899014484163
2 https://conversationswithtyler.com/episodes/peter-thiel-political-theology/
3 https://www.newyorker.com/magazine/2016/10/10/sam-altmans-manifest-destiny
4 https://techcrunch.com/2024/03/02/vc-trae-stephens-says-he-has-a-bunker-and-much-more-in-talk-about-founders-fund-and-anduril/
5 https://www.cato-unbound.org/2009/04/13/peter-thiel/education-libertarian/
6 https://www.businessinsider.com/google-ceo-larry-page-wants-a-place-for-experiments-2013-5
7 https://www.npr.org/2024/02/28/1232564250/billionaire-benioff-buys-hawaii-land-salesforce
8 https://www.wsj.com/tech/salesforce-ceo-marc-benioff-makes-150-million-donation-to-hawaii-hospitals-7b09ef59
9 https://www.cato-unbound.org/2009/04/13/peter-thiel/education-libertarian/
10 https://www.nytimes.com/2024/08/28/magazine/prospera-honduras-crypto.html
11 https://www.nytimes.com/2023/12/12/style/praxis-city-dryden-brown.html
12 https://www.crunchbase.com/organization/praxissociety
13 https://www.wired.com/story/a-lawsuit-from-backers-of-a-startup-city-could-bankrupt-honduras/
14 https://www.state.gov/reports/2022-investment-climate-statements/honduras/
15 https://www.hagerty.senate.gov/press-releases/2022/10/13/hagerty-and-cardin-urge-state-department-to-encourage-honduras-to-honor-legal-guarantees-with-respect-to-u-s-investments/
16 https://www.theguardian.com/society/2023/apr/18/is-elon-musk-creating-a-utopian-city-the-hellish-heavenly-history-of-company-towns
17 https://www.wsj.com/articles/elon-musk-texas-town-52386513

NOTES

18 https://www.nytimes.com/2024/05/24/opinion/elon-musk-spacex-brownsville-texas.html
19 https://newrepublic.com/article/180487/balaji-srinivasan-network-state-plutocrat
20 Author interview with Gil Duran.
21 https://newrepublic.com/article/180487/balaji-srinivasan-network-state-plutocrat
22 https://www.youtube.com/watch?v=PHlcAx-IooY

CHAPTER 11: THE GREAT SOLANO COUNTY LAND GRAB

1 https://www.abc10.com/article/news/local/vacaville/farmers-refuse-sell-to-flannery-associates/103-e02f38f9-8093-43a5-8dc2-79a9b0a98ed6
2 https://fingfx.thomsonreuters.com/gfx/legaldocs/zdpxdejmlpx/Flannery%20Associates%20-%20ED%20California%20-%202023-05-18.pdf
3 https://www.nytimes.com/2023/08/25/business/land-purchases-solano-county.html
4 https://www.nytimes.com/2023/08/25/business/land-purchases-solano-county.html
5 https://x.com/NickMc1717/status/1730042262837674226
6 https://www.nytimes.com/2023/08/29/business/economy/california-land-solano-county.html
7 https://www.businessinsider.com/california-forever-jan-sramek-goldman-sachs-silicon-valley-city-future-2024-4
8 https://www.wane.com/news/who-is-behind-flannery-associates-the-mystery-california-land-buyers/amp/
9 https://www.youtube.com/watch?v=PHlcAx-IooY
10 Author interview with Nick McConnell.
11 https://eastsolanoplan.com/
12 https://www.thereporter.com/2024/03/29/california-forever-fund-uc-davis-agriculture-research/
13 https://www.thereporter.com/2024/05/16/california-forever-announce-employer-commitments/
14 https://www.thereporter.com/2024/04/18/california-forever-study-outlines-solano-gap/
15 https://www.kqed.org/news/11984830/california-forever-shells-out-2m-in-campaign-to-build-city-from-scratch
16 https://www.theguardian.com/education/2006/aug/17/schools.alevels3
17 https://web.archive.org/web/20090206083409/http://nicube.com/files/Nicube-The-Gateway.pdf
18 https://web.archive.org/web/20090206083409/http://nicube.com/files/Nicube-The-Gateway.pdf
19 https://www.standard.co.uk/hp/front/party-boy-jan-is-youngest-rising-star-in-square-mile-6758772.html
20 https://www.fnlondon.com/articles/sramek-quits-goldman-sachs-20110503
21 https://www.efinancialcareers.com/news/2011/04/has-jan-sramek-quit-goldman-for-entrepreneurship
22 https://nymag.com/intelligencer/2009/12/meet_jan_sramek_the_22-year-ol.html
23 http://anjool.co.uk/

24 https://www.independent.co.uk/news/uk/crime/stockbroker-anjool-malde-died-amid-prankmessage-investigation-1901268.html
25 https://www.thetimes.com/article/hidden-torment-of-a-champagne-suicide-jrv6tojjjxf
26 https://find-and-update.company-information.service.gov.uk/company/06833101/filing-history
27 https://medium.com/@jan_sramek
28 https://www.youtube.com/watch?v=PHlcAx-IooY
29 https://x.com/pmarca/status/1514106295770509320
30 https://a16z.com/rebuilding-the-california-dream/
31 https://www.forbes.com/sites/davidjeans/2024/04/19/gundo-bros-silicon-valley-military/?sh=387dd84752c9
32 https://www.nytimes.com/2023/11/30/business/solano-county-california-forever-city.html
33 Author interview with Jan Sramek.
34 https://www.youtube.com/watch?v=PHlcAx-IooY
35 https://www.theguardian.com/us-news/article/2024/jul/22/california-forever-silicon-valley-city-ballot-withdrawn
36 Author interview with Nick McConnell.

CHAPTER 12: IT'S FREE MONEY

1 https://nypost.com/2022/05/16/eric-adams-blockchain-for-birth-certificates-way-of-the-future/
2 https://www.coindesk.com/business/2021/11/09/citycoins-plan-for-nyccoin-is-welcomed-by-mayor-elect-adams/
3 https://podcasts.apple.com/us/podcast/beware-the-crypto-mayor/id1483871507?i=1000551061231
4 https://podcasts.apple.com/us/podcast/beware-the-crypto-mayor/id1483871507?i=1000551061231
5 https://www.brookings.edu/articles/debunking-the-narratives-about-cryptocurrency-and-financial-inclusion/
6 https://www.nytimes.com/2025/02/19/nyregion/eric-adams-quid-pro-quo.html
7 https://www.nytimes.com/2024/08/17/style/alex-karp-palantir.html
8 https://x.com/rabois/status/1331712288781344768
9 https://fortune.com/2020/11/17/keith-rabois-investor-silicon-valley-loses-another-tech-icon/
10 https://x.com/rabois/status/1474463658541412354
11 https://www.bizjournals.com/southflorida/news/2021/04/22/edmund-irvine-sells-miami-beach-spec-mansion.html
12 https://therealdeal.com/miami/2024/03/06/david-sacks-linked-to-23m-venetian-islands-sale/
13 https://www.wsj.com/articles/ken-griffin-moving-citadel-from-chicago-to-miami-following-crime-complaints-11655994600
14 https://www.reuters.com/business/hedge-fund-citadel-move-headquarters-miami-chicago-2022-06-23/

NOTES

15 https://fortune.com/2024/02/13/florida-jeff-bezos-600-million-ultra-high-net-worth-individuals-nirvana/
16 https://www.bloomberg.com/news/articles/2022-12-14/ftx-us-planned-miami-headquarters-move-before-bankruptcy
17 https://x.com/FrancisSuarez/status/1574799835777179650
18 https://www.nba.com/news/miami-heat-home-arena-gets-temporary-name-after-ftx-collapse
19 https://x.com/FrancisSuarez/status/1360241507878522883
20 https://www.sfchronicle.com/bayarea/article/Miami-tries-to-woo-Bay-Area-tech-workers-firms-15961992.php
21 https://www.miamitimesonline.com/news/local/mayor-francis-suarez-running-for-president-despite-being-under-investigation-for-possible-corruption/article_0687c4b8-0b04-11ee-a56c-f7d28c2df210.html
22 https://www.foxbusiness.com/technology/miamicoin-could-revolutionize-the-way-governments-are-funded-mayor-suarez
23 https://qz.com/2165639/miamis-mayor-backed-miamicoin-then-its-price-dropped-95-percent
24 https://www.local10.com/news/local/2023/03/22/mayor-defends-miamicoin-for-funding-citys-525m-rental-assistance-program/
25 https://protos.com/dodgy-cryptos-miamicoin-and-nyccoin-finally-get-delisted/
26 https://www.youtube.com/watch?v=YuJjYiYM4R0

CHAPTER 13: THE CRYPTO SWAMP

1 https://www.nbcnews.com/politics/2024-election/ron-desantis-presidential-campaign-twitter-problems-rcna86123
2 https://www.flgov.com/eog/news/press/2023/governor-ron-desantis-signs-first-nation-legislation-protect-against-government
3 https://www.fbba.io/understanding-floridas-cbdc-ban/
4 https://www.cnn.com/2022/12/01/politics/joel-greenberg-sentencing/index.html
5 https://www.nbcnews.com/politics/politics-news/former-jesus-christ-superstar-actor-acquitted-jan-6-charges-rcna93956
6 https://x.com/bankoferyka/status/1346823249691336708
7 https://www.miaminewtimes.com/news/miamis-eryka-gemma-remains-a-crypto-queen-despite-past-proud-boy-ties-19094875
8 https://witi.com/conferences/2019/fortlauderdale/speakers.php

CHAPTER 14: THE TAP TURNS OFF

1 https://www.nytimes.com/2025/01/17/opinion/marc-andreessen-trump-silicon-valley.html
2 https://www.wsj.com/articles/silicon-valley-bank-svb-financial-what-is-happening-299e9b65
3 https://x.com/Jason/status/1634702300345438208
4 https://x.com/Jason/status/1634792355294515200

5   https://x.com/DavidSacks/status/1634292056821764099
6   https://fortune.com/2023/03/30/how-did-silicon-valley-bank-fail-whatsapp-chats-messages-twitter/
7   https://x.com/DavidSacks/status/1635053976612933634

CHAPTER 15: THE COMPANIES SUCK

1   https://techcrunch.com/2025/02/10/ai-driven-ads-take-the-field-during-2025-super-bowl/
2   https://x.com/naval/status/1852922757249704039
3   https://x.com/EpsilonTheory/status/1853072969171423337
4   https://techcrunch.com/2024/11/22/y-combinator-often-backs-startups-that-duplicate-other-yc-companies-data-shows-its-not-just-ai-code-editors/
5   https://www.theverge.com/2024/8/14/24220658/google-eric-schmidt-stanford-talk-ai-startups-openai
6   https://time.com/6317661/eric-schmidt-drones-warfare-voices/
7   https://www.bloomberg.com/news/articles/2024-10-30/ex-google-ceo-schmidt-urges-us-army-to-replace-tanks-with-drones
8   https://www.972mag.com/israel-gaza-drones-ai/
9   https://www.972mag.com/lavender-ai-israeli-army-gaza/
10 https://www.goldmansachs.com/images/migrated/insights/pages/gs-research/gen-ai--too-much-spend,-too-little-benefit-/TOM_AI%202.0_ForRedaction.pdf
11 https://www.wsj.com/business/energy-oil/three-mile-islands-nuclear-plant-to-reopen-help-power-microsofts-ai-centers-aebfb3c8
12 https://www.statista.com/statistics/277501/venture-capital-amount-invested-in-the-united-states-since-1995/
13 https://www.wsj.com/finance/banks-sell-5-5-billion-of-x-loans-after-investor-interest-surges-4b84f89c
14 https://x.com/danprimack/status/1826069352246116826
15 https://x.com/chamath/status/1826362058121576955
16 https://www.wsj.com/articles/spac-king-chamath-palihapitiya-shuttering-two-spacs-after-failing-to-find-deals-11663674342
17 https://x.com/bigblackjacobin/status/1826385946562158858
18 https://www.cnn.com/2023/09/06/tech/huawei-mate-60-pro-phone/index.html
19 https://www.washingtonpost.com/technology/2025/01/04/huawei-export-controls-us-china-trade-chips-telecommunications/

CHAPTER 16: TIKTOK, CHINA, AND THE MONEYMAN OF THE MOMENT

1   https://www.axios.com/local/salt-lake-city/2024/05/06/senator-romney-antony-blinken-tiktok-ban-israel-palestinian-content; https://www.middleeasteye.net/news/us-tiktok-ban-linked-israel-china-insiders-reveal
2   https://www.washingtonpost.com/technology/2020/09/18/wechat-ban-faq/
3   https://trumpwhitehouse.archives.gov/presidential-actions/executive-order-addressing-threat-posed-tiktok/

NOTES

4 https://www.aclu.org/news/national-security/secret-court-opinion-reveals-mystery-tech-firm
5 https://www.theverge.com/2017/1/28/14428262/google-sergey-brin
6 https://www.washingtonpost.com/politics/2024/05/14/trump-donors-tech-jacob-helberg/?utm_source=pocket_saves
7 https://mma.prnewswire.com/media/2384252/FILE_7154.pdf?p=pdf
8 https://www.politico.com/news/2022/12/22/eric-schmidt-joe-biden-administration-00074160
9 Schmidt, who had asked the class not to quote him, later had the discussion removed from YouTube, but I found an audio-only recording that someone had shared online.
10 https://archive.ph/mLKx9
11 https://github.com/ociubotaru/transcripts/blob/main/Stanford_ECON295%E2%A7%B8CS323_I_2024_I_The_Age_of_AI%2C_Eric_Schmidt.txt
12 https://www.axios.com/2024/03/08/trump-claims-tiktok-ban-would-only-help-enemy-facebook
13 https://www.politico.com/news/2024/06/10/billionaires-learned-to-stop-worrying-and-love-trump-00162219
14 Author interview with Arielle Klagsbrun.
15 Author interview with Arielle Klagsbrun.
16 https://www.nytimes.com/2024/06/20/us/politics/timothy-mellon-trump-donation.html
17 https://www.opensecrets.org/elections-overview/biggest-donors
18 https://www.propublica.org/article/jeff-yass-susquehanna-tiktok-tax-avoidance
19 https://www.youtube.com/watch?v=Cfu_oWAuusg
20 https://www.phillymag.com/news/2016/11/15/thinkfest-jeff-yass-school-vouchers/
21 https://www.youtube.com/watch?v=mcDiN5gIrNo
22 https://fortune.com/2024/11/09/timothy-mellon-net-worth-top-donor-trump-campaign-elon-musk/
23 https://www.nbcnews.com/meet-the-press/meetthepressblog/vivek-ramaswamy-flip-flops-tiktok-rcna105062
24 https://www.congress.gov/bill/118th-congress/house-bill/7521
25 https://www.nytimes.com/2024/03/24/business/jeff-yass-shares-trump-media-merger.html
26 https://www.inquirer.com/business/jeff-yass-susquehanna-international-group-donald-trump-shares-20240508.html

CHAPTER 17: THE ROAD TO VANCE

1 https://www.bbc.com/news/articles/c3gw58wv4e9o
2 https://x.com/DavidSacks/status/1812253290803200272
3 https://x.com/shaunmmaguire/status/1812283594737619181
4 https://x.com/VivekGRamaswamy/status/1812277655271809243
5 https://x.com/elonmusk/status/1812279046715363494
6 https://x.com/VivekGRamaswamy/status/1812281734278345079

7 https://x.com/shaunmmaguire/status/1812338986683433168
8 https://x.com/elonmusk/status/1812341031373009346
9 https://x.com/shaunmmaguire/status/1798189194604634250
10 https://x.com/shaunmmaguire/status/1812284185937125484
11 https://x.com/shaunmmaguire/status/1812277653292171636
12 https://x.com/shaunmmaguire/status/1812275547516576071
13 https://www.wsj.com/politics/policy/elon-musk-political-donations-stephen-miller-desantis-39464294
14 https://www.wsj.com/politics/elections/elon-musk-has-said-he-is-committing-around-45-million-a-month-to-a-new-pro-trump-super-pac-dda53823
15 https://x.com/JamesDowell2/status/1760554891502661694
16 https://x.com/zebulgar/status/1757904339148919079
17 https://x.com/zebulgar/status/1812928216262451586?lang=en
18 https://x.com/elonmusk/status/1812932793250509144
19 https://x.com/VivekGRamaswamy/status/1812929198433964249
20 https://x.com/chamath/status/1812930312697225282
21 https://www.opensecrets.org/political-action-committees-pacs/fairshake-pac/C00835959/summary/2024
22 https://www.followthecrypto.org/
23 https://www.politico.com/news/2024/06/26/vance-crypto-00164859
24 https://www.cato-unbound.org/2009/04/13/peter-thiel-education-libertarian/
25 https://www.buzzfeednews.com/article/rosiegray/peter-thiel-donald-trump-white-nationalist-support
26 https://theintercept.com/2023/03/23/peter-thiel-jeff-thomas/
27 https://www.washingtonpost.com/technology/2023/11/12/silicon-valley-billionaire-donors-presidential-candidates/
28 https://www.cnbc.com/2024/06/27/peter-thiel-says-if-you-hold-a-gun-to-my-head-ill-vote-for-trump.html
29 https://www.youtube.com/watch?v=WToLZYlV6aA
30 https://youtu.be/euzxpbBOju8?si=zV2B8k-smZVkrFul
31 https://www.theatlantic.com/politics/archive/2023/11/peter-thiel-2024-election-politics-investing-life-views/675946/
32 https://www.msnbc.com/all-in/watch/trump-s-right-hand-guy-the-man-behind-project-2025-and-the-maga-dating-app-214614085835
33 https://thelampmagazine.com/blog/how-i-joined-the-resistance
34 https://thelampmagazine.com/blog/how-i-joined-the-resistance
35 https://www.nbcnews.com/politics/2024-election/secretive-conservative-donor-group-meets-draw-2024-plans-call-trump-rcna148899
36 https://www.nytimes.com/2024/07/17/technology/jd-vance-tech-silicon-valley.html
37 https://x.com/autismcapital/status/1852087988475564090?s=46&t=sXqcqguxdxpor12Cj4raIQ
38 https://www.cnn.com/2024/07/17/politics/kfile-jd-vance-abortion-comments
39 https://www.vice.com/en/article/jd-vance-suggests-people-in-violent-marriages-shouldnt-get-divorced/

40. https://www.reuters.com/world/us/jd-vance-once-compared-trump-hitler-now-they-are-running-mates-2024-07-15/
 41. https://x.com/NatConTalk/status/1455700807144415232

CHAPTER 18: DIDN'T THE LAST GUY GO TO PRISON?

 1. https://x.com/SBF_FTX/status/1347964322459262977?lang=en
 2. https://twitter.com/elonmusk/status/1591822387267665921
 3. https://twitter.com/DavidSacks/status/1684747280447164416
 4. https://www.justice.gov/usao-sdny/pr/united-states-attorney-announces-charges-against-ftx-founder-samuel-bankman-fried
 5. https://www.brennancenter.org/our-work/research-reports/citizens-united-explained
 6. "Zero to One" by Peter Thiel.
 7. https://www.forbes.com/sites/michaeldelcastillo/2020/10/29/leaked-tai-chi-document-reveals-binances-elaborate-scheme-to-evade-bitcoin-regulators/
 8. https://www.warren.senate.gov/oversight/letters/warren-grassley-probe-cftc-chair-behnams-interactions-and-meetings-with-sam-bankman-fried
 9. https://www.coindesk.com/business/2022/11/02/divisions-in-sam-bankman-frieds-crypto-empire-blur-on-his-trading-titan-alamedas-balance-sheet/
 10. https://twitter.com/cz_binance/status/1589283421704290306
 11. https://twitter.com/cz_binance/status/1589283430684319744
 12. https://x.com/binance/status/1590449161069268992
 13. https://x.com/binance/status/1590449164932243456
 14. https://x.com/SBF_FTX/status/1590709166515310593
 15. https://x.com/SBF_FTX/status/1590709197502812160
 16. https://apnews.com/article/sam-bankman-fried-ftx-second-trial-b01fae9f9dd69f2ac2e8bbda21d277ff
 17. Bankman-Fried sentencing hearing transcript, March 28, 2024.
 18. Bankman-Fried sentencing hearing transcript, March 28, 2024.
 19. Bankman-Fried sentencing hearing transcript, March 28, 2024.
 20. Bankman-Fried sentencing hearing transcript, March 28, 2024.
 21. Bankman-Fried sentencing hearing transcript, March 28, 2024.
 22. https://www.reuters.com/legal/ftxs-singh-agrees-plead-guilty-us-criminal-charges-lawyer-says-2023-02-28/
 23. https://www.justice.gov/usao-sdny/pr/former-ftx-executive-ryan-salame-sentenced-90-months-prison
 24. https://apnews.com/article/ftx-sam-bankman-fried-ryan-salame-crypto-f999baec34226d277bff373a8077d565
 25. https://x.com/rsalame7926/status/1820884772127961304
 26. https://x.com/rsalame7926/status/1820503049145639414
 27. https://x.com/rsalame7926/status/1820503301949198502
 28. https://www.citizen.org/news/new-complaint-to-fec-alleges-coinbase-violated-campaign-finance-laws/
 29. https://x.com/brian_armstrong/status/1801011098176405598
 30. https://www.reuters.com/technology/cybersecurity/north-korea-laundered-1475-mln-stolen-crypto-march-say-un-experts-2024-05-14/

31 https://www.wired.com/story/turmoil-black-lives-matter-political-speech-coinbase/
32 https://www.wired.com/story/turmoil-black-lives-matter-political-speech-coinbase/
33 https://x.com/brian_armstrong/status/1268622377182621696
34 https://www.motherjones.com/politics/2023/03/coinbase-racism/
35 https://www.coinbase.com/blog/coinbase-is-a-mission-focused-company
36 https://www.theblock.co/post/79247/coinbase-offers-exit-package-for-employees-not-comfortable-with-its-mission
37 https://www.businessinsider.com/coinbase-employees-leaving-after-memo-banning-activism-2020-10
38 https://bitcoinmagazine.com/culture/trump-is-the-best-choice-for-bitcoin
39 https://www.cnbc.com/2024/06/03/bitcoin-billionaire-michael-saylor-settles-dc-tax-fraud-case-for-40-million.html
40 https://www.nbcnews.com/politics/donald-trump/trump-hails-crypto-largest-bitcoin-conference-rcna163925
41 https://twitter.com/tphillips/status/1816196880050839994
42 https://x.com/nic__carter/status/1817301604627796119
43 https://x.com/nic__carter/status/1817310483445407895
44 https://www.cnbc.com/2024/08/14/schumer-says-crypto-legislation-can-pass-the-senate-this-year-on-crypto4harris-.html

CHAPTER 19: BEST TO BE LOW-KEY

1 https://www.reuters.com/markets/us/how-will-elon-musk-pay-twitter-2022-10-07/
2 https://muskmessages.com/d/42
3 https://www.washingtonpost.com/technology/2023/07/27/twitter-csam-dom-lucre-elon-musk/
4 https://x.com/elonmusk/status/1724908287471272299?lang=en
5 https://www.washingtonpost.com/technology/2024/08/21/elon-musk-x-investors/
6 https://www.cnbc.com/2024/03/20/saudi-arabia-in-talks-with-andreessen-horowitz-to-create-ai-fund.html
7 https://www.vox.com/technology/2023/5/1/23702451/silicon-valley-saudi-money-khashoggi
8 https://x.com/johnhering/status/1845449030085611902
9 https://x.com/johnhering/status/1845451901204058407
10 https://news.bitcoin.com/discuss-crypto-while-promoting-peace-have-lunch-in-paradise-with-roger-ver/
11 https://www.justice.gov/opa/pr/binance-and-ceo-plead-guilty-federal-charges-4b-resolution
12 https://www.forbes.com/sites/thomasbrewster/2024/01/10/elon-musk-fired-80-per-cent-of-twitter-x-engineers-working-on-trust-and-safety/; https://www.npr.org/2022/12/12/1142399312/twitter-trust-and-safety-council-elon-musk
13 https://muskmessages.com/d/42
14 https://www.usatoday.com/story/money/2024/10/02/x-valuation-down-fidelity/75481287007/

NOTES

15 https://muskmessages.com/d/9
16 https://x.com/elonmusk/status/1591224814597189633
17 https://www.judiciary.senate.gov/imo/media/doc/Testimony%20-%20Zatko%20-%202022-09-131.pdf
18 https://www.washingtonpost.com/us-policy/2022/11/01/musk-twitter-treasury-department-review/
19 https://www.linkedin.com/in/ssnasiri/
20 https://www.linkedin.com/posts/ssnasiri_exclusive-armada-lands-40-million-in-funding-activity-7217203909344325632-zqu4?utm_source=share&utm_medium=member_desktop&rcm=ACoAABc1uJoBVWTjxxVk15PkUmS1DfWp3g26RgI
21 https://www.cnn.com/2021/09/02/politics/haines-state-secrets-privilege-court-case/index.html; https://edition.cnn.com/2021/08/04/politics/doj-mbs-lawsuit-vendetta-aljabri/index.html
22 https://www.washingtonpost.com/us-policy/2023/02/06/twitter-musk-treasury-cfius/
23 https://www.washingtonpost.com/us-policy/2023/02/06/twitter-musk-treasury-cfius/

CHAPTER 20: SOMEONE HAS TO WIN

1 https://www.11alive.com/article/news/politics/elections/president-elect-donald-trump-victory-win-speech-full-transcript-mar-a-lago/85-288efe3f-149c-4de1-a046-2072fbcc240e
2 https://www.washingtonpost.com/technology/interactive/2025/elon-musk-business-government-contracts-funding/
3 https://x.com/levie/status/1854733432410325002
4 https://www.washingtonpost.com/business/2024/10/26/elon-musk-immigration-status/
5 https://www.youtube.com/watch?v=cehV3vyT3s8
6 https://www.cnn.com/2024/10/28/us/elon-musk-immigration-washington-post-cec/index.html
7 https://www.washingtonpost.com/business/2024/10/26/elon-musk-immigration-status/
8 https://www.wired.com/story/elon-musk-citizenship-revoked-denaturalized/
9 https://www.bbc.com/news/articles/czd5lod37940
10 https://x.com/elonmusk/status/1855565891280511147
11 https://www.latimes.com/business/story/2022-03-25/black-tesla-employees-fremont-plant-racism-california-lawsuit
12 https://www.mercurynews.com/2024/08/16/teslas-fremont-car-factory-blockbuster-racism-lawsuit-to-go-before-a-jury-next-year/
13 https://www.mercurynews.com/2023/04/03/tesla-racism-lawsuit-elon-musks-firm-to-pay-3-2-million-after-137-million-award-tossed/
14 https://x.com/elonmusk/status/1854791544374804784
15 https://www.washingtonpost.com/politics/2024/11/06/democrats-kamala-harris-loss/

16 https://www.theverge.com/2017/6/1/15726292/elon-musk-trump-advisory-council-paris-climate-decision
17 https://twitter.com/elonmusk/status/1815230942400696410
18 https://www.wsj.com/politics/policy/elon-musk-political-donations-stephen-miller-desantis-39464294
19 "Next to Hughes: Behind the Power and Tragic Downfall of Howard Hughes by His Closest Advisor" by Robert Maheu.
20 https://www.wsj.com/politics/policy/elon-musk-political-donations-stephen-miller-desantis-39464294
21 https://www.wired.com/story/canvassers-elon-musk-america-pac-fired-stranded-michigan-mistreatment/
22 https://www.cnn.com/2024/11/04/media/elon-musk-election-x-misinformation-trump-harris/index.html
23 https://www.opensecrets.org/news/2024/10/pro-trump-dark-money-network-tied-to-elon-musk-behind-fake-pro-harris-campaign-scheme
24 https://www.404media.co/this-is-exactly-how-an-elon-musk-funded-pac-is-microtargeting-muslims-and-jews-with-opposing-messages/
25 https://talkingpointsmemo.com/edblog/elon-musks-fake-sites-and-texts-impersonating-the-harris-campaign
26 https://www.bloomberg.com/news/features/2024-09-13/behind-the-trump-crypto-project-is-a-self-described-dirtbag-of-the-internet
27 https://www.npr.org/2025/01/23/g-s1-44341/trumps-entry-into-crypto-opens-new-doors-for-those-seeking-political-influence
28 https://www.worldlibertyfinancial.com/us/token-sale-terms-and-conditions
29 https://www.cnbc.com/2024/10/17/trump-crypto-project-allows-ex-president-family-to-make-75percent-of-revenue.html
30 https://www.cnbc.com/2024/10/17/trump-crypto-project-allows-ex-president-family-to-make-75percent-of-revenue.html
31 https://www.coindesk.com/business/2024/10/31/trumps-crypto-business-slashes-fundraise-goal-by-90-after-lackluster-sales/
32 https://www.politico.com/news/2024/10/23/howard-lutnick-trump-transition-scrutiny-00184985
33 https://www.cnbc.com/2024/11/05/cryptos-245-million-campaign-finance-operation-funded-non-crypto-ads.html
34 https://www.cnbc.com/2024/11/05/cryptos-245-million-campaign-finance-operation-funded-non-crypto-ads.html

CHAPTER 21: ELECTION DAY

1 https://www.realclearpolitics.com/video/2024/11/06/msnbcs_joy_reid_this_was_a_historic_flawlessly_run_campaign_kamala_harris_had_every_prominent_celebrity_voice.html
2 https://www.washingtonpost.com/politics/2025/01/31/elon-musk-trump-donor-2024-election/
3 https://www.nytimes.com/2024/11/13/us/politics/musk-trump-transition-mar-a-lago.html

NOTES

4. https://www.followthecrypto.org/elections/VA-H-10
5. https://www.nytimes.com/2022/04/10/us/jared-kushner-saudi-investment-fund.html
6. https://www.nytimes.com/2023/03/30/us/politics/jared-kushner-qatar-united-arab-emirates.html
7. https://abcnews.go.com/US/special-counsel-subpoenaed-trump-organization-potential-foreign-business/story?id=99523066
8. https://www.axios.com/2024/11/07/trump-elon-musk-business-tax-cuts
9. https://finance.yahoo.com/news/elon-musk-net-worth-surges-190121037.html?guccounter=1
10. https://edition.cnn.com/2024/11/07/investing/billionaires-net-worth-trump-win/index.html
11. https://www.axios.com/2024/11/07/trump-project-2025-second-term-agenda
12. https://x.com/emiliemc/status/1854240350371766571
13. https://techcrunch.com/2024/11/18/sam-altman-will-co-chair-the-new-mayor-of-san-franciscos-transition-team/
14. https://missionlocal.org/2024/11/michael-moritz-togethersf-sf-elections-november-2024/
15. https://missionlocal.org/2024/11/michael-moritz-togethersf-sf-elections-november-2024/; https://missionlocal.org/2024/11/s-f-ethics-commission-fines-mark-farrell-108k-for-campaign-violations/; https://www.kqed.org/news/12012377/san-franciscos-most-expensive-ballot-measure-prop-d-headed-for-defeat
16. https://www.kqed.org/news/12012377/san-franciscos-most-expensive-ballot-measure-prop-d-headed-for-defeat
17. https://sfstandard.com/2024/11/13/aaron-peskin-san-francisco-progressive-billionaires/
18. https://www.kqed.org/news/12003004/michael-bloomberg-gives-1-million-to-back-mayor-london-breeds-reelection
19. https://www.sfchronicle.com/election/article/sf-supervisor-district-5-dean-preston-19857793.php
20. https://www.theguardian.com/us-news/2024/nov/07/san-francisco-mayor-election
21. Author interview with Gil Duran.
22. https://x.com/garrytan/status/1854048895162347672
23. https://x.com/garrytan/status/1854051361526366503
24. https://www.dailyrepublic.com/news/former-head-of-air-force-air-mobility-joins-california-forever/article_a8ba287e-9e02-11ef-9fb6-233b74789947.html
25. https://www.nbcnews.com/business/economy/economy-if-trump-wins-second-term-could-mean-hardship-for-americans-rcna177807
26. https://x.com/PirateWires/status/1856517841916145756 https://archive.ph/hTScX
27. https://edition.cnn.com/2024/11/14/politics/elon-musk-doge-trump/index.html
28. https://www.pbs.org/newshour/politics/trump-announces-musk-and-ramaswamy-will-lead-outside-advisory-group-department-of-government-efficiency
29. https://www.nbcnews.com/business/economy/economy-if-trump-wins-second-term-could-mean-hardship-for-americans-rcna177807

30 https://edition.cnn.com/2024/11/14/politics/elon-musk-doge-trump/index.html
31 https://www.wsj.com/world/russia/musk-putin-secret-conversations-37e1c187
32 https://x.com/ianbremmer/status/1579941475613229056?lang=en
33 https://eprints.qut.edu.au/253211/1/A_computational_analysis_of_potential_algorithmic_bias_on_platform_X_during_the_2024_US_election-4.pdf
34 https://x.com/JeffBezos/status/1854184441511571765
35 https://x.com/JeffBezos/status/1854184441511571765
36 https://www.nytimes.com/2024/11/09/technology/tech-employee-activism-trump.html
37 https://www.reuters.com/world/us/trump-son-don-jr-joining-venture-capital-firm-1789-capital-sources-say-2024-11-12/
38 https://x.com/sundarpichai/status/1854207788290850888
39 https://www.forbes.com/sites/richardnieva/2024/11/12/google-trump-antitrust/
40 https://x.com/elonmusk/status/1854220837420695729
41 https://www.wsj.com/politics/elections/trump-family-election-cash-bonanza-2f5f8714?st=k8deQk
42 https://www.nytimes.com/2024/12/14/technology/trump-tech-amazon-meta-openai.html

EPILOGUE

1 https://www.npr.org/2025/01/15/nx-s1-5258510/biden-farewell-address
2 https://bidenwhitehouse.archives.gov/briefing-room/speeches-remarks/2025/01/15/remarks-by-president-biden-in-a-farewell-address-to-the-nation/
3 https://www.bloomberg.com/news/articles/2025-04-26/elon-musk-s-xai-holdings-is-in-discussions-to-raise-20-billion

List of Figures

Page 102: Tweet by Naval Ravikant, a venture capitalist, https://x.com/naval/status/1345564424770240513 [Most recently accessed July 3, 2025]

Page 142: 1776 Returns document created by Jan. 6 plotters, https://www.documentcloud.org/documents/22060615-1776-returns/ [Most recently accessed July 3, 2025]

Page 143: Jan 6 investigation interview with Samuel Armes, https://www.govinfo.gov/app/details/GPO-J6-TRANSCRIPT-CTRL0000916110

Page 144: 1776 Returns document

Page 146: Government interview with Samuel Armes, https://www.govinfo.gov/app/details/GPO-J6-TRANSCRIPT-CTRL0000916110

Page 146: ibid

Page 147: ibid

Page 148: ibid

Page 149: Law and Crime News, "Oath Keepers Member Accused in Jan. 6 Capitol Attack Opts Out of Having a Lawyer, Tells Judge He Will Represent Himself", Published December 1, 2022, https://lawandcrime.com/u-s-capitol-breach/oath-keepers-member-accused-in-jan-6-capitol-attack-opts-out-of-having-a-lawyer-tells-judge-he-will-represent-himself/ [Accessed July 3, 2025]

Page 151: 1776 Returns document

Index

a16z *see* Andreessen Horowitz (a16z)
Abdulaziz, Omar   54, 57
Abouammo, Ahmad   47, 52–3, 53
Ackman, Bill   xix, 233–4
Activision   21
Adams, Eric   130–1, 133
Adams, Scott   44
Adelson, Miriam   188, 259
Agarwal, Sachin   100
AGI (artificial general intelligence)   12, 80, 164
Al Ahmed, Ali   46–7, 51, 52, 55, 57
AI (artificial intelligence)   xxix, 11–12, 80, 105, 163–70
   and the 2024 election   261
   Project Maven   15
   and the Trump administration   272–3
Alameda Research   200, 208–9, 210, 211, 215, 216
All-In (podcast)   63, 64–5, 66, 73
Alpha Parties   121–2
Alphabet   269
Alsuwaidi, Ahmed   236
Alternative for Germany (AfD)   83
Altman, Sam   xxix, 103
Alwaleed bin Talal, Prince   47, 49, 53–4, 54, 224, 235, 236
Alzabarah, Ali   47, 53
Amazon   20, 167
   see also Bezos, Jeff
"America Loves Crypto Tour"   257
America PAC   186, 230, 251–2, 267

American dynamism   20
Andreessen Horowitz (a16z)   20, 26, 31, 154
   and Saudi money   48
   and the Trump administration   272
Andreessen, Marc   25–31, 37, 71
   and Facebook   25
   on protest movements   157
   and Solano County/California Forever   114, 124, 125
   and Donald Trump   187
Anduril Industries   18–19
Anoke v. Twitter   59, 227
anti-capitalist activists   157
Antifa   184
Apple   16, 38, 50, 123, 135
Armes, Samuel   141–8, 150
Armstrong, Brian   218–19, 257
Arnold v. X Corp   35–6
Arpinum   94–5
Arrillaga, John, Sr.   26
Al Asaker, Bader   54–5, 56, 238
Asparouhov, Delian   186
assassination attempts, Donald Trump   183–5, 248
Atkins, Paul   272
Austin, *see also* Snailbrook (TX)
Austin (TX)   91, 92–3, 94–6
authoritarianism   x, 11, 20, 81, 87–8, 178, 246
   and Peter Thiel   189–93
Axelrod, David   246

INDEX

Bankman-Fried, Sam   xxx, 154, 156, 158, 159, 198, 199–217
 and Elon Musk   234
Bannon, Steve   1
Beeks, James   147–50
Bek, Nassr Haj Ali   236–7
Benioff, Marc   105
Bezos, Jeff   105, 135, 267–8, 270
 see also Amazon
Biden, Joe   184, 247
 farewell address   271
 Protecting Americans from Foreign Adversary Controlled Applications Act   181
 and the tech industry   14–15
 Tweet   41
Binance   206–7, 209–10, 211, 231–2, 235
Bitcoin   81, 131, 136, 153, 207, 217
 and Congress   219
 and elections   220
 and freedom   140
 Nashville conference   220–1
Black Lives Matter   6, 7, 35, 157, 218, 267
Bloomberg, Mike   131–2, 133, 263
Board of Education (San Francisco, CA)   65–6, 71, 86
Bond, Michelle   216
The Boring Company   34, 36
bots   232, 239, 249
Boudin, Chesa   xxvi, 66–7, 71
Breed, London   87, 88, 89, 262
 and homelessness   98, 100
Breitbart, Andrew   3030
Bremmer, Ian   68, 266–7
Brin, Sergey   105, 173, 269, 270
Burgum, Doug   81, 85
Bush, George W.   9–10
Butler (PA)   183–5, 248
ByteDance   178–9

Calacanis, Jason   35, 71, 72, 80
 and Silicon Valley Bank   160, 161
 and Twitter   234
calculation problem   105
California Forever   115–28, 263
Callin (podcast platform)   69, 158

campaign-finance law   204–5, 212, 217, 250, 252, 262
Cantor Fitzgerald   256–7
Carlson, Tucker   28, 67, 109, 183, 252
 and 1789 Capital   268
Carmona, Tonantzin   133
Carter, Nic   222
Catz, Safra   3, 173
CBDCs (central bank digital currencies)   140–1
CFIUS *see* Committee on Foreign Investment in the United States (CFIUS)
Chafkin, Max   60–1
Chain.com   152–5
charter cities   105, 107, 109–11, 192, 231
chatbots   xxvii, 163
China   11–12
 and AI   105, 169
 and Alameda   216
 and fentanyl   70
 OKCoin   131
 and security   17–18
 TikTok   21, 171–82
Choi, Emilie   262
Cicero Institute/Research   94–6, 96, 98–100
Citadel Securities   91, 135
Citizens for Sanity   185, 251
Citizens United v. FEC   205
City of Grants Pass v. Johnson   98
city supervisors   78, 81
CityCoins   130–1, 132–3, 137–8
climate change   12, 91, 151, 202
 Jan Sramek on   122, 127
 and Donald Trump   248
Club for Growth   176, 178
Clubhouse   68–9
Coinbase   216–19, 257, 262
Colby, Elbridge   17–18
Collison brothers   123, 126
Committee on Foreign Investment in the United States (CFIUS)   115, 238
Commodity Futures Trading Commission (CFTC)   205, 207–8, 258
conspiracism/conspiracy theories   xxiii–xxiv, xxvi, 70, 157

and the Cicero Institute   96
and Joe Lonsdale   100
and Maguire   185
and Elon Musk   243, 249
and Sovereign Citizen   149
and Twitter   40, 42, 45
conspiracy
  and Sam Bankman-Fried   202, 204, 215, 216
  and James Beeks   150
  and the Oath Keepers   148
  and Solano County   115–16, 127
content moderation, Twitter   37–8, 40
corporatism   31, 109
Covello, Jim   167
Covid-19   xxvii, 7–8, 69–70, 156
Craft Ventures   8, 62, 71, 73, 83, 160, 234
Crooks, Thomas Matthew   183
cryptocurrency   88, 105–6, 130–8
  and the   2024 election   260, 262
  and politics   187–8, 198
  and Donald Trump   217–23, 254–8
  see also Bankman-Fried, Sam

Daniel B. & Florence E. Green Foundation   236
dark money   60, 86–7, 203, 263
Davis, Steve   36, 265
decarcerationism   67
defense
  and AI   166
  and Silicon Valley   9–22
Defense Department   20–1
defense tech   13, 20, 103–4, 124, 175, 266
Democratic County Central Committee (DCCC)   85, 87
Democrats   248, 257
  and the   2024 election   245–6, 247, 248
Denver (CO)   134
Department of Government Efficiency (DOGE)   250, 264–5, 272–3, 274
DeSantis, Ron   31, 75
  and the "1776 Returns" document   151
  and CBDCs   140–1

on cryptocurrency   139–40
and Disney   74
homeless law   98
and Elon Musk   xxv–xxvi, 251
and David Sacks   72
and Twitter   72–3
digital currencies   140, 206, 220, 254
disinformation   37, 39, 180, 238, 240
Disney   xxiv, 38, 42, 74, 75
Dorsey, Jack   31, 39, 55, 57, 228, 235
drones   166
Duran, Gil   78–81, 82, 90, 111, 263

East Solano Plan   118, 128
education
  JD Vance on   197
  Jeffrey Yass on   179–80
  see also Board of Education
eight8VC   94, 235–6
Eisenhower, Dwight D.   271
election law   251
Ellison, Caroline   204, 210, 213
Ellison, Larry   3, 167
  and TikTok   172
  and Twitter   224, 235
espionage see spies
Ethereum   154
exits   102–12

Facebook   4, 18, 25, 192
see also Zuckerberg, Mark
Fairshake PAC   187–8, 217, 219, 220
Farrell, Mark   89, 262
FBI
  and Amazon's facial-recognition tool   20
  and California Forever   115
  and developer in Florida   137
spies in Twitter   47, 53, 55, 57
Federal Reserve   157–9
fentanyl   70
Fidelity   233
Flannery Associates   113–18, 127
For You feeds   41
Founders Fund   18, 19, 20
  and Saudi money   48
  and Silicon Valley Bank   160
France   83–4

free speech 31, 74
  and Elon Musk 225
  and Saudi Arabia 47, 51–2
  and TikTok 174
  and Twitter 34, 37, 39, 44, 45
FTX 26, 136, 154, 159
  see also Bankman-Fried, Sam
Fuentes, Nick 40, 43

G64 Ventures 233
Gabbard, Tulsi 75
Gaetz, Matt 144
Garamendi, John 115
Gascón, George 74
Gates, Bill 151
Gates, Bill and Melinda 50
Gellman, Barton 5, 192
Gemma, Eryka (Erika Gemma Flores) 143, 145, 150–1
Gensler, Gary 81, 159, 222, 256, 260
Germany 83
Girard, René 195
Glacier Ventures 233
Google 269–70
  and AI 165, 167
  and defense tech 15–16
governance 104–5
government contracts xxvi, 6, 20, 174, 272
  and Elon Musk 241
  Palantir 2
  Qwest 10
Gracias, Antonio 35, 36, 234, 265
Grants Pass (OR) 98–100
Great Replacement Theory xxiv, 226
Greenberg, Joel 144
Greene, Marjorie Taylor 38
Griffin, Ken 91, 135
GrowSF 78, 263
Groypers 40, 43

Hamilton family 116
Harris, Kamala 221, 222, 245–6, 268
  Elon Musk on 252–3
Hashemi, Nader 49, 50–1
Helberg, Jacob 83–4
  and defense tech 13–14, 21
  and national security 175
  and TikTok 174, 180
  and Donald Trump 185
  and the Trump administration 272
Hering, John 230
Herro, Chase 254
Hill and Valley Forum 13–14
Hoffman, Reid 14, 234
homelessness 95–6, 98–101
Honduras 106–9, 111
Horowitz, Ben 187, 229
Huawei 169
Hughes, Howard 250
Hyperloop 50

identity politics xviii, xxvii, 69, 84, 191, 245, 273
Illston, Susan 227
immigration 226, 242, 244, 247, 249, 269
  and the Alternative for Germany party 83
  and crime 186, 247
  France 84
immunity 9, 14, 56, 104, 261
intelligence agencies 2, 13, 15, 173
interest rates 157–9
  zero-interest-rate policy (ZIRP) xxx, 6, 158–9, 162
Israel 15–16, 166–7

Al Jabri, Saad 56
Janssens, Olivier 230–1
January 6 Committee 142–8
January 6 riot 141, 147, 150
J.A.S. Ventures 236
Jenkins, Brooke 67, 87
Jobs, Laurene Powell 114, 126
Judis, John B., *The Emerging Democratic Majority* 73

Kaplan, Lewis 201, 212, 214
Karp, Alex 2, 12–13, 134
Kennedy, Robert F., Jr. 31
Khan, Lina 168, 181, 187, 260
Khashoggi, Jamal 48, 56
Khosla, Vinod 174, 248
Klagsbrun, Arielle 177–8
Krasner, Larry 251–2

Kratsios, Michael   272
Krishnan, Sriran   35, 272
Kull, James   72
Kupor, Scott   272
Kushner, Jared   1, 229, 261

Larsen, Chris   87, 88–9
lawfare   42, 117, 225
laws   104–5
  campaign-finance   204–5, 212, 217, 250, 252
  election   251
  lottery   251–2
lawsuits
  and Disney   42
  and FTX   216
  and Jamaal Khashoggi   56
  and Joe Lonsdale   92
  and MBS   56
  and Media Matters   59
  and Elon Musk   39, 45, 237
  and Ripple   88
  and Solano County   115–17, 127
  and Tesla   25, 42, 243–4
  and Twitter   34, 42, 57, 58–9
  Anoke v. Twitter   59, 227
  and X   226, 237
  Arnold v. X Corp   35–6
Le Pen, Marine   84
Leone, Doug   3
Levie, Aaron   242, 243, 244
LibsOfTikTok   43
Litani   233
Lonsdale, Joe   72
  8VC   236
  and America PAC   186
  and Austin   92–6, 98–101
  and charter cities   107
  and DOGE   272
lotteries   250–2, 267
Luckey, Palmer   18–20
Lucre, Dom   225
Lurie, Daniel   89, 262, 263
Lutnick, Howard   256–7

McConnell, Nick   117, 128
Maguire, Shaun   175, 183–5
Mahmood, Bilal   89, 263

Malde, Anjool   121–2
Mar-a-Lago (FL)   14, 196, 260, 267, 270
Mather, Thomas   113, 126, 127
MBS *see* Mohammed bin Salman, Crown Prince (MBS)
Media Matters   42, 59
Mellon, Timothy   178, 259
Mercer, Rebekah   3, 268
Mercer, Robert   3
#MeToo   6, 157
Miami (FL)   91
  and cryptocurrency   130, 132, 133–8
  and the political culture   139–55
Miami Heat   136, 152, 154
MiamiCoin   130, 132, 137–8
Microsoft   20–1, 21, 167
Middle East   261
  investment money   xxviii, 31, 168, 228–30, 235
  see also Saudi Arabia
Miley, Kara   137
Miller, Stephen   185, 251
mimetic rivalry theory   195
Minihan, Mike   263–4
misinformation   253
Mnuchin, Steven   181
model legislation   96–8
Mohammed bin Salman, Crown Prince (MBS)   47, 49–50, 54–5, 56, 224, 228–9, 235, 237–8
Moreno, Bernie   257
Moritz, Michael   86, 87, 89, 114, 262
Moulton, Seth   17–18
Moy, Catherine   117, 124
Mubadala   236
Mudge   58, 235
Mukasey, Marc   212–13
Murphy, Chris   238
Musk, Elon   xxiii, 23, 102
  and Sam Bankman-Fried   202, 234
  The Boring Company   34, 36
  children   xxx, 43
  citizenship   242–3
  compared to the Network State concept   112
  dealings with foreign governments   55–6
  and Ron DeSantis   xxv–xxvi, 251
  and Disney   75

INDEX

and DOGE 264–5, 272, 273–4
and John Hering 230
on immigration 243
and MAGA 64
and MBS' tour of US 50
and national security 175
and PayPal 62
political views 83
rightward shift xxiii–xxiv
on San Francisco 64
Snailbrook (TX) 109–10
SpaceX 25, 34, 36, 110
and Donald Trump 6, 32, 181, 183, 185–6
2024 election 241, 248–54, 259–62, 264–7, 270
on Ukraine 68
on unions 25
wealth 29
woke mind virus xxiv, xxx, 7, 83
xAI 168, 229, 272, 273–4
see also Twitter/X
Musk, James 36, 41
Musk, Kimbal 242–3

Nacchio, Joseph 10
Nashville (TN) 220–1
Nasiri, Sean 236
National Labor Relations Board (NLRB) 25, 237
National Rally (NR) party (France) 84
national security 190
and TikTok 171–2, 181
National security Agency 10
Neighbors for a Better San Francisco 71, 80, 85, 86, 87
Network State concept 78–9, 80, 90, 111–12
New Right 195–6
New York City, and cryptocurrency 130–2, 133, 138
Newsom, Gavin 64
and homelessness 98–9, 101, 163
recall xxvi, 64–5
"Nextdoor Election" 70
Nixon, Richard 197
nondisclosure agreements (NDAs) 93–4
and America PAC 252

North Korea 218
NYCCoin 131–2, 133, 138

Oath Keepers 147, 148, 150
Obama, Barack 10
Oberndorf, William 67, 85
O'Connor, Reed 59
oligarchs/oligarchy 27, 84, 265, 271–2
Ongweso, Edward 70
OpenAI xxix, 164, 167
Oracle 3, 167
outrage, politics of 63

Page, Larry 104
Palantir 2, 12–13, 18, 22, 92, 95, 134, 190
Palihapitiya, Chamath 63, 64, 168–9, 185, 186
PayPal 4, 62–3, 206
PayPal Mafia xx, 62–3, 186, 189–90
Pelosi, Paul 40
Pence, Mike 1, 151
Pennsylvania, and the 2024 election 251
Perez, Edward 44–5
Perkins, Tom 28–9
Peskin, Aaron 81, 85, 89, 262
Phillips, Todd 221
Phoenix Project 86–7
Pichai, Sundar 269–70
podcasts
  All-In 63, 64–5, 66, 73
  and Callin 69
  The FinReg Pod 131
politics of outrage 63
populism xxvi, 24–5, 29, 30–1, 45, 81
Poulson, Jack 21
Preston, Dean 85, 87, 89, 263
professional-managerial class (PMC) 27–8, 29, 30
Progress 2028 253
Project 2025 6, 192, 253, 262
Project Maven 15
Próspera 107–9
Protecting Americans from Foreign Adversary Controlled Applications Act 181
protest movements 157

Proud Boys 141, 142, 145, 150
Purple Good Government PAC 72
Putin, Vladimir 68, 266

Q Tetris holding LLC 229
Al Qahtani, Saud 52
Qatar 228, 229, 235, 261
Qwest 10

Rabois, Keith 14, 61–2, 73
  move to Florida 134
  and PayPal 62
racism 38, 44, 65, 74
  anti-white 75
  and the Great Replacement
    Theory xxiii
  Jean-Marie Le Pen 84
  Elon Musk on 83
  and the "Nextdoor Election" 70
  and South Africa 23
  Tesla lawsuit 243–4
Raichik, Chaya 43
Ramaswamy, Vivek xiii–xxii, 31, 158
  on assassination attempt of
    Trump 184
  and China 24
  and DOGE 264–5, 272
  running for president xx–xxi, 29–30
  and George Soros 24
  on TikTok 180
  Truths: The Future of America First 264
  and JD Vance 186
reactionary utopians xxii–xxxi
recalls xxvii
  Chesa Boudin 66–7
  George Gascón 74
  Gavin Newsom 64–5
  San Francisco Board of Education 65–6, 86
Reporters Committee for Freedom of the
  Press (RCFP) 59, 226, 226–7
Republican Party 31
Reynolds, Susan Dyer 71, 79, 80, 263
Ripple Inc 88, 187
Roatan *see* Honduras
Rockbridge Network 194, 268
Roivant xiv–xv
Rometty, Ginni 173

Roos, Nicolas 214
Roosevelt, Franklin D. 237
Roth, Yoel 38–9
Rumble (video platform) 69, 158
Sacks, David 23, 158
  on Sam Bankman-Fried 202
  on Biden's Ukraine policy 241
  on Covid-19 policies 8
  and Ron DeSantis xxvi, 251
  and Florida 134
  and national security 175
  net worth 73
  and PayPal 62
  and political donations/
    fundraising xxvi–xxvii, 31, 64, 72–3
  political views 68–70, 73–6
  and the Republican Party 31
  and San Francisco 60–2, 63, 64–7
  and Silicon Valley Bank 160–2
  The Diversity Myth 60–1
  and Donald Trump 81, 183, 185, 189
  and the Trump administration 272
  and Twitter 35, 43, 234
  and JD Vance 194–5

Al Sadhan, Abdulrahman 47, 55, 57
Al Sadhan, Areez 47, 52, 54
Salame, Ryan 215–16
San Francisco (CA) 60–7, 70–6, 77
  and the 2024 election 262–3
  and political billionaires 77–90
San Francisco police 88–9
Saudi Arabia 228–9, 237–8
  and Andreessen Horowitz 28
  and Donald Trump 261
  and Twitter/X 46–59, 235–6, 238–9
Schmidt, Eric 10–11, 165, 166
  and exits 103
  and national-security 175–6
school board recall 65–6, 71, 86
Schumer, Chuck 222–3
seasteading 107, 192
Securities and Exchange Commission
  (SEC) 205, 255–6, 258, 272
  and Sam Bankman-Fried 159
  and Binance 232
  and cryptocurrency 207–8
  and Ripple Inc 88

INDEX

and Tesla 42
Donald Trump on 81, 221
  and Twitter 224
  and Vy 230
Sequoia Capital 3, 175, 185, 230, 235
seventeen1789 Capital 268
seventeen seventy "1776 Returns" 142–3, 144–5, 150–1
Silicon Valley, defense tech 9–22
Silicon Valley Bank (SVB) 159–62
Singh, Nishad 215
Snailbrook (TX) 109–10
Solano County (CA) 113–28
Soros, George 66, 67, 79, 253
  and Duran 79, 80
  Elon Musk on 42
  and Vivek Ramaswamy 24
Soros Foundation 119
South Africa 23
Southern District of New York's District Attorney's Office 202–3, 212
Sovereign Citizen movement 149
SpaceX 25, 34, 36, 110
SPACs (special purpose acquisition companies) 168–9
Special Competitive Studies Project (SCSP) 11
spies, and Twitter 47, 52–8, 235
Sramek, Jan 113, 119–28, 263–4
Srinivasan, Balaji 78–9, 80, 111
charter cities 107
stablecoins 159, 209, 256
Stand with Crypto Alliance PAC 257
Stanford University
  and John Arrillaga, Jr. 26
  and Joe Lonsdale 92
  and Keith Rabois 61–2
  and David Sacks 60
  and Peter Thiel 4, 14, 60, 191
Stanley, Patrick 130
Starbase 110
Stephens, Trae 20, 103–4
stock market 4, 42, 262
Stroppa, Andrea 232–3
Suarez, Francis
  cryptocurrency 130, 132, 136, 141
  and Eryka Gemma 150
  and David Sacks 72

subscriptions 40–1
surveillance 10, 88–9, 172, 173
Susquehanna International Group 178, 182

T. One Holdings LLC 236
"Tai Chi strategy" 206–7
Tamas, Alexander 229, 230
Tan, Garry 77–9, 82, 90, 263
  endorsements for mayor of San Francisco 89
  and GrowSF 87
Tandler, Michelle 71
Tarrio, Enrique 142–3, 145, 150
Tech Transparency Project (TTP) 10–11
Teixeira, Ruy, *The Emerging Democratic Majority* 73
Tesla 7–8, 25, 36, 42–3, 243–4
Tether 256–7
Thapliyal, Deepak 152–4
Thiel, Peter xxi, xxvi, 5–8, 23
  and the 2024 election 266
  and authoritarianism 189–93
  "The Education of a Libertarian" 104, 106
  and exits 103, 105–6
  and Facebook 4, 192
  and Florida 135
  and MBS' US tour 50
  and PayPal 62, 206
  political views 74–5
  and David Sacks 60
tech executive meeting with Donald Trump 1–4
The Diversity Myth 60–1
  and Donald Trump 2, 5, 32, 188–9, 190–1, 193
  and JD Vance 5–6, 186, 191, 193–6
TikTok 21, 81, 165, 171–82
Times Tech Guild 21
TogetherSF 86, 87
Tornado Cash 218
Travis Air Force Base (CA) 114, 125, 264
Trump, Donald
  assassination attempts 183–5
  and cryptocurrency 217–23, 254–8
  Bitcoin 81, 219–20, 221–2
  and the Hill and Valley Forum 14

   meeting with tech industry
     executives 1–4
   and Elon Musk xxiii, xxiv
   and David Sacks 31–2
   and Saudi Arabia 261
   and the SEC 81
   and Peter Thiel 2, 5, 32, 188–9,
     190–1, 193
   and TikTok 170, 171
twenty2024 election 240–58
   election day 259–70
Twitter account 38, 39
   and JD Vance 73, 195, 196–7
   and Jeffrey Yass 176–9, 180, 181–2
Trump, Donald, Jr. 268
Trump, Melania 270
trust and safety 233
TSMC 17–18
Twitter Spaces xxvi
Twitter/X xxv, xxviii, 31, 33–45, 224–5
   and the 2024 election 259, 267
   after the 2024 election 273–4
   blue checks xxv
   and free speech 225
   investors 224–39
   and David Sacks 67
   and Saudi Arabia 46–59, 235
   and Saudi money xxviii, 46–59, 235
   and the Silicon Valley Bank 161
   Twitter becoming 41–5

UAE 48, 229–30, 235, 236, 261
Uber 48, 238
Ukraine 68, 166, 176, 266
unions 21, 25, 30
University of Austin 94
University of Michigan 236
US Marshals Service 217

Vance, JD 182, 185–8, 190–1, 193–8, 260
   and Vivek Ramaswamy xx
   and the Rockbridge Network 268

   and David Sacks 73, 81
   and Peter Thiel 5–6, 186, 191, 193–6
   and Donald Trump 73, 195, 196–7
Vays, Tone 150
Ver, Roger 231
Vy Capital 229–30, 235

war on terror 9–10, 190
Washington Post, and Jeff Bezos 267–8
Web 3 26, 131
White, Molly 188, 217
White Stork 166, 176
Winklevoss, Tyler and Cameron, and America PAC 186
Winston, Ali 86
"woke mind virus" xxiv, xxx, 7, 83, 248, 250
wokeness xxvii, xxviii, 30, 80
   anti- 31, 251, 266
   and DOGE 273
   and Tulsi Gabbard on 75
   and Vivek Ramaswamy on xviii
   and David Sacks on 68
Wolfe, Josh 21
World Liberty Financial 254–8

X *see* Twitter/X
xAI 168, 229, 272, 273–4

Y Combinator 77, 103, 122
Yarvin, Curtis 108, 190, 195, 229, 266
Yass, Jeffrey 176–82

Zelensky, Volodymyr 266
zero-interest-rate policy (ZIRP) xxx, 6, 158–9, 162
Zhao, Changpeng 209–11, 231–2
Zip2 242
Zones for Employment and Economic Development (ZEDE) 106–7
Zuckerberg, Mark 105, 173, 186
see also Facebook